# The Vegan Cook from Around The World

The Best 300 Traditional Recipes for Eating Vegan. Vegan kitchen from USA, Mexico, Indian, Europe and More. Easy and Delicious Vegan Recipes for Lunch and Dinner

*by*

Martin Giuck

## Contents
**INTRODUCTION** ................................................................................................ 11
**AMERICAN RECIPES** ....................................................................................... 17
   **NUTS & SEEDS GRANOLA** ............................................................................ 17
   **CHIA SEED PORRIDGE** ................................................................................. 17
   **BISCUITS WITH GRAVY** ................................................................................ 17
   **BAGELS** ........................................................................................................... 18
   **BLUEBERRY WAFFLES** .................................................................................. 19
   **BANANA PANCAKES** ..................................................................................... 19
   **PUMPKIN MUFFINS** ...................................................................................... 19
   **HASH BROWNS** ............................................................................................. 20
   **BANANA BREAD** ........................................................................................... 20
   **SOURDOUGH BREAD** ................................................................................... 20
   **PEANUT BUTTER SANDWICH** ..................................................................... 21
   **STRAWBERRY & APPLE SALAD** .................................................................. 21
   **MIXED BERRIES SALAD** ............................................................................... 21
   **ASPARAGUS & PEAS SALAD** ....................................................................... 22
   **CAULIFLOWER WITH HORSERADISH SAUCE** ........................................... 22
   **POTATO CASSEROLE** ................................................................................... 22
   **GLAZED VEGETABLES** ................................................................................. 23
   **BEETS & FENNEL SOUP** .............................................................................. 23
   **BEANS & VEGGIES SOUP** ............................................................................ 23
   **VEGGIE STEW** .............................................................................................. 24
   **VEGGIE JAMBAYLA** ..................................................................................... 24
   **VEGGIE GUMBO** .......................................................................................... 25
   **VEGGIE POT PIE** .......................................................................................... 25
   **CHICKPEAS PATTIES WITH GRAVY** ........................................................... 26
   **SPICY BAKED BEANS** .................................................................................. 26
   **MOLASSES BAKED BEANS** ......................................................................... 27
   **BEANS & OATS LOAF** .................................................................................. 27
   **RICE, LENTIL & OATS LOAF** ....................................................................... 28

- LENTILS WITH MACARONI ............................................................................. 28
- NUT ROAST DINNER ..................................................................................... 29
- MAC N' CHEESE ............................................................................................ 29
- BAKED PUMPKIN MAC & CHEESE ............................................................... 29
- MACARONI SALAD ........................................................................................ 30
- CORNBREAD ................................................................................................. 30
- FRENCH FRIES .............................................................................................. 30
- AVOCADO FRIES ........................................................................................... 31
- ONION RINGS ................................................................................................ 31
- HUSH PUPPIES ............................................................................................. 31
- GRANOLA BARS ............................................................................................ 32
- APPLE COOKIES ........................................................................................... 32
- CHOCOLATE COOKIES ................................................................................ 33
- FROZEN VANILLA YOGURT .......................................................................... 33
- PEANUT BUTTER FUDGE ............................................................................. 33
- CHICKPEAS FUDGE ...................................................................................... 33
- WALNUT BROWNIES ..................................................................................... 34
- CINNAMON DONUTS ..................................................................................... 34
- MINI BLACKBERRY PIES ............................................................................... 35
- CHOCOLATE CUPCAKES .............................................................................. 35
- RED VELVET CAKE ........................................................................................ 36
- APPLE PIE ...................................................................................................... 36

MEXICAN RECIPES ............................................................................................ 38
- BEANS & POMEGRANATE SALAD ................................................................ 38
- BEANS & CORN SALAD ................................................................................. 38
- BEANS & MANGO SALAD .............................................................................. 38
- MIXED BEANS SALAD ................................................................................... 39
- BBBQ TOFU & BEANS SALAD ....................................................................... 39
- VEGETARIAN TACO BOWL ............................................................................ 39
- RICE, BEANS & CORN BOWLS ..................................................................... 40
- TEMPEH BURRITO BOWL ............................................................................. 40
- SQUASH WITH CORN .................................................................................... 40
- TOFU BURRITO BOWLS ................................................................................ 40

| | |
|---|---|
| STUFFED AVOCADO | 41 |
| BEANS & WALNUT BURGERS | 41 |
| BEANS & OATS BURGERS | 42 |
| SPINACH QUESADILLAS | 42 |
| VEGGIE TACOS | 42 |
| BLACK BEANS ENCHILADAS | 43 |
| BEANS & PINEAPPLE ENCHILADAS | 43 |
| LENTIL SOUP | 44 |
| PASTA, BEANS & CORN SOUP | 44 |
| RICE & BEANS SOUP | 44 |
| HOMINY & VEGGIES STEW | 45 |
| LENTIL CHILI | 45 |
| CHICKPEAS & ZUCCHINI CHILI | 45 |
| BEANS WITH SALSA | 45 |
| BEANS IN BEER SAUCE | 46 |
| BLACK BEANS CHILI | 46 |
| BEANS & SWEET POTATO CHILI | 46 |
| BEANS & CORN CHILI | 47 |
| TWO BEANS CHILI | 47 |
| THREE BEANS CHILI | 47 |
| BEANS & CORN CASSEROLE | 48 |
| BEANS PIE | 48 |
| CORN CASSEROLE | 49 |
| RICE PAELLA | 49 |
| RICE WITH SALSA | 50 |
| RICE WITH TOMATO | 50 |
| TOMATO SALSA | 50 |
| MANGO & AVOCADO SALSA | 51 |
| TOMATILLO SALSA | 51 |
| AVOCADO GUACAMOLE | 51 |
| SWEET BUNS | 51 |
| WALNUT COOKIES | 52 |
| SOPAPILLA | 52 |

| | |
|---|---:|
| APPLE CHIMICHANGAS | 53 |
| CHOCOLATY SWEET POTATO PUDDING | 53 |
| RICE PUDDING | 53 |
| VANILLA FLAN | 54 |
| CHOCOLATE BROWNIES | 54 |
| DULCE DE LECHE CREPE CAKE | 55 |
| CHOCOLATE CAKE | 55 |
| CHURRO CINNAMON CHEESECAKE | 55 |
| **ITALIAN RECIPES** | **57** |
| TOMATO SALAD | 57 |
| MIXED VEGGIE SALAD | 57 |
| VEGGIE NOODLES SALAD | 57 |
| BEANS SALAD | 58 |
| PASTA SALAD | 58 |
| STUFFED ZUCCHINI | 58 |
| BURGERS WITH MUSHROOM SAUCE | 59 |
| BEET SOUP | 59 |
| TOMATO BASIL SOUP | 59 |
| MUSHROOM SOUP | 60 |
| ZUCCHINI SOUP | 60 |
| MIXED VEGGIE SOUP | 60 |
| LENTIL SOUP | 61 |
| BEANS & SPINACH SOUP | 61 |
| THREE BEANS SOUP | 61 |
| BEANS, FARRO & KALE STEW | 62 |
| BARLEY & LENTIL STEW | 62 |
| ZOODLES WITH TOMATOES | 63 |
| SQUASH WITH FRUIT | 63 |
| LENTIL CASSEROLE | 63 |
| BEANS & TOMATO BAKE | 63 |
| BARLEY & MUSHROOM BAKE | 64 |
| ASPARAGUS RISOTTO | 64 |
| BAKED RISOTTO | 65 |

| | |
|---|---|
| RICE & BEANS IN SAUCE | 65 |
| RICE & LENTIL CASSEROLE | 65 |
| PASTA WITH TOMATOES | 66 |
| PASTA WITH ASPARAGUS | 66 |
| PASTA WITH MUSHROOMS | 66 |
| PASTA WITH VEGGIES | 67 |
| PASTA WITH BOLOGNESE SAUCE | 67 |
| SPAGHETTI WITH BEANS BALLS | 68 |
| PASTA & CHICKPEAS CURRY | 68 |
| PASTA CASSEOLE | 68 |
| CIABATTA BREAD | 69 |
| FOCACCIA | 70 |
| HERBS BREAD | 70 |
| SUN-DRIED TOMATO BREAD | 71 |
| HERBED FLATBREAD | 71 |
| LEMON SORBET | 71 |
| BERRIES GRANITA | 72 |
| COFFEE GRANITA | 72 |
| ALMOND BRITTLE | 72 |
| COCONUT MACAROONS | 72 |
| TIRAMISU | 73 |
| VANILLA PANNA COTTA | 73 |
| CHOCOLATE PANNA COTTA | 73 |
| FIG CAKE | 74 |
| BANANA CAKE | 74 |
| MAPLE BAKED PEAR | 75 |
| **CHINESE RECIPES** | **76** |
| DRAGON FRUIT SALAD | 76 |
| PAPAYA & CARROT SALAD | 76 |
| SAUTEED GREEN BEANS | 76 |
| GARLICKY BROCCOLI | 77 |
| GENERAL TSO CAULIFLOWER | 77 |
| EGGPLANT IN SAUCE | 77 |

| | |
|---|---|
| VEGGIES IN SAUCE | 78 |
| VEGGIES STIR FRY | 78 |
| GENERAL TSO TOFU | 79 |
| GLAZED TOFU | 79 |
| TOFU WITH BROCCOLI | 80 |
| TOFU WITH MUSHROOMS | 80 |
| TOFU WITH GREEN PEAS | 81 |
| TOFU WITH VEGGIES | 81 |
| TOFU & RICE SALAD | 81 |
| TOFU CHOW MEIN | 82 |
| TOFU & VEGGIE HOT POT | 82 |
| TOFU & BAMBOO SHOOT SOUP | 82 |
| TOFU & GREENS SOUP | 83 |
| SWEET & SOUR TEMPEH | 83 |
| TEMPEH WITH VEGGIES | 84 |
| CRISPY FRIED NOODLES | 84 |
| SESAME NOODLES | 84 |
| NOODLES & VEGGIE SOUP | 85 |
| RICE NOODLES WITH SNOW PEAS | 85 |
| NOODLES WITH TOFU | 86 |
| PINEAPPLE & CORN HOT POT | 86 |
| VEGGIE CHOW MEIN | 86 |
| VEGGIE LO MEIN | 87 |
| VEGGIE FRIED RICE | 87 |
| TOFU FRIED RICE | 87 |
| STICKY RICE BALLS | 88 |
| FRIED SESAME BALLS | 88 |
| BANANA FRITTERS | 89 |
| TAPIOCA PUDDING | 89 |
| SOY PUDDING | 89 |
| MANGO PUDDING | 90 |
| ALMOND JELLY | 90 |
| MANGO ICE CREAM | 90 |

## INDIAN RECIPES ........................................................................................................................92
### CILANTRO CREPES ............................................................................................................92
### SAVORY PANCAKES ..........................................................................................................92
### TOMATO OMELET .............................................................................................................92
### TOMATO & CUCUMBER SALAD .......................................................................................93
### WARM CHICKPEAS SALAD ...............................................................................................93
### VEGGIE BURGERS .............................................................................................................93
### VEGGIES & CASHEWS BURGERS .....................................................................................94
### LENTIL BURGERS ..............................................................................................................94
### SPICED POTATOES ............................................................................................................94
### COCONUT SPINACH ..........................................................................................................95
### SPICED OKRA .....................................................................................................................95
### OKRA & TOMATO CURRY .................................................................................................95
### BANANA CURRY .................................................................................................................96
### EGGPLANT CURRY .............................................................................................................96
### SWISS CHARD CURRY .......................................................................................................97
### SPINACH & POTATO CURRY ............................................................................................97
### CABBAGE WITH POTATOES .............................................................................................97
### CAULIFLOWER WITH GREEN PEAS .................................................................................98
### POTATOES WITH CAULIFLOWER ....................................................................................98
### THREE VEGGIES CURRY ...................................................................................................99
### MIXED VEGGIE COMBO ....................................................................................................99
### VEGETARIAN BALLS IN GRAVY .......................................................................................99
### LENTIL CURRY..................................................................................................................100
### CHICKPEAS CURRY ..........................................................................................................100
### CHICKPEAS WITH POTATO ............................................................................................101
### RED KIDNEY BEANS CURRY ..........................................................................................101
### MIXED BEANS CURRY .....................................................................................................102
### TOMATO RICE ..................................................................................................................102
### RICE WITH PEAS ..............................................................................................................103
### RICE WITH CARROTS ......................................................................................................103
### RICE WITH VEGGIES ........................................................................................................103
### NAAN .................................................................................................................................104

| | |
|---|---|
| CHAPATI (FLATBREAD) | 104 |
| SEMOLINA HALWA | 104 |
| CARROT HALWA | 105 |
| NUTTY MILK PUDDING | 105 |
| VERMICELLI PUDDING | 106 |
| CARROT PUDDING | 106 |
| RICE PUDDING | 106 |
| **BRITISH RECIPES** | **108** |
| OATS & CHIA PUDDING | 108 |
| TOFU & ARUGULA SCRAMBLE | 108 |
| CHOCOLATE PANCAKES | 108 |
| POTATO PANCAKES | 109 |
| CHOCOLATE WAFFLES | 109 |
| ENGLISH MUFFINS | 109 |
| WHOLE-GRAIN BREAD | 110 |
| GRAPEFRUIT, BEET & CARROT SALAD | 110 |
| VEGGIE SALAD | 111 |
| ROASTED VEGGIE SALAD | 111 |
| GLAZED BRUSSELS SPROUT | 111 |
| CABBAGE WITH LEEK | 112 |
| MUSHROOM WITH LEEKS | 112 |
| VEGGIES WITH VEGAN SAUSAGE | 112 |
| MUSHROOM SOUP | 112 |
| POTATO & LEEK SOUP | 113 |
| VINEGAR BLACK-EYED PEAS | 113 |
| LENTIL SOUP | 113 |
| IRISH STEW | 114 |
| RICE & VEGGIE STEW | 114 |
| YORKSHIRE STEW | 114 |
| VEGGIE CASSEROLE | 115 |
| SAUSAGE VEGGIES & BEANS | 115 |
| MINI SHEPHERD PIES | 116 |
| BARLEY & LENTIL SHEPHERD PIE | 116 |

YORKSHIRE PUDDING .................................................................................................... 117

STRAWBERRIES WITH CREAM ................................................................................... 117

BANOFFEE PIE ................................................................................................................. 117

BLUEBERRY SCONES ..................................................................................................... 118

CHOCOLATE CUPCAKES ............................................................................................... 118

CHERRY CRUMBLE ........................................................................................................ 119

PEACH COBBLER ............................................................................................................ 119

BLACKBERRY & BANANA CRUMBLE ....................................................................... 120

APPLE CRISP .................................................................................................................... 120

BLUEBERRY CRUMBLE ................................................................................................. 120

FRENCH RECIPES ............................................................................................................... 121

CREPES .............................................................................................................................. 121

FRENCH TOAST ............................................................................................................... 121

FRENCH BREAD .............................................................................................................. 122

CROISSANTS .................................................................................................................... 122

MUSHROOM & BROCCOLI QUICHE ........................................................................... 123

SPINACH & MUSHROOM QUICHE .............................................................................. 123

POTATO SALAD .............................................................................................................. 124

NICOISE SALAD .............................................................................................................. 124

LENTIL SALAD ................................................................................................................ 124

FRENCH ONION SOUP ................................................................................................... 125

POTATO SOUP ................................................................................................................. 125

PASTA E FAGIOLI ........................................................................................................... 126

BAKED VEGGIE STEW .................................................................................................. 126

TEMPEH & BEANS STEW .............................................................................................. 127

GLAZED CARROTS ......................................................................................................... 127

GARLIKY POTATOES ..................................................................................................... 127

SCALLOPED POTATOES ................................................................................................ 128

GREEN BEANS WITH SHALLOT .................................................................................. 128

MUSHROOM BOURGUIGNON ...................................................................................... 129

VEGGIE COQ AU VIN ..................................................................................................... 129

RATATOUILLE ................................................................................................................. 129

CHICKPEA RATATOUILLE ............................................................................................ 130

- ONION GALETTE .................................................................................................... 130
- MUSHROOM GALETTE ......................................................................................... 131
- SPINACH GRATIN ................................................................................................... 131
- POTATO GRATIN .................................................................................................... 132
- BEANS & VEGGIE CASSEROLE .......................................................................... 132
- BERRIES COMPOTE ............................................................................................... 133
- RASPBERRY MOUSSE ........................................................................................... 133
- BANANA MOUSSE .................................................................................................. 133
- CRÈME BRULEE ...................................................................................................... 134
- CHOCOLATE POT DE CREME ............................................................................ 134
- ALMOND FINANCIERS ......................................................................................... 134
- BLUEBERRY FINANCIERS ................................................................................... 134
- APPLE TART ............................................................................................................ 135
- CHERRY CLAFOUTIS ............................................................................................ 135

CONVERSION TABLES .................................................................................................. 137

CONCLUSION .................................................................................................................... 139

INDEX .................................................................................................................................. 140

# INTRODUCTION

**What is a Vegan Diet?**

A vegan diet is one that abstains from all animal products, including meat, dairy, eggs, and honey. While there are many different reasons why someone might choose to adopt a vegan lifestyle, the most common motivation is a concern for animal welfare. By abstaining from animal products, vegans can help to reduce the demand for these items, and ultimately help to promote a more humane treatment of animals. In addition to ethical concerns, some vegans also believe that plant-based diets are healthier for both people and the planet. They argue that raising animals for food requires large amounts of land, water, and other resources and that eating meat can contribute to health problems such as heart disease and obesity. Whatever the reasons for choosing a vegan diet, it is important to ensure that you get all the nutrients your body needs. This can be accomplished by carefully selecting vegan-friendly foods that are rich in protein, iron, calcium, and other essential nutrients.

Proponents of veganism believe it is a more ethical way of eating that reduces animal harm. They also argue that a vegan diet has many health benefits, including lower heart disease and obesity rates. In addition, vegans claim that a plant-based diet is more sustainable than one that includes animal products. While there is some debate about the exact definition of a vegan diet, it generally includes vegetables, fruits, grains, beans, and nuts. Some vegans also consume dairy and meat substitutes made from tofu, tempeh, or seitan.

**The Vegan Moment**

A vegan diet eliminates all animal products, including eggs, dairy, and honey. People who follow a vegan diet consume only plant-based foods, such as fruits, vegetables, grains, and nuts. While some people choose to become vegan for health reasons, others do so for ethical or environmental reasons. The vegan movement has grown in recent years, with more and more people adopting veganism as a lifestyle.

The word vegan was coined in 1944 by Donald Watson, founder of the Vegan Society in England. At the time, he defined it as "the doctrine that man should live without exploiting animals." Today, the definition of veganism has evolved to encompass a more holistic approach to living that seeks to avoid all forms of exploitation, injustice, and cruelty to sentient beings. This includes abstaining from eating animal products and using and supporting products and services that do not involve animal exploitation or harm. In recent years, there has been a growing movement of people who are choosing to live a vegan lifestyle. This "vegan moment" is fueled by a growing awareness of veganism's ethical, environmental, and health benefits. As more people learn about the many reasons for going vegan, the vegan movement will likely continue to grow.

Veganism is a way of living that excludes all forms of animal exploitation and cruelty, whether for food, clothing or any other purpose. At its core, veganism is about respect for animals. It rejects the commodification of animals and the notion that they are here for us to use as we see fit. Instead, vegans believe that animals should be free to live their lives according to their own nature. This ethical commitment leads many vegans to seek out plant-based alternatives to animal-derived products. For example, instead of eating eggs, vegans may eat tofu scramble; instead of wearing leather shoes, they may wear canvas sneakers; and instead of using honey, they may use agave nectar. We can reduce our reliance on animal agriculture by choosing vegan options and help create a more just and compassionate world.

**Importance of a Vegan Diet**

A vegan diet excludes all animal products, including meat, dairy, eggs, and honey. While there are many different reasons why people choose to follow a vegan diet, the two most common motives are ethical concerns for animals and environmental sustainability. From an ethical standpoint, veganism is rooted in the belief that all sentient beings have a right to life and freedom from exploitation. For vegans, this means abstaining from all forms of animal husbandry, including both livestock farming and the consumption of animal products. In addition to sparing the lives of animals, vegans also believe that this lifestyle helps to protect the environment.

Animal agriculture is a leading cause of deforestation, water pollution, and habitat loss, so by choosing plant-based foods, vegans can help to reduce their impact on the planet. In addition to being more environmentally friendly, a vegan diet can also be healthier than one that includes animal products. Vegans tend to consume more fruits and vegetables than non-vegans, which means they take in more vitamins, minerals, and antioxidants. Additionally, vegan diets are typically lower in saturated fat and cholesterol than diets that include meat and dairy. For these reasons, veganism is often touted as a way to improve overall health and wellness. Whether motivated by ethical concerns or a desire for better health, more and more people are choosing to adopt a vegan lifestyle.

A vegan diet is one that excludes all animal products, including meat, eggs, dairy, and honey. While some people choose a vegan diet for ethical reasons, there are also many health benefits associated with this way of eating. Studies have shown that a vegan diet can help to control weight. In addition, a vegan diet is often rich in fiber, antioxidants, and other essential nutrients for good health. For these reasons, choosing a vegan diet can be a healthy and delicious way to improve your overall health.

A vegan diet excludes all animal products. Vegans also avoid using any products that are made from animals, such as leather and wool. There are many reasons why someone might choose to follow a vegan diet. It is a moral or ethical choice for some people, as they believe that all animals should be treated with respect and compassion. Others may choose veganism for health reasons, as a vegan diet can lower the risk of heart disease, diabetes, and some types of cancer. Some people also follow a vegan diet for environmental reasons, as producing animal products requires a significant amount of land, water, and other resources. Whatever the reason, following a vegan diet can have many benefits for both individuals and the planet.

**Benefits of a Vegan Diet**
A vegan diet is one that excludes all animal products, including meat, dairy, eggs, and honey. While some people choose to follow a vegan diet for ethical reasons, there are also a number of health benefits associated with this way of eating. For example, vegans tend to have lower cholesterol and blood pressure levels and are at reduced risk for heart disease and type 2 diabetes. In addition, a vegan diet is often high in fiber and antioxidants, which can help to protect against certain types of cancer. Furthermore, vegans tend to have a lower body mass index (BMI) than people who eat animal products, making them less likely to experience obesity-related health problems. Overall, following a vegan diet offers a number of potential health benefits. One of the main health benefits of a vegan diet is that it tends to be lower in saturated fat and cholesterol than diets that include animal products. This can lead to a lower risk of heart disease and other chronic conditions such as obesity and type 2 diabetes. Additionally, vegans tend to consume more fiber and antioxidants than non-vegans, which can further reduce the risk of chronic disease.

A vegan diet is one that abstains from all animal products, including meat, dairy, eggs, and honey. While this may seem like a restrictive way of eating, it can actually be quite beneficial for both your health and the environment. Studies have shown that vegans tend to have lower levels of cholesterol and blood pressure, as well as a lower risk of developing heart disease, type 2 diabetes, and certain types of cancer. Furthermore, veganism is environmentally friendly, as it requires less land and water than traditional farming methods. In fact, the United Nations has recommended that everyone adopt a vegan diet in order to help combat climate change. So, vegan diet not only helps improve health and but also helps in reducing the carbon footprint thus improving the planet.

**Weight Loss**
A vegan diet can be an effective weight-loss tool, as it eliminates many high-calorie animal products from your diet. Studies have shown that a vegan diet can help you lose weight and maintain a healthy body mass index (BMI). Additionally, veganism has been associated with lower rates of obesity, heart disease, and type-2 diabetes. While some people may worry that a vegan diet won't provide enough nutrients, there are many nutrient-rich plant-based foods that can easily be incorporated into your meals. These include fruits, vegetables, legumes, nuts, and seeds. With a little planning, it is easy to get all the nutrients you need on a vegan diet.

A vegan diet can be very effective for weight loss. By eliminating animal products from your diet, you automatically cut out a lot of high-fat, high-calorie foods. This can lead to weight loss even without counting calories or making any other changes to your diet. In addition, vegan diets tend to be high in fiber and low in refined carbs, both of which are beneficial for weight loss. Fiber helps keep you feeling full longer and can help reduce cravings, while refined carbs can cause blood sugar spikes that lead to hunger and cravings. As a result, following a vegan diet can help you lose weight healthily and sustainably.

**Regulates Blood Sugar Level**
A vegan diet can be extremely beneficial for those who are struggling to regulate their blood sugar levels. By removing all animal products from your diet, you can minimize the sugar and fat you consume. In addition, plant-based foods are generally high in fiber, which helps slow down sugar absorption into the bloodstream. This can be especially beneficial for those who are suffering from diabetes or prediabetes. While a vegan diet may require some adjustments, it can ultimately lead to better blood sugar control and improved overall health.

A vegan diet can be beneficial for people who are looking to lower their blood sugar levels. This is because a vegan diet is typically high in fibre and low in sugar. Fibre helps to regulate blood sugar levels by slowing down the rate at which glucose is absorbed into the bloodstream. This can help to prevent blood sugar spikes after meals, and over time, can help to lower overall blood sugar levels. Additionally, a vegan diet is often naturally low in sugar, as most sweets and processed foods contain animal products. This means that people following a vegan diet are less likely to experience the blood sugar spikes that can occur after eating sugary foods. As a result, a vegan diet can be an effective way to lower blood sugar levels and improve overall health.

**Improved Kidney Function**
there are also many health benefits associated with this way of eating. One area of improvement is kidney function. A study published in the Journal of Renal Nutrition found that a plant-based diet was associated with higher estimated glomerular filtration rates (eGFR) and better kidney function. The study participants who ate the most vegetables, fruits, and tofu had the best results. In addition to improving kidney function, a vegan diet has also been shown to lower blood pressure and cholesterol levels, two risk factors for heart disease.
The kidneys filter the blood and remove waste from the body. A vegan diet can help improve kidney function by providing the body with more nutrients and fiber. Fiber helps to keep the gastrointestinal tract clean and helps the body to absorb nutrients better. In addition, a vegan diet is often lower in sodium and fat, which can help reduce the risk of high blood pressure and obesity, both of which can lead to kidney damage. As a result, a vegan diet can be an important part of maintaining healthy kidney function. A vegan diet can help reduce the chances of developing kidney diseases. This is because a vegan diet is rich in antioxidants and fiber, which can help to protect the kidneys from damage.

**Lower Risk of Cardiovascular Complications**
A vegan diet has been shown to help Lower risks of cardiovascular complications. This type of diet includes no animal products, including meat, poultry, fish, eggs, and dairy. A vegan diet is high in fiber, antioxidants, and phytochemicals. All of these nutrients work together to help protect the heart and blood vessels from damage. They also help to Lower cholesterol levels and keep blood pressure under control. In addition, a vegan diet can help to reduce inflammation throughout the body. Inflammation is a major risk factor for heart disease and stroke. By following a vegan diet, you can help to Lower your risks of developing cardiovascular complications.
A vegan diet can help to decrease the risk of strokes and heart attacks. This is because a vegan diet is typically lower in saturated fats and cholesterol than a non-vegan diet. Saturated fats and cholesterol can contribute to the buildup of plaque in the arteries, leading to stroke or heart attack. A vegan diet is also often higher in fiber than a non-vegan diet, and fiber can help to reduce cholesterol levels. In addition, a vegan diet is typically rich in antioxidants, which can protect against plaque formation in the arteries.

**Lowers Cholesterol Levels**
one potential benefit is that it can help to lower cholesterol levels. Studies have shown that vegans tend to have lower total cholesterol and LDL ("bad") cholesterol levels than omnivores (those who eat both animal and plant foods). This may be due to the fact that vegan diets are typically lower in saturated fat and cholesterol than omnivorous diets. Additionally, vegan diets often contain more fiber than omnivorous diets, and fiber has been shown to help reduce cholesterol levels. This diet can help lower cholesterol levels by reducing the amount of saturated fat consumed. Saturated fat is found in animal products such as meat and dairy, and it can raise cholesterol levels. By eliminating these foods from your diet, you can help to keep your cholesterol levels in check. In addition to lowering cholesterol levels, a vegan diet can also help to improve heart health in other ways. For example, it can promote weight loss and help to lower blood pressure. A vegan diet can help lower cholesterol levels for several reasons. First, vegan diets are typically lower in saturated fats than other diets. Saturated fats are known to increase cholesterol levels, so by reducing the amount of saturated fats you consume, you can also reduce your cholesterol levels. Additionally, vegan diets often contain more fiber than other diets. Fiber helps to remove cholesterol from the body, and it can also help to reduce the absorption of cholesterol from food. Finally, vegan diets tend to be higher in antioxidants than other diets. Antioxidants help to protect the LDL ("bad") cholesterol from oxidation, which can lead to a buildup of plaque in the arteries.

**Promotes Healthy and Radiant Skin**
While a vegan diet has many benefits, one of the most visible is the improvement it can have on your skin. Because a vegan diet is rich in fruits and vegetables, it provides your skin with essential vitamins and minerals, as well as antioxidants that help to protect against damage from free radicals. In addition, a vegan diet is typically low in inflammatory foods that can contribute to breakouts and other skin problems. As a result, those who follow a vegan diet often experience an improvement in the overall health and appearance of their skin.
The vegan diet is rich in antioxidants and other essential nutrients for maintaining healthy skin. For example, vitamin C helps to protect the skin from damage caused by free radicals, while vitamin E helps to keep the skin hydrated and youthful-looking. In addition, a vegan diet is also low in fat and sugar, which can contribute to dull, lackluster skin. In addition, a vegan diet can also help to reduce inflammation, as it is typically low in pro-inflammatory omega-6 fatty acids. Moreover, a vegan diet can help to promote healthy skin by providing the body with essential nutrients like vitamin C, zinc, and vitamin E.

**Reduced Inflammation**
Inflammation is a natural response of the body to protect itself from harm, but chronic inflammation can lead to a number of serious health problems. Vegan diets have been shown to help reduce inflammation by decreasing the levels of pro-inflammatory compounds in the body. In addition, vegan diets are rich in antioxidants, which help to protect the body against cellular damage caused by inflammation. As a result, a vegan diet may be an effective way to reduce inflammation and improve overall health.
A vegan diet has been shown to help reduce chronic inflammation. This may be due to the fact that vegan diets tend to be high in antioxidants and fiber and low in saturated fat. Moreover, some studies have suggested that certain components of a vegan diet, such as omega-3 fatty acids, may have anti-inflammatory properties. Inflammation can be reduced by avoiding trigger foods such as red meat and dairy. In addition, plant-based foods are rich in anti-inflammatory nutrients such as antioxidants and omega-3 fatty acids. Studies have shown that plant-based diets are associated with lower levels of inflammatory biomarkers, such as C-reactive protein (CRP) and interleukin-6 (IL-6). The anti-inflammatory effects of a vegan diet are thought to be due, in part, to the higher intake of antioxidants and phytochemicals. These nutrients scavenge harmful toxins and byproducts that can damage cells and lead to inflammation. Furthermore, plant-based diets tend to be lower in saturated fat and omega-6 fatty acids, which are thought to promote inflammation. In contrast, they are higher in omega-3 fatty acids, which have anti-inflammatory properties.

**Anti-Aging Qualities**
Studies have shown that a plant-based diet can help to reduce the signs of aging, both internally and externally. One of the main reasons for this anti-aging effect is the high levels of antioxidants found in plant-based foods. Antioxidants help to protect cells from damage, and as we age, our cells become increasingly susceptible to oxidative stress.
By including plenty of antioxidants in your diet, you can help to reduce this damage and keep your cells healthy for longer. Foods particularly high in antioxidants include berries, green leafy vegetables, and nuts. In addition to the antioxidant content, a vegan diet is also rich in other nutrients that are essential for skin health, such as vitamin C, beta-carotene, and zinc. These nutrients help to promote collagen production, fight free radicals, and keep the skin hydrated – all important factors in maintaining a youthful appearance.

**Reduced Joint Pain**
A vegan diet may help to reduce the pain and inflammation associated with osteoarthritis and rheumatoid arthritis. These conditions are both caused by an overactive immune system, and a vegan diet has been shown to help regulate the immune system. In addition, a vegan diet is rich in antioxidants, which can help to reduce inflammation. There are also a number of other nutrients in a vegan diet that are beneficial for joint health, including vitamin C, magnesium, and omega-3 fatty acids. While there is no cure for either osteoarthritis or rheumatoid arthritis, a vegan diet may help to alleviate some of the symptoms.
One of the most surprising findings is that a vegan diet can help to reduce joint and bone pain. This is thought to be because a vegan diet is rich in antioxidants and phytochemicals, which help reduce inflammation in the body. Studies have also shown that following a vegan diet can help improve bone density, making it an ideal way to eat for those at risk of developing osteoporosis.

**Lower risks of Cognitive Impairment**
Studies have shown that people who consume a plant-based diet are less likely to develop Alzheimer's disease and other forms of dementia. This may be because a vegan diet is high in antioxidants and phytochemicals, which protect the brain from damage. Furthermore, a vegan diet is typically low in saturated fats and cholesterol, which are known to contribute to cognitive decline.
Numerous studies have shown that a diet rich in fruits and vegetables can help to protect against cognitive decline. This is likely because these foods are packed with nutrients essential for brain health, including antioxidants and vitamins. In addition, a vegan diet tends to be low in saturated fats, which have been linked to cognitive decline. Furthermore, many plant-based foods contain compounds that have been shown to boost brain function, such as omega-3 fatty acids and flavonoids. As a result, following a vegan diet is a good way to reduce the risk of cognitive impairment.

**Why go the Vegan Way?**
The vegan diet is gaining popularity for a variety of reasons. People may choose to follow a vegan diet for health, environmental, or ethical reasons. Veganism is a plant-based diet that excludes all animal products, including eggs, dairy, and honey. Vegans also avoid using animal-derived products in clothing, cosmetics, and other goods. Some people choose to follow a vegan diet for health reasons. They may believe that it is the best way to meet their nutritional needs or that it will reduce their risk of developing certain chronic diseases. Others adopt a vegan lifestyle for environmental reasons. They may believe that animal agriculture is a leading cause of climate change or that producing plant-based foods requires less land and water than producing meat. Finally, some people

become vegans for ethical reasons. They may object to the way animals are treated in the food industry or feel that it is wrong to kill animals for food. Whatever the reason, more and more people are choosing to follow a vegan diet.

So, why go vegan? There are a number of reasons why people choose to adopt a vegan lifestyle. For some, it is a way to reduce their impact on the environment. The livestock industry is a major contributor to greenhouse gas emissions, deforestation, and water pollution. By eliminating animal products from their diet, vegans can help to slow down the rate of climate change. Others go vegan for health reasons. A well-balanced vegan diet can lower your risk of heart disease, stroke, diabetes, and some forms of cancer. And last but not least, many people choose veganism as a way to show compassion for animals. Animals raised for food are typically kept in cramped and unnatural conditions and are subjected to painful procedures such as castration and tail docking. By going vegan, you can help spare animals from this suffering.

Of course, switching to a vegan lifestyle is not always easy. It takes effort and commitment to learn how to cook delicious vegan meals and to find replacements for all your favorite animal-based products. But if you are willing to put in the work, going vegan can be an incredibly rewarding experience. Not only will you be doing your part to help improve the planet and protect animals, but you'll also be doing something good for your own health and wellbeing.

**Vegan Diet Food List**
A vegan diet can be a healthy and delicious way to eat, but it is important to ensure that you get all the nutrients your body needs. To that end, here is a list of vegan diet food staples that will help you to meet the nutritional needs of the body:
- Whole grains: brown rice, quinoa, oats, barley, millet, etc.
- Legumes & Beans: lentils, peas, beans etc.
- Soy Products: tofu, tempeh, etc.
- Vegetables: leafy greens, broccoli, cauliflower, zucchini, squash, carrots, tomatoes, potatoes, turnip, sweet potatoes, etc.
- Fruits: bananas, apples, peach, mango, pineapple, watermelon, oranges, berries, etc.
- Nuts and seeds: almonds, walnuts, cashews, pistachios, flaxseeds, chia seeds, sunflower seeds, pumpkin seeds, etc.
- With these foods as part of your vegan diet food list, you'll be sure to get the fiber, protein, vitamins, and minerals your body needs to function at its best.

**Foods to Avoid on Vegan Diet**
The vegan diet excludes all animal products, including dairy, eggs, and honey. This means that vegans must be careful about what they eat to ensure they get all the nutrients they need. Here is a list of food to avoid on a vegan diet:
- Dairy products: milk, cheese, butter, yogurt, cream etc.
- Eggs: whole eggs and egg whites
- Honey
- Animal-based ingredients: gelatin, whey, casein, carmine, shellac
- Some plant-based ingredients: white sugar (refined with bone char), palm oil (may be refined with chemicals that are tested on animals)

Vegans must also be careful about food containing hidden animal products. For example, some brands of bread or pasta may be made with eggs, and some soups or sauces may contain beef or chicken broth. Always read the ingredient label carefully before buying any food product.

**Refrigerator Staples that are Vegan Friendly**
There are a few key ingredients that every vegan kitchen should have on hand. These staples will make it easy to whip up delicious and healthy meals without worrying about finding vegan-friendly ingredients. Some of the most important staples to stock your fridge include plant-based milk, tofu, vegetables, fruit, and condiments.

Finding food that meets their dietary requirements can sometimes be challenging for vegans. However, several fridge staples are both vegan-friendly and delicious. For example, tofu is an excellent source of protein and can be used in a variety of dishes. It can be marinated and grilled, stir-fried with vegetables, or even used to make a vegan version of scrambled eggs. Similarly, tempeh is another excellent option for vegans. It is made from fermented soybeans and has a slightly nutty flavor. Tempeh can be used much the same as tofu and makes an excellent addition to any meal. Finally, lentils are another key ingredient in many vegan dishes. They are highly versatile and can be used to make soups, stews, and even burgers.

**Food Options to Replace the Animal-Based Ingredients**
People might want to cut animal-based ingredients out of their diet for many reasons. Perhaps they are concerned about the welfare of animals, or they may want to reduce their carbon footprint. For this reason, plenty of food options are available to replace animal-based ingredients. For example, you could try almond milk or soy milk instead of milk. These milk alternatives are often just as tasty as the real thing and come with the added benefit of being cruelty-free. Tofu and tempeh are excellent options if you are looking for a meat replacement. Both of these products are made from soybeans and can be cooked in various ways. If you are not a fan of soy, there are also many plant-

based meat replacements on the market made from ingredients like peas and wheat. With so many delicious and nutritious options available, there's no need to consume animal-based products.

**Cuisines**
Several cuisines are vegan-friendly. Italian cuisine, for example, offers a wide variety of plant-based dishes. Many Indian and Chinese dishes can also be easily made vegan. In addition, there are many vegan-friendly American, Mexican, French, British, Indian and Chinese dishes. With a little bit of planning, it is easy to find vegan-friendly options no matter what your taste buds crave.

**FAQs about the Vegan Diet Plan**
Considering a vegan diet? You're not alone. An increasing number of people are choosing to eliminate animal products from their diets for a variety of reasons. Some do it for health reasons, while others are motivated by environmental concerns or animal welfare issues. Whatever your reason, switching to a vegan diet can be a big change. Here are answers to some frequently asked questions that may help you as you make the transition.

Individuals choose to follow a vegan diet for many different reasons. Some want to improve their health, while others want to reduce their impact on the environment. Whatever the reason, it is important to ensure that you get all the nutrients your body needs. Here are some frequently asked questions about vegan diets:

1. What is a vegan diet?
A vegan diet is one that excludes all animal products, including meat, dairy, eggs, and honey.

2. What are the benefits of a vegan diet?
Vegans tend to have lower levels of cholesterol and saturated fat, as well as higher levels of fiber and antioxidants. This combination of nutrients can lead to a number of health benefits, including lower risk of heart disease, obesity, and type II diabetes.

3. Is a vegan diet healthy?
A vegan diet can be healthy if it is well-planned and includes a variety of nutritious foods. However, it is important to note that some processed vegan foods (such as veggie burgers and french fries) may not be as healthy as whole plant foods (such as fruits and vegetables). As with any diet, it is important to ensure you get all the nutrients your body needs. If you have any concerns about your health, be sure to speak with your doctor before making any changes to your diet.

4. How do I make sure I'm getting all the nutrients I need on a vegan diet?
There are a few key nutrients that vegans need to be aware of: protein, iron, calcium, vitamin B12, and omega-3 fatty acids. You can get most of these nutrients from plant-based sources, but you may need to supplement with vitamin B12 or omega-3s.

5. What are some good plant-based sources of protein?
Soybeans and tofu are excellent sources of protein for vegans, as well as legumes such as lentils and beans. Nuts and seeds are also high in protein, as well as healthy fats and minerals.

6. What are some good plant-based sources of iron?
Dark leafy green vegetables such as spinach and Swiss chard are great sources of iron for vegans. Other good sources include beans, lentils, tofu, tempeh, and quinoa. Fortified foods such as breakfast cereals and plant-based milks can also be helpful in meeting your iron needs.

7. What are some good plant-based sources of calcium?
Calcium-rich foods for vegans include kale, collard greens, broccoli, Brussels sprout, oranges, almonds, Brazil nuts, tahini, and fortified plant-based milks.

8. What are some good plant-based sources of omega-3 fatty acids?
Omega-3 fatty acids are found in flaxseeds, chia seeds, hemp seeds, walnuts, and soybeans. You can also find them in fortified foods such as plant-based milks and some brands of tofu. Vegans can also supplement with algae-based DHA supplements if desired.

# AMERICAN RECIPES

### NUTS & SEEDS GRANOLA
**Prep Time: 15 mins. | Cook Time: 28 mins. | Serves: 8**

- ½ C. unsweetened coconut flakes
- 1 C. raw almonds
- 1 C. raw cashews
- ¼ C. raw sunflower seeds, shelled
- ¼ C. raw pumpkin seeds, shelled
- ¼ C. coconut oil
- ½ C. maple syrup
- 1 tsp. vanilla extract
- ½ C. golden raisins
- ½ C. black raisins
- Salt, as required

1. Preheat your oven to 275 °F. Line a large-sized baking sheet with parchment paper.
2. In a food processor, add the coconut flakes, almonds, cashews, and seeds and pulse until finely chopped.
3. Meanwhile, in a medium-sized non-stick pan, add the oil, maple syrup, and vanilla extract and cook for 3 minutes over medium-high heat stirring continuously.
4. Remove from the heat and immediately stir in the nut mixture.
5. Transfer the mixture to the prepared baking sheet and spread it out evenly.
6. Bake for approximately 25 minutes, stirring twice.
7. Remove the pan from the oven and immediately stir in the raisins.
8. Sprinkle with a little salt.
9. With the back of a spatula, flatten the surface of the mixture.
10. Set aside to cool completely.
11. Then, break into even chunks.
12. Serve with your choice of non-dairy milk and fruit topping.

Per Serving:
Calories: 382 | Fat: 25g | Carbs: 37.9g | Fiber: 3.5g | Protein: 7.3g

### CHIA SEED PORRIDGE
**Prep Time: 10 mins. | Serves: 2**

- 1 C. unsweetened almond milk
- 1/3 C. chia seeds
- 1 tsp. vanilla liquid stevia
- 1 tsp. vanilla extract
- Pinch of salt
- ¼ C. fresh strawberries, hulled and sliced

1. Place all the ingredients except the strawberries in a bowl and whisk them until well combined.
2. Refrigerate the mixture for at least 10 minutes before serving.
3. Top the mixture with strawberry slices and serve.

Per Serving:
Calories: 218 | Fat: 13.8g | Carbs: 21.3g | Fiber: 16.9g | Protein: 8.6g

### BISCUITS WITH GRAVY
**Prep Time: 20 mins. | Cook Time: 18 mins. | Serves: 6**

**For Biscuits**
- 1 C. unsweetened cashew milk
- 1 tbsp. fresh lemon juice
- 2½ C. unbleached all-purpose flour plus more for dusting
- 1 tbsp. baking powder
- ½ tsp. baking soda
- Pinch of salt
- 4 tbsp. chilled vegan butter
- 1-2 tbsp. olive oil

- **For Gravy**

- ✓ 5 tbsp. olive oil
- ✓ 7 tbsp. all-purpose flour
- ✓ ½ tsp. lemon-pepper seasoning
- ✓ 1/8 tsp. ground nutmeg
- ✓ Pinch of garlic powder
- ✓ 4 C. unsweetened cashew milk
- ✓ Salt and ground black pepper, as required

1. For biscuits: preheat your oven to 425 °F. Arrange a rack in the center of oven.
2. Line a baking sheet with parchment paper.
3. In a mug, blend the cashew milk and lemon juice. Set aside for about 10 minutes.
4. In a medium-sized-sized bowl, blend the flour, baking powder, baking soda and salt.
5. With a pastry blender, cut in the chilled butter until the mixture becomes crumbly.
6. Add in the cashew milk mixture and mix until just combined.
7. Place the dough onto a lightly floured surface and with your hands, pat into a 1-inch thick circle.
8. With your floured fingers, gently flatten the dough into ¾-inch thickness.
9. With a 2½-inch floured cookie cutter, cut in the biscuits.
10. Arrange the biscuits onto the prepared baking sheet in a single layer and brush the top of each with a little olive oil.
11. Bake for approximately 15-18 minutes.
12. Meanwhile, for gravy: in a medium-sized-sized saucepan, heat oil over medium-high heat and cook the flour for about 2-3 minutes, stirring continuously.
13. Add the seasoning, nutmeg and garlic powder and stir to combine.
14. Slowly add the milk, stirring continuously and bring to a gentle simmer.
15. Adjust the heat to medium and cook for about 10 minutes, stirring continuously.
16. Stir in salt and black pepper and remove from the heat.
17. Remove the baking sheet of biscuits from oven and set aside for about 10-15minutes.
18. Split each biscuit and serve with the topping of gravy.

Per Serving:
Calories: 407| Fat: 18g| Carbs: 55.7g| Fiber: 2.7g| Protein: 7.4g

## BAGELS

**Prep Time: 20 mins.| Cook Time: 27 mins.| Serves: 8**

- ✓ 2¾ tsp. active dry yeast, crumbled
- ✓ 1 tbsp. white sugar
- ✓ 1 1/3 C. lukewarm water, divided
- ✓ 4 C. all-purpose flour
- ✓ 2 tsp. salt
- ✓ 2½ tbsp. vegetable oil, divided
- ✓ 2-3 tbsp. coconut cream
- ✓ 3-4 tbsp. poppy seeds

1. In a small-sized bowl, add the yeast, sugar and 1/3 C. of lukewarm water and stir until dissolved completely. Set aside for about 5 minutes.
2. In a large-sized bowl, mix together the flour and salt.
3. Make a well in the center of flour mixture.
4. In the well of flour mixture, place the yeast mixture and 2½ tbsp. of vegetable oil and then cover the yeast with flour.
5. Add the remaining 1 C. of water and stir until well combined.
6. With your hands, knead until a smooth dough forms.
7. Grease a bowl with remaining vegetable oil.
8. Place the dough into the oiled bowl and cover with a damp tea towel.
9. Place the bowl a warm place for about 45 minutes or until doubled in size.
10. Uncover the bowl and with your hands, punch down the dough well.
11. Divide the dough into 8 equal-sized pieces and shape each into a round ball.
12. Place the dough balls onto a parchment paper-lined baking sheet.
13. Cover with a damp tea towel and set aside for about 5-10 minutes.
14. Preheat your oven to 430 °F. Line a large-sized baking sheet with parchment paper.
15. Pace a large-sized saucepan of water over medium-high heat and bring to a boil and
16. With the back of a wooden spoon, press a (1½-inch) wide hole through the center of each dough ball.
17. Carefully place the bagels into the saucepan of boiling water and cook for about 45-60 seconds per side.
18. With a slotted spoon, transfer the bagels onto a wire rack to drain.
19. Arrange the bagels onto the prepared baking sheet in a single layer.
20. Brush the top of each bagel with cream lightly and sprinkle with poppy seeds.
21. Bake for approximately 22-25 minutes.
22. Remove the baking sheet of bagels from oven and place onto a wire rack to cool completely before serving.

Per Serving:
Calories: 301| Fat: 7.3g| Carbs: 50.7g| Fiber: 2.4g| Protein: 7.7g

## BLUEBERRY WAFFLES
**Prep Time: 10 mins.| Cook Time: 40 mins.| Serves: 8**

- 1¼ C. all-purpose flour
- 3 tbsp. granulated white sugar
- 2 tsp. baking powder
- ¼ tsp. salt
- 1¼ C. unsweetened almond milk
- 2 tbsp. coconut oil, melted
- 1 tsp. vanilla extract
- 3 oz. fresh blueberries
- Olive oil cooking spray
- 4 tbsp. maple syrup

1. In a large-sized bowl, mix together the flour, sugar, baking powder, cinnamon and salt.
2. Add the almond milk,, coconut oil and vanilla and mix until just combined.
3. Gently fold in the blueberries.
4. Preheat the waffle iron and then grease it with cooking spray.
5. Place the desired amount of the mixture into the preheated waffle iron and cook for about 4-5 minutes or until golden brown.
6. Repeat with the remaining mixture.
7. Serve warm with the drizzling of =maple syrup.

Per Serving:
Calories: 185| Fat: 4.2g| Carbs: 35.3g| Fiber: 1g| Protein: 2.3g

## BANANA PANCAKES
**Prep Time: 15 mins.| Cook Time: 8 mins.| Serves: 2**

- ¼ C. rolled oats
- ¼ C. arrowroot flour
- ½ tsp. baking powder
- ¼ tsp. baking soda
- 1/8 tsp. ground cinnamon
- ¼ C. unsweetened almond milk
- 4 tbsp. aquafaba (liquid from the can of chickpeas)
- 2 tsp. almond butter
- ½ banana, peeled and mashed well
- 1/8 tsp. vanilla extract
- 1 tsp. olive oil
- ½ banana, peeled and sliced

1. In a large-sized bowl, add the flour, oats, baking soda, baking powder and cinnamon and mix well.
2. In another bowl, add the alone milk, aquafaba, almond butter, mashed banana and vanilla and beat until well combined.
3. Add the flour mixture and mix until well combined.
4. In a large-sized frying pan, heat the oil over medium-low heat.
5. Add half of the mixture and cook for about 1-2 minutes.
6. Flip the side and cook for 1-2 minutes more.
7. Repeat with the remaining mixture.
8. Serve with the topping of banana slices.

Per Serving:
Calories: 244| Fat: 12.7g| Carbs: 26.6g| Fiber: 4.6g| Protein: 9.8g

## PUMPKIN MUFFINS
**Prep Time: 10 mins.| Cook Time: 25 mins.| Serves: 12**

- 2 C. all-purpose flour
- 2/3-¾ C. white sugar
- 1 tsp. baking soda
- 1 tsp. baking powder
- 3 tsp. ground cinnamon
- Pinch of salt
- 1 (15-oz.) can pumpkin puree
- 1/3 C. unsweetened almond milk
- 1/3 C. unsweetened applesauce
- 2 tsp. vanilla extract

1. Preheat your oven to 350 °F. Line 12 cups muffin tin with paper liners.
2. In a large-sized bowl, mix together the flour, sugar, baking soda, baking powder, cinnamon and salt.
3. Add the pumpkin puree, almond milk, applesauce and vanilla extract and mix until just combined.
4. Place the mixture into the prepared muffin cup evenly.
5. Bake for approximately 20-25 minutes or until a toothpick inserted in the center comes out clean.
6. Remove the muffin tin from oven and place onto a wire rack to cool for about 10 minutes.
7. Carefully invert the muffins onto a wire rack to cool completely before serving.

Per Serving:
Calories: 137| Fat: 0.4g| Carbs: 31.5g| Fiber: 2g| Protein: 2.6g

## HASH BROWNS
**Prep Time: 15 mins.| Cook Time: 12 mins.| Serves: 4**

- ✓ 1 lb. Russet potatoes, scrubbed and grated
- ✓ ¼ tsp. garlic powder
- ✓ ¼ tsp. onion powder
- ✓ Salt, as required
- ✓ ¼ C. extra-virgin olive oil

1. In a fine-mesh sieve, rinse the grated potato until the water runs clear.
2. Drain the potatoes well.
3. Through a clean tea towel, remove the moisture from the potatoes completely.
4. Transfer potato into a bowl with garlic powder, onion powder and salt and mix well.
5. In a large-sized cast-iron skillet, heat the olive oil over medium heat and place the potatoes.
6. With a spatula, spread the potatoes in an even layer and then press them down.
7. Cook for about 2 minutes without stirring.
8. Stir the potatoes gently and again, press them down.
9. Cook for about 2 minutes.
10. Cook for about 6-8 minutes or until the potatoes are golden brown and crispy, stirring and pressing after every 2 minutes.
11. Meanwhile, line a plate with a couple of layers of paper towels to absorb excess oil, and set it near the stove.
12. Transfer the hash browns onto paper towels-lined plate to drain.
13. Serve hot.

Per Serving:
Calories: 187| Fat: 12.7g| Carbs: 18.1g| Fiber: 2.8g| Protein: 2g

## BANANA BREAD
**Prep Time: 15 mins.| Cook Time: 1 hr.| Serves: 8**

- ✓ 1 tbsp. chia seeds
- ✓ 3 tbsp. water
- ✓ 1½ C. oats
- ✓ 1 C. millet flour
- ✓ ¼ C. rice protein powder
- ✓ 1 tsp. baking powder
- ✓ 1 tsp. baking soda
- ✓ 2 tsp. ground cinnamon
- ✓ ½ tsp. salt
- ✓ 3 medium, very ripe bananas, peeled and mashed
- ✓ 1 C. unsweetened soy milk
- ✓ ½ C. unsweetened applesauce
- ✓ ¼ C. maple syrup
- ✓ 1 tsp. vanilla extract
- ✓ ½ C. walnuts, crushed and divided
- ✓ 1/3 C. unsweetened coconut, shredded

1. Preheat your oven to 350 °F.
2. Line a bread loaf pan with parchment paper.
3. In a bowl, add the chia seeds and water and mix well.
4. Refrigerate for about 15 minutes.
5. In a large-sized bowl, add the oats, flour, protein powder, baking powder, baking soda, cinnamon and salt and mix well.
6. In another bowl, add the bananas, soy milk, applesauce, maple syrup and vanilla extract and beat until well combined.
7. Add the flour mixture and mix until well combined.
8. Add the chia seed mixture and mix until well combined.
9. Gently fold in ¼ C. of walnuts and coconut.
10. Place the mixture into the prepared loaf pan evenly and sprinkle with remaining walnuts.
11. Bake for approximately 55-60 minutes or until a wooden skewer inserted in the center comes out clean.
12. Remove the bread pan from oven and place onto a wire rack to cool for about 10 minutes.
13. Carefully invert the bread onto the wire rack to cool completely before slicing.
14. Cut the bread loaf into the desired-sized slices and serve.

Per Serving:
Calories: 292| Fat: 8.5g| Carbs: 46.8g| Fiber: 6.4g| Protein: 10.6g

## SOURDOUGH BREAD
**Prep Time: 30 mins.| Cook Time: 45 mins.| Serves: 10**

**For Starter**
- ✓ 2 C. warm water
- ✓ 2¼ tsp. active dry yeas
- ✓ 3½ C. all-purpose flour
- ✓ 2 tbsp. white sugar

**For Bread**
- ✓ 4 C. all-purpose flour
- ✓ 2 tsp. salt
- ✓ 1¼ C. water

1. For starter: place water and yeast in a glass bowl and mix until dissolved completely.
2. Let it rest for 2-3 minutes.
3. In the bowl of yeast mixture, place remaining ingredients and mix until well combined.
4. With a kitchen wrap, cover the bowl loosely and set aside in a dark place at room temperature for 5 days, stirring after every 12 hours
5. On day 5, stir the starter well.
6. For bread: place 1 C. of starter, flour, salt and water in the bowl of a stand mixer and mix on low speed for 10 minutes.
7. Place the dough into a large-sized, floured bowl and wrap with a kitchen towel.
8. Sprinkle the top with some flour and place in a warm place to rise for about for 12 hours.
9. Place the dough onto a floured surface and, with your hands, knead for 3-5 minutes.
10. Now, place the dough into a bowl and sprinkle with some flour.
11. Place the bowl of dough in a warm place to rise again for about for 4 hours.
12. Preheat your oven to 475°F.
13. Place the dough into a parchment paper-lined large cast-iron Dutch oven.
14. With a knife, score the top of the bread.
15. Cover the pan with lid and bake for approximately 30 minutes.
16. Remove the lid and bake for additional 15 minutes or until a wooden skewer inserted in the center comes out clean.
17. Remove the loaf pan from oven and place onto a wire rack to cool for about 10 minutes.
18. Next, invert the bread onto the wire rack to cool completely before slicing.
19. Cut the bread into desired-sized slices and serve.

Per Serving:
Calories: 353| Fat: 1g| Carbs: 74.3g| Fiber: 2.7g| Protein: 10g

## PEANUT BUTTER SANDWICH
**Prep Time: 10 mins.| Cook Time: 3 mins.| Serves: 1**

- ✓ 2 vegan bread slices
- ✓ 1 tbsp. peanut butter
- ✓ 1 banana, peeled and sliced
- ✓ ½ tsp. ground cinnamon
- ✓ 1 tbsp. olive oil

1. Arrange the bread slices onto a plate.
2. Spread peanut butter on one side of each bread slice.
3. Place banana slices over one bread slice and sprinkle with cinnamon.
4. Cover with remaining bread slice, peanut butter side down
5. In a frying pan, heat the oil over medium heat and cook the sandwich for about 1½ minutes per side or until golden brown.
6. Transfer the sandwich onto a plate.
7. Cut the sandwich into half diagonally and serve.

Per Serving:
Calories: 435| Fat: 24.9g| Carbs: 52g| Fiber: 7.9g| Protein: 11.8g

## STRAWBERRY & APPLE SALAD
**Prep Time: 15 mins.| Serves: 4**

- ✓ 4 C. romaine lettuce, torn
- ✓ 2 apples, cored and sliced
- ✓ 1 C. fresh strawberries, hulled and sliced
- ✓ ¼ C. walnuts, chopped
- ✓ 3 tbsp. olive oil
- ✓ 2 tbsp. fresh lime juice
- ✓ 1 tbsp. agave nectar

1. In a salad bowl, place all ingredients and toss to coat well.
2. Serve immediately.

Per Serving:
Calories: 218| Fat: 15.5g| Carbs: 25.2g| Fiber: 5.1g| Protein: 2.8g

## MIXED BERRIES SALAD
**Prep Time: 15 mins.| Serves: 4**

- ✓ 1 C. fresh strawberries, hulled and sliced
- ✓ ½ C. fresh blackberries
- ✓ ½ C. fresh blueberries
- ✓ ½ C. fresh raspberries
- ✓ 6 C. fresh arugula
- ✓ 2 tbsp. olive oil
- ✓ Salt, as required

1. In a salad bowl, place all ingredients and toss to coat well.
2. Serve immediately.

Per Serving:
Calories: 105| Fat: 7.6g| Carbs: 10.1g| Fiber: 3.6g| Protein: 1.6g

## ASPARAGUS & PEAS SALAD

**Prep Time: 15 mins.| Cook Time: 4 mins.| Serves: 6**

- ¾ lb. asparagus, trimmed and cut into 2-inch pieces
- 2 C. frozen green peas
- 2 C. fresh pea shoots, cut in half
- ½ C. fresh mint, roughly chopped
- 1-2 tsp. lemon zest, grated
- 2 tbsp. fresh lemon juice
- 1 tbsp. extra-virgin olive oil
- Salt and ground black pepper, as required

1. In a large-sized saucepan of boiling water, add the asparagus and cook for about 2-3 minutes.
2. With a slotted spoon, remove the asparagus from pan and place into a bowl of ice water for about 1 minute.
3. Drain the asparagus and set aside.
4. In the same pan of boiling water, add the green peas and cook for about 1 minute.
5. With a slotted spoon, remove the green peas from the pan and place into a bowl of ice water for about 1 minute.
6. Drain the green peas and set aside.
7. In a large-sized salad bowl, add the asparagus, green peas and remaining ingredients and toss to coat.
8. Serve immediately.

Per Serving:
Calories: 85| Fat: 2.7g| Carbs: 12g| Fiber: 4.9g| Protein: 4.8g

## CAULIFLOWER WITH HORSERADISH SAUCE

**Prep Time: 15 mins.| Cook Time: 35 mins.| Serves: 6**

**For Sauce**
- 2/3 C. raw cashews, soaked in warm water for 30 minutes and drained
- ½ C. unsweetened almond milk
- 1 tbsp. fresh lemon juice
- 4 tbsp. fresh horseradish, peeled and finely grated
- 1 tbsp. Dijon mustard
- 2½ tsp. white wine vinegar
- Salt and ground black pepper, as required

**For Cauliflower Steaks**
- 2 large heads cauliflower, cut into ½-¾-inch-thick steaks
- ¼ C. olive oil
- ¼ C. fresh lemon juice
- 2 tbsp. white wine vinegar
- 1 tbsp. tahini
- 3 tbsp. fresh parsley, chopped
- 1 garlic clove, minced
- Salt and ground black pepper, as required

1. For sauce: in a high-power blender, add soaked cashews, almond milk, and lemon juice and pulse on high speed until smooth and creamy.
2. Transfer the pureed cashew mixture into a bowl.
3. Add the horseradish, mustard, vinegar, salt, and black pepper and whisk until well combined.
4. Refrigerate for at least 1 hour.
5. For cauliflower steaks: arrange the cauliflower steaks into a large-sized baking dish.
6. For marinade: in a bowl, whisk together the olive oil, lemon juice, vinegar, tahini, parsley, garlic, salt and black pepper.
7. Place the marinade over the cauliflower steaks evenly.
8. Refrigerate to marinate for 30 minutes, spooning the marinade over the cauliflower steaks after every 10 minutes.
9. Preheat your oven to 400 °F. line a large-sized baking tray sheet with parchment paper.
10. Remove the cauliflower steaks from marinade and arrange onto the prepared baking sheet in a single layer.
11. Bake for approximately 30-35 minutes or until golden brown and tender, flipping once after 15-minutes.
12. Remove the baking sheet from oven and set aside to cool slightly.
13. Serve with the topping of horseradish sauce.

Per Serving:
Calories: 215| Fat: 17.5g| Carbs: 12.3g| Fiber: 3.5g| Protein: 5g

## POTATO CASSEROLE

**Prep Time: 20 mins.| Cook Time: 1 hr. 5 mins.| Serves: 4**

- 1 C. raw cashews
- 6-7 medium potatoes, thinly sliced
- 1 C. unsweetened almond milk
- 2 tsp. apple cider vinegar
- 1 tbsp. cornstarch

23

- ✓ 1 tsp. Dijon mustard
- ✓ ½ tsp. onion powder
- ✓ Salt and ground black pepper, as required
- ✓ 1 onion, thinly sliced
- ✓ ¼-½ C. vegan cheese

1. In a heatproof bowl, place the cashews and cover with boiling water.
2. Set aside for about 15 minutes.
3. Preheat your oven to 390 °F.
4. Drain the cashews completely and place into a high-power blender.
5. Add almond milk, vinegar, cornstarch, mustard, onion powder, salt and black pepper and pulse until smooth.
6. In a large-sized bowl, add potato slices and pour ¼ of the sauce mixture and stir to combine.
7. Arrange the potato and onion slices into a baking dish and top with the remaining sauce evenly.
8. Sprinkle with cheese evenly.
9. With a piece of foil, cover the baking dish tightly and bake for approximately 35 minutes.
10. Remove the foil and bake for approximately 30 minutes.
11. Serve immediately.

Per Serving:
Calories: 466| Fat: 18.4g| Carbs: 67.6g| Fiber: 10.1g| Protein: 11.8g

## GLAZED VEGETABLES

**Prep Time: 15 mins.| Cook Time: 25 mins.| Serves: 6**

- ✓ 4 carrots, peeled and cut into 1-inch cubes
- ✓ 2 sweet potatoes, peeled and cut into 1-inch cubes
- ✓ 2 parsnips, peeled and cut into 1-inch cubes
- ✓ 2 bell peppers, seeded and cut into 1-inch pieces
- ✓ 2 tbsp. olive oil
- ✓ 12 cherry tomatoes
- ✓ 10 oz. smoky sweet glaze

1. Preheat your oven to 400 °F.
2. In a large-sized bowl, add the carrots, sweet potatoes, parsnips, bell peppers and oil and toss to coat well.
3. Place the vegetables onto a large-sized baking sheet and spread in an even layer.
4. Roast for about 15 minutes, stirring occasionally.
5. Remove the baking sheet from oven and add in tomatoes.
6. Drizzle the vegetables with glaze evenly and stir to combine.
7. Roast for about for 10 minutes.
8. Serve hot.

Per Serving:
Calories: 227| Fat: 1g| Carbs: 53.2g| Fiber: 7.8g| Protein: 3.9g

## BEETS & FENNEL SOUP

**Prep Time: 15 mins.| Cook Time: 1¼ hrs.| Serves: 4**

- ✓ 2 lb. beets, peeled and cut into 1½-inch chunks
- ✓ 1 fennel bulb, sliced thinly
- ✓ 2 garlic cloves, minced
- ✓ 1 (1-inch) piece fresh ginger, minced
- ✓ 2 tbsp. coconut oil
- ✓ 3 C. vegetable broth
- ✓ 1 tbsp. cornstarch
- ✓ 1 bay leaf
- ✓ ½ tsp. salt

1. In a large-sized soup pan, melt coconut oil over medium heat and cook the fennel for about 5-6 minutes, stirring frequently.
2. Add the garlic and ginger and cook for about 3-4 minutes, stirring continuously.
3. Meanwhile, in a small-sized bowl, mix together the cornstarch and broth.
4. In the pan, add the beets, broth mixture, bay leaf and salt and bring to boil.
5. Adjust the heat to low and simmer, covered for about 1 hour.
6. Remove the soup pan from heat and with an immersion blender, blend the soup until smooth.
7. Serve hot.

Per Serving:
Calories: 217| Fat: 8.4g| Carbs: 30.2g| Fiber: 6.5g| Protein: 8.3g

## BEANS & VEGGIES SOUP

**Prep Time: 15 mins.| Cook Time: 30 mins.| Serves: 6**

- ✓ 1½ tbsp. extra-virgin olive oil
- ✓ 1 large onion, chopped

- 2-3 garlic cloves, minced
- 1 (32-oz.) carton vegetable broth
- 5-6 C. broccoli, roughly chopped
- 2 C. frozen green peas, thawed
- 1 (15-oz.) can Great Northern beans, drained and rinsed
- 1 C. unsweetened rice milk
- ½ C. fresh parsley, chopped
- 2 tbsp. fresh lemon juice

1. In a large-sized soup pan, heat the oil over medium heat and sauté the onion for about 4-5 minutes.
2. Add the garlic and sauté for about 1 minute.
3. Add the broth and roughly chopped broccoli and bring to a boil.
4. Cover the soup pan and simmer for about 8-10 minutes.
5. Add the beans and half the green peas and cook for about 3-4 minutes.
6. Remove the soup pan and with an immersion blender, blend until smooth.
7. Return the pan over low heat and stir in the remaining green peas, rice milk, finely chopped broccoli, parsley, lemon juice, salt and black pepper.
8. Cook for about 5 minutes.
9. Serve hot.

Per Serving:
Calories: 185| Fat: 5.3g| Carbs: 26.8g| Fiber: 9.5g| Protein: 11.8g

## VEGGIE STEW

**Prep Time: 15 mins.| Cook Time: 40 mins.| Serves: 6**

- ½ C. plus 1 tbsp. all-purpose flour, divided
- Salt and ground black pepper, as required
- 2 bags beefless tips
- 2 tbsp. plus 1 tsp. olive oil, divided
- 1 large onion, chopped
- ¼ C. red wine vinegar
- 4 Yukon gold potatoes, chopped
- 3 medium carrots, peeled and sliced
- 6 C. vegetable broth
- 1 tsp. dried thyme
- 2 bay leaves
- 1 C. fresh mushrooms, sliced
- 1 C. fresh green peas, shelled

1. In a bowl, blend the ½ C. flour, salt and black pepper.
2. Add beefless tips and toss to coat well.
3. In a Dutch oven, heat 2 tbsp. of oil over medium-low heat and sear the beef tips for about 5 minutes or until browned completely.
4. With a slotted spoon, transfer the beef tips into a bowl and set aside.
5. In the same pan, heat remaining oil over medium heat and sauté onion for about 5 minutes.
6. With a slotted spoon, transfer the onion into a bowl and set aside.
7. Add vinegar and scrape to loosen the browned bits from bottom.
8. Stir in the potatoes, carrots, broth, thyme, bay leaves, and remaining flour and bring to a boil.
9. Add the beefless tips and onion and stir to combine.
10. Adjust the heat to low and simmer, covered for about 10 minutes.
11. Add in the mushrooms and cook for about 5 minutes.
12. Add in the green peas, salt and black pepper and cook for about 5 minutes.
13. Serve hot.

Per Serving:
Calories: 382| Fat: 10.7g| Carbs: 46.4g| Fiber: 7.2g| Protein: 26g

## VEGGIE JAMBAYLA

**Prep Time: 20 mins.| Cook Time: 25 mins.| Serves: 6**

- 1-2 tbsp. grapeseed oil
- 2 carrots, peeled and chopped
- 2 bell peppers, seeded and chopped
- ½ of red onion
- 6 garlic cloves, minced
- 1 (14-oz.) can diced tomatoes
- 2 tbsp. soy sauce
- 3 tsp. dried oregano
- 2 tsp. dried thyme
- 2 tsp. paprika
- 2 tsp. ground cumin
- 2 tsp. garlic powder
- 2 tsp. onion powder
- 1/8 tsp. ground black pepper
- 2 (14-oz.) cans kidney beans
- 2 C. cooked rice
- 4 vegan sausages
- 2 tbsp. tahini

1. In a large-sized saucepan, heat oil over medium-high heat and cook the carrots, bell peppers, onion, and garlic for about 5 minutes.
2. Add the tomatoes and cook for about 5 minutes.
3. Add the soy sauce and spices and stir to combine.

4. Add the beans, cooked rice and vegan sausages and cook for about 5-10 minutes.
5. Add in the tahini and cook for about 1-2 minutes.
6. Serve hot.

Per Serving:
Calories: 331| Fat: 5.8g| Carbs: 52.8g| Fiber: 15.9g| Protein: 17.3g

## VEGGIE GUMBO
**Prep Time: 20 mins.| Cook Time: 50 mins.| Serves: 4**

- ½ C. vegan butter
- 2/3 C. all-purpose flour
- 2 medium green bell peppers, finely chopped
- 2 celery stalks, finely chopped
- 1 medium onion, finely chopped
- 2 C. vegetable broth
- 1 (15-oz.) can kidney beans, drained
- 1 (14-oz.) can diced tomatoes
- 1 C. mixed frozen vegetables
- 1 medium head cauliflower, cut into florets
- 5 C. fresh cremini mushrooms, sliced
- 1 tbsp. garlic, crushed
- 1 tbsp. Cajun seasoning
- ½ tsp. liquid smoke
- 1 bay leaf
- Salt and ground black pepper, as required

1. In a heavy-bottomed saucepan, melt vegan butter over medium-low heat and stir in the all-purpose flour.
2. Cook for about 10-15 minutes, stirring continuously.
3. Stir in the bell pepper, celery and onion and cook for about 4-5 minutes.
4. add the broth, beans, tomatoes, frozen veggies, cauliflower, mushrooms, garlic, Cajun seasoning, liquid smoke and bay leaf and stir to combine well.
5. Adjust the heat to medium-high and bring to a boil.
6. Adjust the heat to low and simmer, covered for about 15-20 minutes, stirring occasionally.
7. Stir in the salt and black pepper and serve hot.

Per Serving:
Calories: 422| Fat: 5g| Carbs: 76.4g| Fiber: 10.2g| Protein: 32.2g

## VEGGIE POT PIE
**Prep Time: 20 mins.| Cook Time: 1 hr.| Serves: 8**

- ½ C. raw cashews, soaked for 30 minutes and drained
- 2½-3 C. vegetable broth, divided
- 2 tbsp. vegetable oil, divided
- 4 garlic cloves, thinly sliced
- 2 medium carrots, peeled and cut into ½-inch pieces
- 2 celery stalks, cut into ½-inch pieces
- 1 large onion, thinly sliced
- Salt and ground black pepper, as required
- 8 oz. Cremini mushrooms, sliced
- 2 medium potatoes
- ½ C. dry white wine
- 8 oz. butternut squash, peeled, seeded and cubed
- 2 tbsp. fresh sage, minced
- 1 tbsp. fresh thyme, minced
- 1 tsp. fresh rosemary, minced
- 14-16 oz. tofu, pressed, drained and cubed
- 2 tbsp. fresh parsley, finely chopped
- 1 puff pastry sheet, thawed

1. Preheat your oven to 425 °F. arrange a rack in the center of oven.
2. For cashew cream: in a high-power blender, add the cashews and ½ C. of broth and pulse until smooth. Set aside.
3. In a 10-inch ovenproof skillet, heat 1 tbsp. of the oil over medium heat and sauté the garlic for about 40-60 seconds.
4. Add the carrots, celery and onions with a Pinch of salt and black pepper and sauté for about 5 minutes.
5. Add the potatoes and mushrooms and sauté for about 2-3 minutes.
6. Add the wine and cook for about 3-4 minutes, stirring frequently.
7. Add the butternut squash and herbs and sauté for about 1 minute.
8. Add the cashew cream and the remaining broth and bring to a boil.
9. Adjust the heat to low and simmer for about 5 minutes.
10. Stir in the tofu, parsley, salt and black pepper and remove from the heat.
11. Roll out the puff pastry into the size that will cover the skillet.
12. With a knife, make 1-inch slits in the puff pastry.
13. Carefully place the puff pastry over the top of veggie mixture to cover it.
14. Brush the top of pastry with remaining oil.
15. Bake for approximately 30-35 minutes.
16. Serve hot.

Per Serving:
Calories: 423| Fat: 23.2g| Carbs: 36.5g| Fiber: 4.5g| Protein: 16.5g

## CHICKPEAS PATTIES WITH GRAVY
**Prep Time: 20 mins. | Cook Time: 10 mins. | Serves: 4**

**For Patties**
- 1 tbsp. ground flaxseeds
- 3 tbsp. water
- 1 (14-oz.) can chickpeas, rinsed, drained and pat dried
- 1 C. fresh parsley
- 1 scallion, rough chopped
- 1 garlic clove, peeled
- Salt and ground black pepper, as required
- 1 large carrot, peeled and rough chopped
- 4 oz. fresh mushrooms, sliced
- ¼ C. all-purpose flour plus more for coating
- ¼ C. vegan panko breadcrumbs
- 3-4 tbsp. olive oil
- ¼ C. unsweetened almond milk

**For Gravy**
- 1 tsp. olive oil
- 2 tbsp. all-purpose flour
- 1½ C. unsweetened almond milk
- Salt and ground black pepper, as required

1. In a small-sized bowl, blend the flaxseeds and water. Set aside for at least 10 minutes.
2. In a food processor, add the chickpeas, parsley, scallion, garlic, salt and black pepper and pulse until a coarse mixture.
3. Transfer the chickpeas mixture into a large-sized bowl.
4. In the processor, add the carrots and mushrooms and pulse until finely minced.
5. Transfer the carrot mixture into the bowl with chickpea mixture.
6. Add the flax mixture, flour and breadcrumbs and mix until well combined.
7. Make equal-sized balls from the mixture.
8. In 2 shallow bowls, place the extra flour and almond milk respectively.
9. Coat the balls in flour, then dip into almond milk and again, coat with flour.
10. In a non-stick skillet, heat oil over medium-high heat.
11. Place the balls into the skillet, 1 at a time with and with a spatula, press into a patty.
12. Cook for about 3-5 minutes per side.
13. Meanwhile, for gravy: in another noon-stick frying pan, heat oil over medium-low heat and stir in the flour.
14. Cook for about 1 minute, stirring continuously.
15. Add about ¼ C. of the almond milk and whisk until smooth.
16. Add the remaining almond milk, salt and black pepper and cook for about 3-5 minutes or until thickened, stirring continuously.
17. Serve the patties with the topping of gravy.

Per Serving:
Calories: 315 | Fat: 14.9g | Carbs: 34.2g | Fiber: 7g | Protein: 8.4g

## SPICY BAKED BEANS
**Prep Time: 15 mins. | Cook Time: 2 hrs. 10 mins. | Serves: 4**

- ¼ lb. dry lima beans, soaked overnight and drained
- ¼ lb. dry red kidney beans, soaked overnight and drained
- 1¼ tbsp. vegetable oil
- 1 small onion, chopped
- 4 garlic cloves, minced
- 1 tsp. dried thyme, crushed
- ½ tsp. ground cumin
- ½ tsp. red pepper flakes, crushed
- ¼ tsp. paprika
- 1 tbsp. balsamic vinegar
- 1 C. canned tomato sauce
- 1 C. vegetable broth
- Salt and ground black pepper, as required
- 2 tbsp. fresh parsley, chopped

1. In a large-sized pan of boiling water, add the beans over high heat and bring to a boil.
2. Adjust the heat to low and simmer, covered for about 1 hour.
3. Drain the beans well.
4. Preheat your oven to 325 °F.
5. In a large-sized ovenproof pan, heat the oil over medium heat and cook the onion for about 8-9 minutes, stirring frequently.
6. Add the garlic, thyme and red spices and sauté for about 1 minute.
7. Add the cooked beans and remaining ingredients and immediately remove from the heat.
8. Cover the pan and transfer into the oven.

9. Bake for approximately 1 hour.
10. Serve with the garnishing of cilantro.

Per Serving:
Calories: 205| Fat: 5.4g| Carbs: 29.9g| Fiber: 7.4g| Protein: 10.9g

### MOLASSES BAKED BEANS
**Prep Time: 15 mins.| Cook Time: 2 hrs. 20 mins.| Serves: 6**

- 6 C. water
- 1 lb. dry navy beans, soaked overnight and drained
- 1 bay leaf
- Pinch of baking soda
- 1 yellow onion, peeled and chopped
- 1/3 C. molasses
- ¼ C. dark brown sugar
- 1 tsp. dry mustard powder
- Salt and ground black pepper, as required

1. Preheat your oven to 300 °F.
2. In a large-sized Dutch oven, add the water, beans, bay leaf, and baking soda over high heat and bring to a boil.
3. Adjust the heat to medium and cook for about 10 minutes.
4. Drain the beans, reserving cooking liquid.
5. In the Dutch oven, add the remaining ingredients with the beans and stir to combine.
6. Add reserved cooking liquid to cover the beans mixture.
7. Cover the Dutch oven and transfer into the oven.
8. Bake for approximately 1 hour.
9. Uncover and stir in some of the reserved cooking liquid, if needed.
10. Bake, covered, for about 1 hour.
11. Next, increase the temperature of oven to 350°F.
12. Bake uncovered for approximately 20-30 more minutes.
13. Discard the bay leaf and serve hot.

Per Serving:
Calories: 246| Fat: 0.2g| Carbs: 67.4g| Fiber: 24.4g| Protein: 16.4g

### BEANS & OATS LOAF
**Prep Time: 25 mins.| Cook Time: 1¼ hrs.| Serves: 10**

- 1 (15-oz.) can chickpeas
- 2 tsp. olive oil
- 1 medium onion, finely chopped
- 1 tbsp. dried Italian seasoning
- Salt and ground black pepper, as required
- ½ C. low-sodium vegetable broth
- 1/3 C. ketchup
- 2 tbsp. vegan Worcestershire sauce
- 2 (15-oz.) cans black beans, drained and rinsed
- 1 C. rolled oats, roughly ground
- 1 C. cornmeal
- 3 tbsp. liquid smoke
- 1 C. BBQ sauce

1. Preheat your oven to 350 °F. Line a 9-inch bread pan with parchment paper.
2. Drain the can of chickpeas, reserving ½ C. of liquid.
3. Then rinse the chickpeas well.
4. In a large-sized skillet, heat oil over medium-low heat and sauté the onions with Italian seasoning, salt and black pepper for about 5 minutes.
5. Add in broth, ketchup and Worcestershire sauce and stir to combine.
6. Remove from the heat and set aside.
7. In a food processor, add chickpeas and 15 oz. of black beans and pulse until creamy.
8. Transfer the pureed beans into a large-sized bowl.
9. In the clean food processor, add the remaining black beans and pulse until chopped into small pieces.
10. Transfer the chopped beans into the bowl with the pureed beans mixture.
11. In the bowl of beans mixture, add oats, cornmeal, liquid smoke and reserved ½ C. of chickpeas liquid and mix until well combined.
12. Add cooked onion mixture and gently stir to combine.
13. Place the mixture into the prepared loaf pan evenly.
14. Spread BBQ sauce on top of the loaf evenly.
15. Bake for approximately 70 minutes.

16. Remove from the oven and place the loaf pan onto a wire rack for about 10 minutes.
17. Carefully invert the loaf onto a platter.
18. Cut into desired-sized slices and serve.

Per Serving:
Calories: 305| Fat: 3.4g| Carbs: 57.6g| Fiber: 11.4g| Protein: 12.2g

### RICE, LENTIL & OATS LOAF
**Prep Time: 20 mins.| Cook Time: 1 hr. 50 mins.| Serves: 8**

- 1¾ C. plus 2 tbsp. water, divided
- ½ C. wild rice
- ½ C. brown lentils
- Salt, as required
- ½ tsp. mixed dried herbs
- 1 medium yellow onion, chopped
- 1 celery stalk, chopped
- 6 cremini mushrooms, chopped
- 4 garlic cloves, minced
- ¾ C. rolled oats
- ½ C. walnuts, finely chopped
- ¾ C. ketchup
- ½ tsp. red pepper flakes, crushed
- 1 tsp. fresh rosemary, minced
- 2 tsp. fresh thyme, minced

1. In a pan, add 1¾ C. of the water, rice, lentils, salt and Italian seasoning over medium-high heat and bring to a boil.
2. Adjust the heat to low and simmer, covered for about 45 minutes.
3. Remove from the heat and set aside, covered for at least 10 minutes.
4. Preheat your oven to 350 °F. Line a 9x5-inch loaf pan with parchment paper.
5. In a skillet, heat the remaining water over medium heat and sauté the onion, celery, mushrooms and garlic for about 5 minutes.
6. Remove from the heat and set aside to cool slightly.
7. In a large-sized bowl, add the oats, walnuts, ketchup and fresh herbs and mix until well combined.
8. Add the rice mixture and vegetable mixture and mix well
9. In a high-power blender, add the mixture and pulse until just a chunky mixture forms.
10. Transfer the mixture into the prepared loaf pan evenly.
11. With a piece of foil, cover the loaf pan and bake for approximately 40 minutes.
12. Uncover and bake for 20 minutes more or until top becomes golden brown

13. Remove from the oven and place the loaf pan onto a wire rack for about 10 minutes.
14. Carefully invert the loaf onto a platter.
15. Cut into desired-sized slices and serve.

Per Serving:
Calories: 164| Fat: 5.5g| Carbs: 26.1g| Fiber: 4.8g| Protein: 7.1g

### LENTILS WITH MACARONI
**Prep Time: 15 mins.| Cook Time: 45 mins.| Serves: 6**

- ¾ C. dried brown lentils, rinsed
- 2 tbsp. olive oil
- 6 oz. fresh cremini mushrooms, roughly chopped
- 1 onion, chopped
- 1 red bell pepper, seeded and chopped
- 3 garlic cloves, minced
- 1 (14-oz.) can diced tomatoes
- 1 (14-oz.) can tomato sauce
- 2 tbsp. soy sauce
- ½ tsp. dried oregano
- ½ tsp. dried thyme
- 2 bay leaves
- 1½ tsp. paprika
- 3 C. vegetable broth
- 2 C. uncooked elbow macaroni
- ¼ C. tomato paste
- Salt and ground black pepper, as required

1. In a saucepan of water, add the lentils over high heat and bring to a boil.
2. Cook for about 30-35 minutes or until the lentils are tender.
3. Drain the lentils completely.
4. Meanwhile, in a non-stick skillet, heat olive oil over medium heat and sauté mushrooms for about 5 minutes.
5. Add the onion and sauté for about 5 minutes.
6. Add the bell pepper and garlic and sauté for about 1 minute.
7. Add in the tomatoes, tomato sauce, soy sauce, dried herbs, bay leaves, paprika and broth and stir to combine.
8. Adjust the heat to high and bring to a boil.
9. Add in the pasta and stir to combine.
10. Adjust the heat to low and simmer for about 20 minutes.
11. Stir in the lentils and tomato paste and cook for about 2 minutes.
12. Stir in salt and black pepper and serve hot.

Per Serving:
Calories: 310| Fat: 6.5g| Carbs: 49.3g| Fiber: 11.6g| Protein: 16g

## NUT ROAST DINNER
**Prep Time: 15 mins.| Cook Time: 1½ hrs.| Serves: 6**

- Non-stick cooking spray
- ½ tbsp. olive oil
- 2 onions, chopped
- ½ C. celery stalk, chopped
- 1 tsp. dried rosemary, crushed
- 1 tsp. dried basil, crushed
- ¾ C. pecans, chopped
- ¾ C. walnuts, chopped
- 3 C. vegan breadcrumbs
- 2½ C. soy milk
- Salt and ground black pepper, as required

1. Preheat your oven to 350 °F. Lightly grease a loaf pan with cooking spray.
2. In a large-sized bowl, add all the ingredients and mix until well combined.
3. Transfer the mixture into the prepared loaf pan.
4. Bake for approximately 60-90 minutes or until top become golden brown.
5. Remove from the oven and place the loaf pan onto a wire rack for about 10 minutes.
6. Carefully invert the loaf onto a platter.
7. Cut into desired-sized slices and serve.

Per Serving:
Calories: 501| Fat: 26.3g| Carbs: 52.9g| Fiber: 6.8g| Protein: 16.5g

## MAC N' CHEESE
**Prep Time: 10 mins.| Cook Time: 10 mins.| Serves: 8**

- 16 oz. elbow macaroni
- 1½ C. raw cashews, soaked in water for 2 hours and drained
- ½ of garlic clove, peeled
- ¾ C. water
- 3 tbsp. fresh lemon juice
- ¼ C. nutritional yeast
- ½ tsp. yellow mustard
- ½ tsp. red chili powder
- ¼ tsp. ground turmeric
- Pinch of cayenne powder
- Salt and ground black pepper, as required
- 1/8 tsp. paprika

1. In a pan of lightly salted boiling water, cook the macaroni for about 8-10 minutes.
2. In a high-power blender, add the remaining ingredients except for paprika and pulse until smooth.
3. Drain the macaroni and return into the same pan.
4. Add the cashew sauce and stir to combine.
5. Serve immediately with the sprinkling of paprika.

Per Serving:
Calories: 378| Fat: 13.2g| Carbs: 53.4g| Fiber: 4g| Protein: 13.7g

## BAKED PUMPKIN MAC & CHEESE
**Prep Time: 15 mins.| Cook Time: 55 mins.| Serves: 8**

**For Pumpkin Sauce**
- ¾ C. cashews, soaked in water overnight
- 1 C. pumpkin puree
- 3 garlic cloves
- ¼ C. nutritional yeast
- ¼ tsp. ground nutmeg
- 1½ tsp. Salt
- 2 tbsp. olive oil
- 4¼ C. water

**For Macaroni**
- 12 oz. elbow macaroni
- 2 C. pumpkin, peeled, seeded and chopped
- 1 shallot, finely chopped

**For Topping**
- 1-1½ C. vegan breadcrumbs
- 2 tbsp. olive oil
- ½ tbsp. fresh rosemary, roughly chopped
- Salt and ground black pepper, as required

1. Preheat your oven to 425 °F. Arrange a rack in the middle of oven.
2. For sauce: in a high-power blender, add all ingredients and pulse until smooth and creamy.
3. In the bottom of a casserole dish, place the macaroni, pumpkin, and shallot and mix well.
4. Then spread the macaroni mixture in an even layer.
5. Place the pumpkin sauce over the macaroni mixture evenly and stir to combine.

6. With a piece of foil, cover the casserole dish tightly and bake for approximately 45 minutes.
7. Meanwhile, for topping: in a bowl, add all ingredients and mix well.
8. Remove the casserole dish from oven and stir the mixture well.
9. Top the casserole with breadcrumb mixture and bake for approximately 7-10 minutes.
10. Remove the casserole dish from oven and set aside for about 5 minutes before serving.

Per Serving:
Calories: 398| Fat: 14.9g| Carbs: 56.4g| Fiber: 6.4g| Protein: 12.8g

## MACARONI SALAD
**Prep Time: 15 mins.| Serves: 4**

**For Salad**
- 8 oz. cooked elbow macaroni
- 1 C. celery stalk, chopped
- 1 C. bell pepper, seeded and chopped
- 1/3 C. onion, chopped

**For Dressing**
- ¾ C. vegan mayonnaise
- 2 tbsp. apple cider vinegar
- 1 tbsp. prepared mustard
- 1 tsp. white sugar
- 1 tsp. salt
- ¼ tsp. ground black pepper

1. For salad: in a salad bowl, place all ingredients and mix.
2. For dressing: in another bowl, add all the ingredients and beat until well combined.
3. Pour the dressing over salad and gently stir to combine.
4. Refrigerate for at least 4 hours before serving.

Per Serving:
Calories: 201| Fat: 11.1g| Carbs: 23.3g| Fiber: 2.8g| Protein: 3.8g

## CORNBREAD
**Prep Time: 15 mins.| Cook Time: 28 mins.| Serves: 12**

- 1½ C. oat milk
- 2 tsp. apple cider vinegar
- 1½ C. plus 1 tsp. stone-ground yellow cornmeal, divided
- ¾ C. all-purpose flour
- 1 tbsp. plus 1 tsp. baking powder
- ½ tsp. salt
- 6 tbsp. vegan butter, melted and divided
- ¼ C. extra-virgin olive oil
- ¼ C. agave nectar
- ¼ C. brown sugar
- 1 tbsp. fresh rosemary, finely chopped

1. Preheat your oven to 400 °F. arrange a rack in the middle of oven.
2. In a bowl, blend the oat milk and vinegar. Set aside for about 5-10 minutes.
3. In a large-sized bowl, blend 1½ C. of cornmeal, flour, baking powder, and salt.
4. Make a well in the center of flour mixture.
5. In the well of flour mixture, place oat milk mixture, 4 tbsp. of melted butter, oil, agave nectar and brown sugar and gently mix until just smooth.
6. Gently fold in the rosemary.
7. Set aside for about 10 minutes or up to 1 hour.
8. Place a 10-inch cast-iron skillet into the pre-heated oven to heat up for about 10 minutes.
9. Carefully remove the heated skillet from oven and add in the remaining butter.
10. Now dust the skillet with remaining cornmeal evenly.
11. Place the cornbread batter into the hot skillet evenly.
12. Bake for approximately 25-28 minutes or until a toothpick inserted in the center comes out clean.
13. Remove the skillet from oven and place onto a wire rack for about 15-20 minutes.
14. Cut into desired-sized pieces and serve warm.

Per Serving:
Calories: 190| Fat: 5.5g| Carbs: 34.1g| Fiber: 10.4g| Protein: 3.2g

## FRENCH FRIES
**Prep Time: 15 mins.| Cook Time: 40 mins.| Serves: 4**

- 4 tbsp. canola, divided
- 3 large russet potatoes, cut into strips
- 1 tsp. white sugar
- 1 tsp. oregano

- ✓ 1 tsp. red chili powder
- ✓ ½ tsp. cayenne powder
- ✓ ½ tsp. paprika
- ✓ ½ tsp. onion powder
- ✓ ½ tsp. garlic powder
- ✓ Pinch of ground turmeric
- ✓ Salt and ground black pepper, as required

1. Preheat your oven to 475 °F. grease a baking dish with 3 tbsp. of oil.
2. In a bowl of hot water, place the potato strips for 20 minutes.
3. Drain potatoes and place them onto a paper towel to dry.
4. In a large-sized bowl, add sugar, oregano, spices, salt and black pepper and mix well.
5. Sprinkle 1/3 of the spice mixture in the bottom of the prepared baking dish evenly.
6. In a bowl, add the potato strips, remaining oil and a little spice mixture and toss to coat well.
7. Arrange the potato strips into the baking dish in a single layer.
8. With a piece of foil, cover the baking dish and bake for approximately 5 minutes.
9. Remove the foil and bake for approximately 15-20 minutes.
10. Flip the potato strip and bake for approximately 10-15 minutes more.
11. Remove from the oven and sprinkle with the remaining spice mixture.
12. Serve hot.

Per Serving:
Calories: 326| Fat: 14.5g| Carbs: 45.9g| Fiber: 7.2g| Protein: 49g

## AVOCADO FRIES
**Prep Time: 15 mins.| Cook Time: 25 mins.| Serves: 2**

- ✓ 1 firm avocado, peeled, pitted and cut into slices
- ✓ 2 tbsp. brown rice flour
- ✓ ½ tsp. garlic powder
- ✓ ¼ tsp. salt
- ✓ Pinch of ground black pepper
- ✓ 2 tbsp. soy milk
- ✓ 1/3 C. nutritional yeast

1. Preheat your oven to 350 °F. Line a large-sized baking sheet with parchment paper.
2. In a shallow dish, blend the flour, garlic powder, salt and black pepper.
3. Place the soy milk and nutritional yeast in 2 separate shallow bowls, respectively.
4. Coat each avocado slice in flour, then dip into milk, and finally coat with nutritional yeast.
5. Arrange the avocado slices onto the prepared baking sheet in a single layer.
6. Bake for approximately 25 minutes.
7. Serve hot.

Per Serving:
Calories: 358| Fat: 21.9g| Carbs: 30.2g| Fiber: 14.5g| Protein: 17.5g

## ONION RINGS
**Prep Time: 15 mins.| Cook Time: 10 mins.| Serves: 12**

- ✓ 1 C. beer
- ✓ 1 C. all-purpose flour
- ✓ Pinch of salt and ground black pepper
- ✓ 4 large, sweet onions, sliced into rings
- ✓ Vegetable oil, for deep frying

1. In a medium-sized-sized shallow bowl, mix together the beer, flour, salt, and black pepper.
2. Dip the onion rings in beer mixture evenly.
3. In a Dutch oven, heat oil over medium-high heat and fry the onion rings in 2 batches for about 4-5 minutes per batch or until golden brown.
4. With a slotted spoon, transfer the onion rings onto a paper towel-lined plate to drain.
5. Serve warm.

Per Serving:
Calories: 61| Fat: 0.1g| Carbs: 12.1g| Fiber: 1.1g| Protein: 1.6g

## HUSH PUPPIES
**Prep Time: 15 mins.| Cook Time: 10 mins.| Serves: 10**

- ✓ 2 tbsp. vegan egg replacer
- ✓ 2/3 C. plus ½ C. unsweetened almond milk, divided
- ✓ 1 C. cornmeal
- ✓ ¾ C. all-purpose flour
- ✓ 1 tbsp. white sugar
- ✓ 3 tsp. baking powder
- ✓ ¼ tsp. baking soda
- ✓ 1 tsp. ground cumin
- ✓ 1 tsp. red chili powder
- ✓ Salt, as required
- ✓ ½ C. shallots, chopped
- ✓ 1-2 jalapeño peppers, chopped
- ✓ Vegetable oil, for deep frying

1. In a medium-sized-sized bowl, add the egg replacer powder and 2/3 C. of almond milk and stir until well blended.

2. Add the remaining almond milk and mix well.
3. In a large-sized bowl, add cornmeal, flour, sugar, baking powder, baking soda, cumin, chili powder and salt and mix well.
4. Add the almond milk mixture and mi until just blended.
5. Gently fold in the shallots and jalapeño peppers.
6. In a large-sized Dutch oven, heat oil over medium-high heat.
7. With an ice cream scooper, place the mixture into the oil in 2 batches and fry for about 4-5 minutes or until golden brown completely.
8. With a slotted spoon, transfer the hush puppies onto a paper towels-lined plate to drain.
9. Serve warm.

Per Serving:
Calories: 102| Fat: 1.1g| Carbs: 20.5g| Fiber: 1.5g| Protein: 3.4g

## GRANOLA BARS
**Prep Time: 15 mins.| Cook Time: 30 mins.| Serves: 16**

- Non-stick cooking spray
- 1 tbsp. ground flaxseeds
- 3 tbsp. water
- 1 C. rolled oat
- 1 C. granola
- ½ C. white whole-wheat flour
- ½ C. mixed nut
- 2 tbsp. raisin
- 2 tbsp. dried cherries
- 2 tbsp. dried cranberries
- 3 tbsp. maple syrup
- 3 tbsp. canola oil
- 3 tbsp. brown sugar
- ½ tsp. ground cinnamon

1. Preheat your oven to 325 °F.
2. Line an 8x8x2-inch baking dish with a piece of foil and then grease it with cooking spray.
3. In a small-sized bowl, whisk together the ground flaxseeds and water. Set aside for about 10 minutes.
4. In a large-sized bowl, blend the oats, granola, flour, nuts, raisins, cherries and cranberries.
5. In the bowl of flaxseeds mixture, add the brown sugar, oil, maple syrup and cinnamon.
6. Add the sugar mixture into the bowl of granola mixture and mix until blended thoroughly.
7. Place the bar mixture into the prepared baking dish evenly and with the back of a spoon, smooth the top surface.
8. Bake for approximately 25-30 minutes.

9. Remove the baking dish of bras from oven and set aside to cool completely.
10. Cut into desired-sized bars and serve.

Per Serving:
Calories: 127| Fat: 9.4g| Carbs: 21.6g| Fiber: 3.1g| Protein: 4.3g

## APPLE COOKIES
**Prep Time: 15 mins.| Cook Time: 12 mins.| Serves: 18**

- Non-stick cooking spray
- ¼ C. warm water
- 2 tsp. chia seeds
- 2 C. quick oats, divided
- ½ tsp. baking soda
- ½ tsp. ground cinnamon
- ¼ tsp. ground nutmeg
- ¼ tsp. ground ginger
- ¼ C. golden raisins
- 1 large apple, peeled, cored and chopped
- 4 Medjool dates, pitted and chopped1
- tsp. apple cider vinegar
- 2 tbsp. cold water

1. Preheat your oven to 375 °F. Line a large-sized cookie sheet with parchment paper and then grease it with cooking spray.
2. In a bowl, mix together warm water and chia seeds.
3. Set aside until thickened
4. In a large-sized food processor, add 1 C. of the oats and pulse until finely ground.
5. Transfer the ground oats in a large-sized bowl.
6. Add the remaining oats, baking soda, spices and raisins and mix well.
7. Now in a high-power blender, add the remaining ingredients and pulse until smooth.
8. Transfer the apple mixture into the bowl with oat mixture and mix well.
9. Stir in the chia seeds mixture.
10. Spoon the mixture onto the prepared cookie sheet

in a single layer and with your finger, flatten each cookie slightly.
11. Bake for approximately 12 minutes or until golden brown.
12. Remove from oven and place the cookie sheet onto a wire rack to cool for about 5 minutes
13. Carefully invert the cookies onto wire rack to cool completely before serving.

Per Serving:
Calories: 64| Fat: 0.7g| Carbs: 13.6g| Fiber: 1.8g| Protein: 1.5g

## CHOCOLATE COOKIES
**Prep Time: 15 mins.| Cook Time: 14 mins.| Serves: 6**

- ✓ 2 medium ripe bananas, peeled
- ✓ 1 C. old-fashioned oats
- ✓ 2 scoops collagen protein powder
- ✓ 2 tbsp. unsalted peanut butter
- ✓ 2 tbsp. mini chocolate chips

1. Preheat your oven to 350 °F. Line a large-sized cookie sheet with parchment paper.
2. In a bowl, add bananas and with a fork, mash well.
3. Add the oats, protein powder and peanut butter and mix until blended thoroughly.
4. Gently fold in the chocolate chips.
5. With a cookie scooper, place the cookies onto the prepared cookie sheet about 2-inch apart.
6. With the fingers of your hand, flatten each cookie slightly.
7. Bake for approximately 12-14 minutes or until top of cookies becomes golden brown.
8. Remove the cookie sheet from oven and place onto a wire rack to cool for about 5 minutes.
9. Then invert the cookies onto the wire rack to cool before serving.

Per Serving:
Calories: 140| Fat: 4.7g| Carbs: 21.2g| Fiber: 2.8g| Protein: 4.6g

## FROZEN VANILLA YOGURT
**Prep Time: 15 mins.| Serves: 6**

- ✓ 3 C. coconut yogurt
- ✓ 4-6 drops liquid stevia
- ✓ 1 tsp. vanilla extract
- ✓ ¼ C. fresh strawberries, hulled and sliced

1. In a bowl, add all the ingredients except for strawberries and mix until well combined.
2. Transfer the mixture into an ice cream maker and process according to manufacturer's directions.
3. Transfer the mixture into a bowl and freeze, covered for about 30-40 minutes or until desired consistency.
4. Garnish with strawberry slices and serve.

Per Serving:
Calories: 59| Fat: 2g| Carbs: 7g| Fiber: 0.1g| Protein: 2g

## PEANUT BUTTER FUDGE
**Prep Time: 15 mins.| Serves: 16**

- ✓ 1½ C. creamy, salted peanut butter
- ✓ 1/3 C. coconut oil
- ✓ 2/3 C. powdered sugar
- ✓ ¼ C. vegan protein powder
- ✓ 1 tsp. vanilla extract

1. In a small-sized saucepan, add peanut butter and coconut oil over low heat and cook until melted and smooth.
2. Add sugar and protein powder and mix until smooth.
3. Remove from heat and stir in vanilla extract.
4. Place the fudge mixture into a baking paper-lined 8x8-inch baking dish evenly and with a spatula, smooth the top surface.
5. Freeze for about 30-45 minutes or until set completely.
6. Carefully transfer the fudge onto a cutting board with the help of parchment paper.
7. Cut the fudge into equal-sized squares and serve.

Per Serving:
Calories: 207| Fat: 16.6g| Carbs: 9.5g| Fiber: 3g| Protein: 6.5g

## CHICKPEAS FUDGE
**Prep Time: 15 mins.| Serves: 12**

- ✓ 2 C. cooked chickpeas
- ✓ 8 Medjool dates, pitted and chopped
- ✓ ½ C. almond butter

- ½ C. unsweetened almond milk
- 1 tsp. vanilla extract
- 2 tbsp. unsweetened cocoa powder

1. Line a large-sized baking dish with parchment paper
2. In a food processor, add all the ingredients except cocoa powder and pulse until well combined.
3. Transfer the mixture into a large-sized bowl and stir in the cocoa powder.
4. Transfer the mixture into the prepared baking dish evenly and with the back of a spatula, smooth the top surface.
5. Refrigerate for about 2 hours or until set completely.
6. Cut into desired-sized squares and serve.

Per Serving:
Calories: 176| Fat: 2.7g| Carbs: 33g| Fiber: 7.4g| Protein: 7.45g

## WALNUT BROWNIES

**Prep Time: 15 mins.| Cook Time: 18 mins.| Serves: 10**

- Non-stick cooking spray
- 2 tbsp. flaxseeds meal
- 6 tbsp. water
- 2 C. oats
- 1 C. white whole-wheat flour
- 2 scoops pea protein powder
- ¾ C. brown sugar
- ¼ C. unsweetened cocoa powder
- 1 tsp. baking soda
- 1 tsp. salt
- 2/3 C. applesauce
- 2/3 C. canola oil
- 1 tsp. vanilla extract
- 1/8 C. walnuts, chopped
- 1 tbsp. vegan mini semisweet chocolate chips

1. Preheat your oven to 350 °F. Grease a 9x13-inch baking dish with cooking spray.
2. In a small-sized bowl, add the flaxseeds meal and water and mix well.
3. Set aside for about 5 minutes.
4. In a large-sized bowl, mix together the oats, flour, brown sugar, protein powder, cocoa powder, baking soda and salt.
5. Add the applesauce, oil, vanilla extract and flax mixture and mix until a thick dough forms.
6. Fold in the walnuts and chocolate chips.
7. Place the mixture into the prepared baking dish and with your hands, press to smooth the surface.
8. Bake for approximately 15-18 minutes.
9. Remove from oven and place onto a wire rack to cool completely.
10. Cut into equal-sized brownies and serve.

Per Serving:
Calories: 329| Fat: 18.3g| Carbs: 34.8g| Fiber: 4.3g| Protein: 9.5g

## CINNAMON DONUTS

**Prep Time: 15 mins.| Cook Time: 10 mins.| Serves: 8**

**For Donuts**
- Non-stick cooking spray
- 1 C. all-purpose flour
- ½ C. granulated white sugar
- 1 tsp. baking powder
- ¼ tsp. salt
- ½ tsp. ground cinnamon
- ½ C. plus 2 tbsp. soy milk
- 1 tbsp. vegan butter, melted
- 1 tbsp. applesauce
- 1 tsp. pure vanilla extract

**For Topping**
- ½ C. granulated white sugar
- 1 tsp. ground cinnamon
- ¼ C. vegan butter, melted

1. Preheat your oven to 350 °F. Grease a donut pan with cooking spray.
2. In a large-sized bowl, blend the flour, sugar, baking powder, salt and cinnamon.
3. Add in the soy milk, vegan butter, applesauce and vanilla extract and mix until well combined.
4. Place the mixture into the prepared donut pan evenly.
5. Bake for approximately 9-10 minutes.
6. Remove the donut pan from oven and place onto a wire rack for about 2-3 minutes.
7. Then carefully transfer the donuts onto the wire rack.
8. Meanwhile, for topping: in a bowl, blend the sugar and cinnamon.
9. In another bowl, place the melt the vegan butter.
10. Dip the warm donuts into the melted butter and then sprinkle with cinnamon sugar mixture.
11. Serve immediately.

Per Serving:
Calories: 186| Fat: 0.9g| Carbs: 43.5g| Fiber: 1.6g| Protein: 3.1g

## MINI BLACKBERRY PIES

**Prep Time: 25 mins.| Cook Time: 40 mins.| Serves: 8**

**For Pie Dough**
- 2¼ C. whole-wheat pastry flour plus more for dusting
- 1 tbsp. granulated white sugar
- ½ tsp. salt
- 12 tbsp. frozen vegan butter, cubed
- 4-6 tbsp. ice-cold water
- 1 tbsp. apple cider vinegar

**For Blackberry Jam**
- 2 C. fresh blackberries
- 1 tbsp. fresh lemon juice
- 1 tbsp. maple syrup
- 1½ tsp. tapioca flour

**For Topping**
- 2-3 tbsp. olive oil
- 3-4 tbsp. white sugar

1. For dough: in a food processor, add flour, sugar and salt and pulse until well combined.
2. Add in the butter cubes and pulse until a coarse meal-like mixture is formed.
3. Add in ice-cold water, 1 tbsp. at a time and pulse until dough comes together.
4. Divide the dough into 2 equal-sized round disks and refrigerate for 1 hour.
5. Meanwhile, for blackberry jam: in a saucepan, add blackberries over medium heat and cook for about 8 minutes, stirring occasionally.
6. Adjust the heat to medium-low and with a potato masher, mash the blackberries.
7. Add in lemon juice, maple syrup and tapioca flour and cook for about 3-4 minutes, stirring continuously.
8. Transfer the jam into a heatproof bowl and set aside to cool.
9. Line a large-sized baking sheet with parchment paper.
10. Place the dough portions onto a lightly floured surface and roll each into 1/8-inch thick circle.
11. With a 3½-inch round biscuit cutter, cut each rolled dough circle into 8 circles.
12. Arrange 8 dough circles onto the prepared baking sheet.
13. For top crusts: place remaining 8 dough circles onto a smooth surface and make 4 cuts into each.
14. Place about 1 tbsp. of blackberry jam over 8 dough circles arrange onto the baking sheet.
15. Cover with top dough circles and with your fingers, press edges together.
16. Freeze the baking sheet of pies for about 20-25 minutes.
17. Preheat your oven to 375 °F.
18. Remove the baking sheet of pies from freezer and brush the top of each with oil.
19. Then sprinkle each pie with sugar.
20. Bake for approximately 25-30 minutes or until edges are golden.
21. Remove from the oven and set aside for about 20 minutes before serving.

Per Serving:
Calories: 271| Fat: 5.1g| Carbs: 52.9g| Fiber: 4.9g| Protein: 6.2g

## CHOCOLATE CUPCAKES
**Prep Time: 15 mins.| Cook Time: 20 mins.| Serves: 6**

**For Cuocakes**
- 1 C. water
- 1 C. dates, pitted
- 1 C. oat flour
- 1/3 C. unsweetened cocoa powder
- 1 tbsp. baking powder
- ¼ tsp. salt
- ¼ C. almond milk

**For Topping**
- 2 tbsp. walnuts, chopped

1. For frosting: in a food processor, add all the ingredients and pulse until smooth.
2. Transfer into a bowl and refrigerate to chill for at least 3 hours.
3. Preheat your oven to 350 °F. Line 6 cups of a muffin tin with paper liners.
4. In a food processor, add water and dates and pulse until smooth.
5. In a large-sized bowl, mix together flour, cacao powder, baking powder and salt.
6. Add the almond milk and date paste and beat until well combined.
7. Transfer the mixture into paper muffin cups about ¾ of full.
8. Bake for 25 minutes or until a toothpick inserted in the center comes out clean.
9. Remove the muffin tin from oven and place onto a wire rack to cool for about 10 minutes.
10. Carefully invert the cupcakes onto a wire rack to cool completely before frosting.
11. Spread frosting over each cupcake evenly.
12. Top with walnuts and serve.

Per Serving:
Calories: 351| Fat: 12g| Carbs: 64.1g| Fiber: 9.6g| Protein: 6.7g

## RED VELVET CAKE
**Prep Time: 20 mins.| Cook Time: 20 mins.| Serves: 12**

**For Cake**
- Non-stick cooking spray
- 1 C. soy milk
- 1 tbsp. fresh lemon juice
- 2 C. all-purpose flour, sifted
- 1 C. granulated white sugar
- 1 tbsp. unsweetened cocoa powder, sifted
- 1 tsp. baking soda
- ½ tsp. salt
- ½ C. canola oil
- 1 tbsp. distilled white vinegar
- 2 tsp. vanilla extract
- 1 tsp. red gel food color

**For Frosting**
- 4 C. powdered sugar
- ½ C. vegan butter, softened
- 2-3 tbsp. fresh lemon juice
- 2 tsp. lemon extract

**For Decoration**
- ¼ C. pecans, chopped

1. Preheat your oven to 350 °F. Grease 3 (6-inch) cake pans with cooking spray and then line the bottoms of each with circles of parchment paper.
2. In a small-sized bowl, add the soy milk and lemon juice and mix well. Set aside for about 10 minutes.
3. In a large-sized bowl, blend the flour, white sugar, cocoa powder, baking soda and salt.
4. Add the soy milk mixture, oil, vinegar, vanilla extract and red food color and mix until just combined.
5. Divide the mixture into the prepared cake pans evenly.
6. Bake for approximately 20 minutes or until a toothpick inserted into the center of one of the cakes comes out clean.
7. Remove the cake pans from oven and place onto a wire rack for about 5-10 minutes.
8. Now invert the cakes onto the wire rack to cool completely before frosting.
9. For frosting: in a bowl, add all ingredients and with a wire whisk, beat until thick and smooth.
10. Place 1 cake onto a serving plate, flat side down.
11. With a knife, trim off the top dome of cake to create a flat bottom.
12. Spread some frosting over the top of cake evenly.
13. Place second cake layer on top and spread some frosting on top.
14. Now place the third cake on top.
15. Cover the top and sides of cake with remaining frosting.
16. Decorate with pecans and serve.

Per Serving:

Calories: 434| Fat: 12.3g| Carbs: 79.6g| Fiber: 2.1g| Protein: 4.1g

## APPLE PIE
**Prep Time: 25 mins.| Cook Time: 1 hr.| Serves: 8**

**For Crust**
- 2½ C. all-purpose flour, plus more for dusting
- 1 tbsp. white sugar
- 1 tsp. salt
- 1 C. chilled vegan butter, cubed
- 6 tbsp. ice water
- Non-stick cooking spray

**For Filling**
- 7 granny smith apples, peeled and cored and thinly sliced
- 2 C. plus 1 tsp. white sugar, divided
- 5 tbsp. cornstarch
- 1 tbsp. plus 1 tsp. coconut oil, melted and divided
- 1 tbsp. fresh lemon juice
- 1-2 tsp. lemon zest, grated
- 4 tsp. ground cinnamon, divided
- ½ tsp. salt

1. For crust: in a large-sized bowl, blend the flour, sugar, and salt.
2. With a fork, cut in the butter until a crumbly mixture forms.
3. Slowly add the ice water and until just the dough comes together.
4. Divide the dough in 2 equal-sized portions and then shape each into a disk.
5. With plastic wrap, cover each dough disk and refrigerate for at least 1 hour.
6. Preheat your oven to 350 °F. Grease an 8-inch pie dish with cooking spray.
7. For filling: in a large-sized bowl, add apple slices, 2 C. of sugar, cornstarch, 1 tsp. of coconut oil, lemon juice, zest, 3 tsp. of cinnamon and salt and toss to coat well. Set aside.
8. Place dough disks onto a lightly floured surface and roll each into 1-inch thickness.

9. Arrange 1 rolled dough round into the prepared pie dish and gently press against the bottom and sides.
10. Carefully trim the excess dough around the edges and then with a fork, prick the bottom.
11. Place the apple mixture over the bottom crust and cover with the remaining dough round.
12. Carefully trim the excess dough around the edges and then with a fork, crimp the top and bottom crusts together.
13. Brush the top of the crust with the remaining melted coconut oil and sprinkle with the remaining sugar and cinnamon.
14. With a knife, cut 4 vents in the top crust.
15. Bake for approximately 1 hour, until crust becomes golden brown.
16. Remove the pie dish from oven and set aside for about 10 minutes before serving.

Per Serving:
Calories: 517 | Fat: 3.4g | Carbs: 122g | Fiber: 8.8g | Protein: 6.8g

# MEXICAN RECIPES

### BEANS & POMEGRANATE SALAD
**Prep Time: 15 mins. | Serves: 3**

- 2 C. canned white kidney beans, rinsed and drained
- 1 C. fresh pomegranate seeds
- 1/3 C. scallion (green part), finely chopped
- 2 tbsp. fresh cilantro, chopped
- 1 tbsp. fresh lime juice
- Salt and ground black pepper, as required

1. In a large-sized salad bowl, place all the ingredients and toss to coat well.
2. Serve immediately.

Per Serving:
Calories: 180 | Fat: 0g | Carbs: 35g | Fiber: 14.1g | Protein: 12g

### BEANS & CORN SALAD
**Prep Time: 15 mins. | Serves: 8**

**For Salad**
- 1 (10-oz.) package frozen corn kernels, thawed
- 3 (15-oz.) cans black beans, rinsed and drained
- 2 large red bell peppers, seeded and chopped
- 1 large red onion, chopped

**For Dressing**
- ¼ C. fresh cilantro, minced
- 1 garlic clove, minced
- 1 tbsp. maple syrup
- ½ C. balsamic vinegar
- ½ C. olive oil
- 1 tbsp. fresh lime juice
- 1 tbsp. fresh lemon juice
- ½ tsp. red pepper flakes, crushed
- Salt and ground black pepper, as required

1. For salad: add all the ingredients in a large-sized serving bowl and mix well.
2. For dressing: add all the ingredients in a bowl and beat until well combined.
3. Place the dressing over salad and gently toss to coat well.
4. Serve immediately.

Per Serving:
Calories: 310 | Fat: 14.3g | Carbs: 36.5g | Fiber: 9.5g | Protein: 10.7g

### BEANS & MANGO SALAD
**Prep Time: 20 mins. | Serves: 6**

**For Dressing**
- ¼ C. fresh lime juice
- 2 tbsp. maple syrup
- 1 tbsp. Dijon mustard
- ½ tsp. ground cumin
- 1 tsp. garlic powder
- Salt and ground black pepper, as required
- ½ C. extra-virgin olive oil

**For Salad**
- 2 C. fresh mango, peeled, pitted and cubed
- 2 tbsp. fresh lime juice, divided
- 2 avocados, peeled, pitted and cubed
- Pinch of salt
- 1 C. cooked quinoa
- 2 (14-oz.) cans black beans, rinsed and drained
- 1 (15¼-oz.) can corn, rinsed and drained
- 1 small red onion, chopped
- 1 jalapeño pepper, seeded and finely chopped
- ½ C. fresh cilantro, chopped
- 6 C. romaine lettuce, shredded

1. For dressing: in a high-power blender, add all the ingredients except oil and pulse until well combined.
2. While the motor is running, gradually add the oil and pulse until smooth.
3. For salad: in a bowl, add the mango and 1 tbsp. of lime juice and toss to coat well.
4. In another bowl, add the avocado, a Pinch of salt and remaining lime juice and toss to coat well.
5. In a large-sized serving bowl, add the mango, avocado and remaining salad ingredients and mix.
6. Place the dressing and toss to coat well.

7. Serve immediately.

Per Serving:
Calories: 631| Fat: 33.6g| Carbs: 73g| Fiber: 16.4g| Protein: 15.9g

## MIXED BEANS SALAD
**Prep Time: 15 mins.| Serves: 8**

**For Salad**
- 1½ C. cooked cannellini beans
- 1½ C. cooked red kidney beans
- 1½ C. cooked black beans
- 2 C. cucumber, chopped
- 1 C. onion, chopped
- 1½ C. plum tomato, chopped

**For Dressing**
- 1 garlic clove, minced
- 2 tbsp. shallots, minced
- 2 tsp. lemon zest, grated finely
- ¼ C. fresh lime juice
- 2 tbsp. extra-virgin olive oil
- Salt and ground black pepper, as required

1. For salad: in a large-sized serving bowl, add the couscous and remaining ingredients and stir to combine.
2. For dressing: in another small bowl, add all the ingredients and beat until well combined.
3. Pour the dressing over the salad and gently toss to coat well.
4. Serve immediately.

Per Serving:
Calories: 327| Fat: 4.5g| Carbs: 54.9g| Fiber: 15.4g| Protein: 19.4g

## BBBQ TOFU & BEANS SALAD
**Prep Time: 20 mins.| Cook Time: 30 mins.| Serves: 6**

- 1 (16-oz.) package tofu, pressed, drained and cubed
- 1 C. BBQ sauce, divided
- ½ C. vegan mayonnaise
- ¼ C. soy milk
- 1/8 C. fresh parsley, chopped
- 1 tsp. garlic powder
- Salt and ground black pepper, as required
- 1 (15-oz.) can black beans, drained and rinsed
- 1 C. corn
- 8 C. lettuce, chopped
- 4 medium tomatoes, chopped
- 2 C. carrots, peeled and shredded
- 2 avocados, peeled, pitted and chopped

1. In a bowl, add tofu cubes and ½ C. of BBQ sauce and toss to coat well.
2. Refrigerate to marinade for at least 20-30 minutes.
3. Preheat your oven to 400 °F.
4. Lightly grease a large-sized baking sheet.
5. Remove the tofu cubes from bowl and place onto the prepared baking sheet in a single layer.
6. Bake for approximately 15 minutes.
7. Remove the baking sheet from oven and flip the tofu cubes.
8. Coat the tofu cubes with remaining BBQ sauce lightly.
9. Bake for approximately 10-15 minutes.
10. Remove from the oven and set aside to cool slightly.
11. Meanwhile, for dressing: in a bowl, add mayonnaise, soy milk, parsley, garlic powder, salt, black pepper and 3 tbsp. of BBQ sauce and beat until well combined.
12. Divide beans, corn, lettuce, tomatoes, carrots, avocado and tofu onto serving plates.
13. Drizzle with dressing and serve.

Per Serving:
Calories: 462| Fat: 22.2g| Carbs: 55.2g| Fiber: 14.8g| Protein: 16.4g

## VEGETARIAN TACO BOWL
**Prep Time: 15 mins.| Serves: 2**

- 2 tsp. olive oil
- 1 bell pepper, seeded and chopped
- 1 red onion, sliced
- 1 C. canned black beans, rinsed and drained
- ½ C. frozen corn, thawed
- 3 C. lettuce, chopped
- 1 jalapeño pepper, seeded and minced
- 1 tbsp. fresh lime juice
- ¼ C. salsa

1. Divide the beans, corn, veggies, lettuce and jalapeño pepper into serving bowls.
2. Drizzle with lime juice and serve alongside the salsa.

Per Serving:
Calories: 257| Fat: 6.5g| Carbs: 39.9g| Fiber: 10.2g| Protein: 11g

## RICE, BEANS & CORN BOWLS
**Prep Time: 15 mins.| Serves: 6**

- 1 (15-oz.) cans black beans, rinsed and drained
- 1 (15-oz.) cans corn, drained
- 4 fresh tomatoes, diced
- ½ C. red onion, chopped
- ½ C. fresh cilantro, chopped
- 1 jalapeño pepper, seeded and diced
- 2 tbsp. fresh lime juice
- 1 tbsp. olive oil
- Salt and ground black pepper, as required
- 2 dashes hot sauce
- 6 C. hot cooked brown rice

1. In a serving bowl, add all the ingredients except the rice and mix well.
2. Divide the hot rice in serving bowls and top with the beans mixture evenly.
3. Serve immediately.

Per Serving:
Calories: 391| Fat: 4.9g| Carbs: 77.1g| Fiber: 10.2g| Protein: 13g

## TEMPEH BURRITO BOWL
**Prep Time: 15 mins.| Cook Time: 16 mins.| Serves: 2**

**For Tempe**
- 1 tbsp. avocado oil
- 2 garlic cloves, mince
- 6 oz. tempeh, crumbled
- 1 C. vegetable broth
- 1 tbsp. tomato paste
- ½ tsp. dried oregano
- 2 tsp. red chili powder
- 1 tsp. smoked paprika
- ½ tsp. cayenne powder
- ½ tsp. ground cumin
- Salt and ground black pepper, as required

**For Serving**
- 1 C. cooked wild rice
- 1 roasted sweet potato, cubed
- 1 C. sweet corn
- 1 avocado, peeled, pitted and sliced

1. For tempeh: a large-sized skillet, heat the avocado oil over medium heat and sauté the garlic for about 3 minutes.
2. Add the tempeh broth, tomato paste, oregano and spices and stir to combine.
3. Adjust the heat to medium-low and cook for about 10-15 minutes, stirring frequently.
4. Divide the tempeh, rice, sweet potato, corn and avocado into serving bowls evenly and serve.

Per Serving:
Calories: 607| Fat: 31.2g| Carbs: 67.8g| Fiber: 12.2g| Protein: 23.7g

## SQUASH WITH CORN
**Prep Time: 15 mins.| Cook Time: 35 mins.| Serves: 6**

- 1 onion, chopped
- 4 tsp. olive oil
- 4 medium yellow squashes, cubed
- ½ C. green chilies, chopped
- 1 (16-oz.) can whole kernel corn, drained
- Salt and ground black pepper, as required
- ½ C. vegan cheese, shredded
- ¼ C. unsweetened almond milk

1. In a saucepan, heat the oil and stir fry the onion for about 4-5 minutes.
2. Add the squash and chilies and stir to combine.
3. Cover the pan and cook for about 18-20 minutes.
4. Stir in the corn, salt and black pepper and cook for about 5 minutes
5. Stir in the cheese and almond milk and cook for about 2-3 minutes, stirring frequently.
6. Serve hot.

Per Serving:
Calories: 151| Fat: 6.1g| Carbs: 23.9g| Fiber: 4.9g| Protein: 4.8g

## TOFU BURRITO BOWLS
**Prep Time: 20 mins.| Cook Time: 20 mins.| Serves: 4**

**For Tofu**
- 2 poblano peppers
- ½ C. vegetable broth
- 4 chipotle peppers in adobo sauce
- 2 tbsp. adobo sauce
- 2 tbsp. tomato paste
- 2 garlic cloves, minced
- 1 tsp. ancho chile powder

- ½ tsp. dried oregano, crushed
- ½ tsp. ground cumin
- ½ tsp. salt
- ½ tsp. ground black pepper
- 1 tsp. vegetable oi
- 16 oz. extra-firm tofu, pressed, drained and crumbled

**For Burrito Bowl**
- 2 C. cooked brown rice
- 1½ C. cooked black beans
- ½ C. fresh corn kernels
- 4 C. romaine lettuce, shredded
- 2 avocados, peeled, pitted and chopped
- 1 C. salsa
- ½ C. cashew cheese sauce
- 2 tbsp. fresh cilantro, chopped

1. Preheat the broiler of oven.
2. For tofu: arrange the poblano peppers onto a baking sheet and place broil for about 3-5 minutes per side or until charred.
3. Remove the poblano peppers from oven and set aside to cool.
4. After cooling, peel off the outer skin of peppers and then remove the seeds.
5. In a food processor, add the peppers and remaining ingredients except for oil and tofu and pulse until smooth.
6. In a large-sized non-stick wok, heat oil over medium-high heat and cook the tofu and sauce for about 10 minutes, stirring frequently.
7. Remove the wok from heat.
8. Divide the tofu rice, black beans, corn kernels, lettuce and avocados into serving bowls.
9. Top with the salsa, cheese sauce and cilantro and serve.

Per Serving:
Calories: 623| Fat: 32.5g| Carbs: 66g| Fiber: 16.6g| Protein: 25.4g

## STUFFED AVOCADO
**Prep Time: 15 mins.| Serves: 2**

- 1 large avocado, halved and pitted
- ¾ C. cooked chickpeas
- ¼ C. tomato, chopped
- ¼ C. cucumber, chopped
- ¼ C. onion, chopped
- 1 small garlic clove, minced
- 1 tbsp. fresh cilantro, chopped
- 1½ tbsp. fresh lime juice
- ½ tsp. olive oil

1. With a small-sized spoon, scoop out the flesh from each avocado half.
2. Then, cut half of the avocado flesh into equal-sized cubes.
3. In a large-sized bowl, add avocado cubes and remaining ingredients and toss to coat well.
4. Stuff each avocado half with the chickpeas mixture evenly and serve immediately.

Per Serving:
Calories: 337Fat: 11.9g| Carbs: 32.2g| Fiber: 4.4g| Protein: 7g

## BEANS & WALNUT BURGERS
**Prep Time: 20 mins.| Cook Time: 25 mins.| Serves: 8**

- ½ C. walnuts
- 1 carrot, peeled and chopped
- 1 celery stalk, chopped
- 4 scallions, chopped
- 5 garlic cloves, chopped
- 2¼ C. canned black beans, rinsed and drained
- 2½ C. sweet potatoes, peeled and grated
- ½ tsp. red pepper flakes, crushed
- ¼ tsp. cayenne powder
- Salt and ground black pepper, as required

1. Preheat your oven to 400 °F. Line a baking sheet with parchment paper
2. In a food processor, add the walnuts and pulse until finely ground.
3. Add the carrot, celery, scallion and garlic and pulse until finely chopped.
4. Transfer the vegetable mixture into a large-sized bowl.
5. In the same food processor, add the beans and pulse until chopped.
6. Add 1½ C. of the sweet potato and pulse until a chunky mixture forms.
7. Transfer the bean mixture into the bowl with vegetable mixture.
8. Stir in remaining sweet potato and spices and mix until well combined.

9. Make 8 equal-sized patties from the mixture.
10. Arrange the patties onto the prepared baking sheet in a single layer.
11. Bake for approximately 25 minutes.
12. Serve hot.

Per Serving:
Calories: 300| Fat: 5.5g| Carbs: 49.8g| Fiber: 11.4g| Protein: 15.3g

## BEANS & OATS BURGERS
**Prep Time: 20 mins.| Cook Time: 16 mins.| Serves: 8**

- Non-stick cooking spray
- 1 tbsp. olive oil
- 1 large onion, finely chopped
- 4 garlic cloves, minced
- 1 medium carrot, peeled and shredded
- 2 tsp. red chili powder
- 1 tsp. ground cumin
- Ground black pepper, as required
- 1 (15-oz.) can pinto beans, rinsed and drained
- 1 (15-oz.) can black beans, rinsed and drained
- 1½ C. quick-cooking oats
- 2 tbsp. low-sodium soy sauce
- 2 tbsp. Dijon mustard
- 1 tbsp. ketchup

1. Preheat the grill to medium heat. Grease the grill grate with cooking spray.
2. In a large-sized non-stick skillet, heat oil over medium-high heat and sauté the onion for about 2 minutes.
3. Add the garlic and sauté for about 1 minute.
4. Stir in carrot and spices and cook for about 2-3 minutes, stirring frequently.
5. Remove from heat and set aside.
6. In a large-sized bowl, add both cans of beans and with a potato masher, mash slightly.
7. Add the carrot mixture, oats, soy sauce, mustard and ketchup and mix until well combined.
8. Make 8 patties from the mixture.
9. Place the patties onto the grill and cook, covered for about 4-5 minutes per side or until desired doneness.
10. Serve hot.

Per Serving:
Calories: 356| Fat: 4.5g| Carbs: 61.4g| Fiber: 15.7g| Protein: 19.3g

## SPINACH QUESADILLAS
**Prep Time: 15 mins.| Cook Time: 8 mins.| Serves: 4**

- 4 vegan whole-wheat tortillas
- 1 tbsp. olive oil
- 2 scallions, chopped
- 1¼ C. vegan cheese, grated
- 1 bunch fresh spinach, chopped
- ¼ tsp. garlic salt
- ¼ tsp. red chili powder

1. In a large-sized frying pan, heat the oil over medium heat.
2. Place 1 tortilla in the pan and top with half of the cheese, followed by half of the scallion, half of the spinach, half of the garlic salt and chili powder.
3. Cover with another tortilla and carefully flip it.
4. Cook for about 2-3 minutes.
5. Repeat with the remaining tortillas and filling.
6. Cut each quesadilla into quarters and serve.

Per Serving:
Calories: 177| Fat: 10.5g| Carbs: 17g| Fiber: 4.6g| Protein: 4.5g

## VEGGIE TACOS
**Prep Time: 20 mins.| Cook Time: 16 mins.| Serves: 4**

**For Tortillas**
- ½ C. dry black beans, rinsed and drained
- ¾ C. water
- 1/8 tsp. salt

**For Tacos**
- 1 avocado, peeled, pitted and sliced
- 1 large tomato, sliced
- ½ C. fresh baby greens
- ¼ C. pomegranate seeds
- 1 red chili, seeded and sliced
- 2 scallions, sliced
- ¼ C. peanut butter
- 1 lime, cut into 4 wedges

1. In a large-sized bowl of water, soak the beans for at least 12 hours.
2. Drain the beans and rinse well.
3. In a high-power blender, add beans, water and salt and pulse until smooth.
4. Transfer the beans puree into a bowl.
5. Heat a non-stick skillet over medium heat.
6. Add about 1/3 C. of mixture and wait for about 5-10 seconds.
7. With a metal spoon, spread the mixture into a 7-inch circle and cook for about 2-2½ minutes.
8. Carefully flip the tortilla and cook for about 1 minute.
9. Transfer the tortilla onto a cooling rack to cool completely.

10. Repeat with the remaining mixture.
11. Arrange the tortillas onto a smooth surface.
12. Divide the avocado, tomato, greens, pomegranate seeds, red chili and scallion onto each tortilla.
13. Top with peanut butter and serve alongside the lime wedges.

Per Serving:
Calories: 245| Fat: 18.3g| Carbs: 16.7g| Fiber: 6.8g| Protein: 7.5g

### BLACK BEANS ENCHILADAS
**Prep Time: 20 mins.| Cook Time: 25 mins.| Serves: 6**

- 1 tbsp. canola oil
- 1 medium yellow onion, finely chopped
- 2 garlic cloves, minced
- 3 tbsp. red chili powder
- 2 tsp. cumin powder
- 1 tsp. salt
- 2 C. cooked black bean
- 2 C. tomato puree
- 8 oz. vegan cheese
- ½ C. plus 1 tbsp. fresh cilantro, chopped
- 1 medium jalapeño pepper, seeded and finely chopped
- 12 (5½-inch) corn tortillas, warmed

1. In a skillet, heat the oil over medium heat and sauté the onion and garlic for about 3 minutes.
2. Add the chili powder, cumin and salt and sauté for about 2 minutes.
3. Stir in the beans and tomato puree and bring to a boil.
4. Adjust the heat to low with a potato masher, mash the beans.
5. Simmer for about 5 minutes.
6. Remove the bean mixture from the heat and, through a fine-mesh strainer, strain the mixture, reserving the sauce into a bowl.
7. In another large bowl, add the strained bean mixture, 4 oz. of the vegan cheese, ½ C. of cilantro and jalapeño pepper and mix well.
8. Preheat your oven to 350 °F.
9. In the bottom of a baking dish, spread ½ C. of the sauce evenly.
10. Arrange the tortillas onto a smooth surface.
11. Place about ¼ C. of bean mixture into each tortilla and roll it up tightly.
12. Place the rolled tortillas over the sauce in the baking dish, seam-side down.
13. Brush the ends of each tortilla with some of the remaining sauce.
14. Place the remaining sauce over the enchiladas evenly, followed by the remaining cheese.

15. With a piece of foil, cover the baking dish and bake for approximately 20 minutes.
16. Remove the foil and bake for approximately 2-3 minutes more.
17. Serve warm with the garnishing of remaining cilantro.

Per Serving:
Calories: 462| Fat: 10.4g| Carbs: 76.5g| Fiber: 17.7g| Protein: 21.7g

### BEANS & PINEAPPLE ENCHILADAS
**Prep Time: 15 mins.| Cook Time: 50 mins.| Serves: 8**

- 1 (20-oz.) can pineapple tidbits
- 2 tsp. vegetable oil
- 1 large yellow onion, chopped
- 1 medium red bell pepper, chopped
- 1 (15-oz.) cans black beans, drained and rinsed
- 1 (4½-oz.) can chopped green chiles
- 1 tsp. salt
- ¾ C. fresh cilantro, chopped and divided
- 1 (10-oz.) can mild enchilada sauce
- 8 whole-wheat flour tortillas

1. Preheat your oven to 350 °F. Lightly grease a 13x9-inch baking dish.
2. Drain the can of pineapple, reserving 1/3 C. of juice.
3. In a wok, heat the oil over medium heat and sauté the bell pepper and onion for about 5-6 minutes.
4. Add the beans, pineapple, green chiles and salt and cook for about 3-4 minutes, stirring frequently.
5. Remove from the heat and immediately stir in ½ C. of the cilantro.
6. Arrange the tortillas onto a smooth surface.
7. Place about 1 tbsp. of the enchilada sauce onto each tortilla evenly, followed by ¾ C. of the vegetable mixture.
8. Roll each tortilla like a burrito.
9. In a bowl, add the remaining enchilada sauce and reserved pineapple juice and mix until well combined.
10. In the bottom of the prepared baking dish, arrange the rolled tortillas in a single layer, seam side down.
11. Top with pineapple juice mixture evenly.
12. With a piece of foil, cover the baking dish tightly.
13. Bake for approximately 35-40 minutes.
14. In the last 5-10 minutes of cooking, remove the foil piece.
15. Serve warm with a garnishing of remaining cilantro.

Per Serving:

Calories: 285| Fat: 4.4g| Carbs: 53.6g| Fiber: 8.8g| Protein: 10.1g

## LENTIL SOUP
**Prep Time: 15 mins.| Cook Time: 50 mins.| Serves: 6**

- 2 tbsp. extra-virgin olive oil
- 2 carrots, peeled and chopped
- 2 celery stalks, chopped
- 1 yellow onion, chopped
- 1 red bell pepper, seeded and chopped
- 3 garlic cloves, minced
- 1 tbsp. ground cumin
- ¼ tsp. smoked paprika
- 1 tsp. dried oregano
- 2 C. green lentils, rinsed
- 1 (15-oz.) can diced tomatoes with juices
- 2 (4-oz.) cans chopped green chilies
- 8 C. vegetable broth
- Dash of hot sauce
- Salt and ground black pepper, as required
- 1 avocado, peeled, pitted, and chopped
- 3 tbsp. fresh cilantro, chopped

1. In a large-sized soup pan, heat olive oil over medium heat and sauté the carrots, celery, onion, and bell pepper for about 5 minutes.
2. Add garlic, cumin, paprika, and oregano and sauté for about 1 minute.
3. Add lentils, tomatoes, chilies and broth and bring to a simmer.
4. Adjust the heat to low and simmer for about 30-40 minutes.
5. Stir in hot sauce, salt and black pepper and remove from heat.
6. Serve hot with the garnishing of avocado and cilantro.

Per Serving:
Calories: 430| Fat: 14.8g| Carbs: 53.8g| Fiber: 10.6g| Protein: 23g

## PASTA, BEANS & CORN SOUP
**Prep Time: 15 mins.| Cook Time: 25 mins.| Serves: 4**

- 1 (28-oz.) can diced tomatoes with juice
- 3 C. water
- 1 (15½-oz.) can kidney beans
- 1¼ C. frozen corn
- 1 C. whole-wheat rotini pasta
- ¼ C. wheat germ
- Dash of hot pepper sauce

1. In a large-sized pan, add all the ingredients over high heat and cook until boiling.
2. Now adjust the heat to low and cook for about 18-20 minutes.
3. Serve hot.

Per Serving:
Calories: 258| Fat: 2.1g| Carbs: 48.3g| Fiber: 14.5g| Protein: 13.9g

## RICE & BEANS SOUP
**Prep Time: 15 mins.| Cook Time: 45 mins.| Serves: 6**

- 1 C. long-grain brown rice
- 1 medium onion, chopped
- 4 garlic cloves, minced
- 1 (15-oz.) can pinto beans, drained and rinsed
- 1 (15-oz.) can black beans, drained and rinsed
- 1 (15-oz.) can kidney beans, drained and rinsed
- 1 (15-oz.) can fire-roasted tomatoes
- 1 tbsp. red chili powder
- Salt, as required
- 6 C. vegetable broth

4. Heat a non-stick frying pan over medium-high heat and toast the rice for about 5 minutes, stirring continuously.
5. Transfer the toasted rice into ab bowl and set aside.
6. In a large-sized soup pan, heat the oil over medium-high heat and sauté the onion and garlic for about 4-5 minutes.
7. Add in the toasted rice, beans, tomatoes, red chili powder, salt and broth and bring to a boil.
8. Adjust the heat to low and simmer for about 25-30 minutes.
9. Serve hot.

Per Serving:
Calories: 420| Fat: 3.5g| Carbs: 75.1g| Fiber: 19.4g| Protein: 24.4g

## HOMINY & VEGGIES STEW

**Prep Time: 15 mins.| Cook Time: 55 mins.| Serves: 10**

- 2 (25-oz.) cans hominy, rinsed and drained
- 4 medium carrots, peeled and cut into ½-inch pieces
- 2 medium potatoes, cut into ½-inch pieces
- ¾ medium onion, cut into ¼-inch pieces and divided
- 2 tbsp. garlic, minced
- 2 tsp. ground Mexican oregano
- ½ tsp. ground cumin
- 9 C. water, divided
- 2 poblano chiles, seeded and cut into ¼-inch pieces
- 2 tsp. guajillo chile powder
- 2 tbsp. ancho chile powder
- Salt, as required
- 3 corn tortillas, cut into ¼-inch strips
- ¼ C. fresh cilantro, finely chopped

1. In a large-sized soup pant, add the hominy, carrots, potatoes, 1 C. of onions, garlic, oregano, cumin and 1 C. of water over medium heat and cook for about 10 minutes.
2. Add poblano chiles, chile powders and remaining water and bring to a boil.
3. Adjust the heat to low and simmer for about 30-40 minutes.
4. Stir in the salt and serve hot with the garnishing of tortilla strips and cilantro.

Per Serving:
Calories: 168| Fat: 1.8g| Carbs: 34.7g| Fiber: 6.4g| Protein: 3.8g

## LENTIL CHILI

**Prep Time: 15 mins.| Cook Time: 2 hrs. 10 mins.| Serves: 8**

- 2 tsp. olive oil
- 1 large onion, chopped
- 3 medium carrot, peeled and chopped
- 4 celery stalks, chopped
- 2 garlic cloves, minced
- 1 jalapeño pepper, seeded and chopped
- ½ tbsp. dried thyme, crushed
- 1 tbsp. chipotle chili powder
- ½ tbsp. cayenne powder
- 1½ tbsp. ground coriander
- 1½ tbsp. ground cumin
- 1 tsp. ground turmeric
- Salt and ground black pepper, as required
- 2 tbsp. tomato paste
- 1 lb. red lentils, rinsed
- 8 C. vegetable broth
- 6 C. fresh spinach
- ½ C. fresh cilantro, chopped

1. In a large-sized pan, heat the oil over medium heat and sauté the onion, carrot and celery for about 5 minutes.
2. Add the garlic, jalapeño pepper, thyme and spices and sauté for about 1 minute.
3. Add the tomato paste, lentils and broth and bring to a boil.
4. Adjust the heat to low and simmer for about 2 hours.
5. Stir in the spinach and simmer for about 3-4 minutes.
6. Stir in cilantro and serve hot.

Per Serving:
Calories: 264| Fat: 0.3g| Carbs: 42.8g| Fiber: 19.8g| Protein: 4g

## CHICKPEAS & ZUCCHINI CHILI

**Prep Time: 15 mins.| Cook Time: 1 hr. 10 mins.| Serves: 8**

- 2 tbsp. avocado oil
- 1 medium white onion, chopped
- 1 large red bell pepper, seeded and chopped
- 4 garlic cloves, minced
- 1 tsp. dried thyme
- 1 tbsp. cayenne powder
- Salt, as required
- 2 medium zucchinis, chopped
- 3 C. plum tomatoes, chopped
- 3 C. cooked chickpeas
- 2 C. water

1. In a pan, heat the avocado oil over medium heat and sauté the onion and bell pepper for about 8 to 9 minutes.
2. Add the garlic, thyme, cayenne powder and salt and sauté for about 1 minute.
3. Add in all remaining ingredients and bring to a boil.
4. Now, adjust the heat to low and simmer for about 1 hour or until desired thickness.
5. Serve hot.

Per Serving:
Calories: 147| Fat: 1.9g| Carbs: 28.2g| Fiber: 6.2g| Protein: 6.2g

## BEANS WITH SALSA

**Prep Time: 10 mins.| Cook Time: 11 mins.| Serves: 4**

- ✓ 1 tbsp. canola oil
- ✓ 1 small onion, chopped
- ✓ 1 garlic clove, minced
- ✓ 2 tsp. fresh cilantro, minced
- ✓ 2 (15-oz.) cans pinto beans, rinsed and drained
- ✓ 2/3 C. salsa

1. In a large-sized skillet, heat the oil over medium heat and sauté the onion for about 4-5 minutes.
2. Add the garlic and cilantro and sauté for about 1 minute.
3. Stir in the beans and salsa and cook for about 4-5 minutes or until heated completely.
4. Serve hot.

Per Serving:
Calories: 182| Fat: 3.6g| Carbs: 34.2g| Fiber: 12.6g| Protein: 10.7g

### BEANS IN BEER SAUCE
**Prep Time: 15 mins.| Cook Time: 2 hrs.| Serves: 6**

- ✓ 1 lb. dried pinto bean, rinsed
- ✓ 1 tbsp. olive oil
- ✓ 4 medium tomatoes, chopped
- ✓ 2 medium onions, chopped
- ✓ 1 medium green bell pepper, chopped
- ✓ 2 garlic cloves, chopped
- ✓ 1 (12-oz.) can beer
- ✓ ½ bunch fresh cilantro, chopped
- ✓ 2 jalapeño peppers, seeded and chopped
- ✓ Salt and ground black pepper, as required

1. In a pan, add the beans and enough water to cover over high heat and bring to a boil.
2. Adjust the heat to medium and cook, covered for about 1½-2 hours.
3. Meanwhile, in a large-sized skillet, heat oil over medium heat and cook the tomatoes, bell pepper, onion, and garlic for about 4-5 minutes, stirring frequently.
4. Add in the beer and cook for about 2-3 minutes.
5. In the pan of the beans, add beer mixture, jalapeño peppers, cilantro, salt and black pepper and stir to combine.
6. Serve hot.

Per Serving:
Calories: 341| Fat: 3.5g| Carbs: 58.9g| Fiber: 14.3g| Protein: 17.2g

### BLACK BEANS CHILI
**Prep Time: 15 mins.| Cook Time: 1hr. 10 mins.| Serves: 10**

- ✓ 2 tbsp. canola oil
- ✓ 2 medium onions, chopped
- ✓ 1 large green bell pepper, seeded and chopped
- ✓ 5 garlic cloves, minced
- ✓ 2 tbsp. ground cumin
- ✓ 2 tbsp. ground coriander
- ✓ 1 tsp. ground cinnamon
- ✓ 1 tbsp. dried basil, crushed
- ✓ 1 tbsp. dried oregano, crushed
- ✓ ¼ C. canned tomato puree
- ✓ 4¼ C. vegetable broth
- ✓ 8 C. canned black beans
- ✓ 3 C. tomatoes, chopped
- ✓ Salt and ground black pepper, as required
- ✓ ½ C. fresh cilantro, chopped

1. In a large-sized pan, heat the oil over medium-high heat and cook the onion for about 8-9 minutes, stirring frequently.
2. Add bell pepper, garlic, spices and herbs and sauté for about 1 minute.
3. Add the tomato puree, broth, black beans and tomatoes and bring to a boil.
4. Adjust the heat to low and simmer, covered for about 1 hour.
5. Season with salt and black pepper and serve hot with the garnishing of cilantro.

Per Serving:
Calories: 339| Fat: 6.3g| Carbs: 53.2g| Fiber: 18.7g| Protein: 20.2g

### BEANS & SWEET POTATO CHILI
**Prep Time: 15 mins.| Cook Time: 2 hrs. 10 mins.| Serves: 6**

- ✓ 2 tbsp. olive oil
- ✓ 1 onion, chopped
- ✓ 2 small bell peppers, seeded and chopped
- ✓ 4 garlic cloves, minced
- ✓ 1 tsp. ground cumin
- ✓ 1 tsp. cayenne powder
- ✓ 1 tbsp. red chili powder
- ✓ 1 medium sweet potato, peeled and chopped
- ✓ 3 C. tomatoes, finely chopped
- ✓ 4 C. cooked black beans, rinsed and drained
- ✓ 2 C. vegetable broth
- ✓ Salt and ground black pepper, as required

1. In a large-sized pan, heat the oil over medium-high heat and sauté the onion and bell peppers for about 3-4 minutes.
2. Add the garlic and spices and sauté for about 1 minute.
3. Add the sweet potato and cook for about 4-5 minutes.

4. Add the remaining ingredients and bring to a boil.
5. Adjust the heat to medium-low and simmer covered for about 1½-2 hours.
6. Season with salt and black pepper and remove from the heat.
7. Serve hot.

Per Serving:
Calories: 275| Fat: 7.2g| Carbs: 40.8g| Fiber: 11.2g| Protein: 13.1g

## BEANS & CORN CHILI
**Prep Time: 15 mins.| Cook Time: 50 mins.| Serves: 6**

- 1 tbsp. canola oil
- 1 large white onion, finely chopped
- 1 green bell pepper, seeded and finely chopped
- 5 garlic cloves, minced
- 1 tsp. dried oregano, crushed
- 1½ tsp. red chili powder
- 1 tsp. ground cumin
- 2 (15-oz.) cans black beans, rinsed and drained
- 1 (28-oz.) can whole tomatoes with juice, crushed
- ½ C. mild salsa
- 3 C. frozen corn kernels
- ½ C. vegetable broth
- Salt and ground black pepper, as required
- ¼ C. fresh cilantro, chopped

1. In a large-sized pan, heat oil over medium-high heat and sauté the onion and bell pepper for about 5 minutes.
2. Add the garlic, oregano and spices and sauté for about 1 minute.
3. Add the beans, tomatoes, salsa and broth and bring to a boil.
4. Adjust the heat to low and simmer for about 15-20 minutes.
5. Stir in the corn and simmer for about 5-10 minutes.
6. Stir in the salt and black pepper and remove from the heat.
7. Serve hot with the topping of cilantro.

Per Serving:
Calories: 349| Fat: 5.5g| Carbs: 62.8g| Fiber: 17.9g| Protein: 17.8g

## TWO BEANS CHILI
**Prep Time: 15 mins.| Cook Time: 1¼ hrs.| Serves: 6**

- 2 tbsp. olive oil
- 1 medium yellow onion, peeled and chopped
- 4 garlic cloves, minced
- 1 tsp. ground cumin
- ¼ tsp. ground coriander
- 1 tbsp. red chili powder
- Salt and ground black pepper, as required
- 1 large bell pepper, seeded and chopped
- 2 medium zucchinis, trimmed and chopped
- 3 C. tomatoes, chopped
- 1½ C. canned red kidney beans
- 1½ C. canned white beans
- 2 C. vegetable broth
- ¼ C. fresh cilantro leaves, chopped

1. In a Dutch oven, heat the oil over medium heat and cook the onion for about 8-9 minutes, stirring frequently.
2. Add the garlic, spices, salt, and black pepper. Sauté for about 1 minute.
3. Add the remaining ingredients except for cilantro and bring to a boil.
4. Adjust the heat to low and simmer, covered, for about 1 hour.
5. Serve hot with the garnishing of cilantro.

Per Serving:
Calories: 220| Fat: 6.2g| Carbs: 34.5g| Fiber: 9.6g| Protein: 12.1g

## THREE BEANS CHILI
**Prep Time: 15 mins.| Cook Time: 1 hr.| Serves: 6**

- 2 tbsp. olive oil
- 1 green bell pepper, seeded and chopped
- 2 celery stalks, chopped
- 1 scallion, chopped
- 3 minced garlic cloves
- 1 tsp. dried oregano, crushed
- 1 tbsp. red chili powder
- 2 tsp. ground cumin
- 1 tsp. red pepper flakes, crushed
- 1 tsp. paprika
- 1 tsp. ground turmeric
- 1 tsp. onion powder
- 1 tsp. garlic powder

- ✓ Salt and ground black pepper, as required
- ✓ 1 (28-oz.) can diced tomatoes
- ✓  C. water
- ✓ 1 (16-oz.) can kidney beans, rinsed and drained
- ✓ 1 (16-oz.) can cannellini beans, rinsed and drained
- ✓ 1 (8-oz.) can black beans, rinsed and drained
- ✓ 1 jalapeño pepper, seeded and chopped
- ✓ ¼ C. pita chips, crushed

1. In a large-sized pan, heat the oil over medium heat and cook the bell peppers, celery, scallion and garlic for about 8-10 minutes, stirring frequently.
2. Add the oregano, spices, salt, black pepper, tomatoes and water and bring to a boil.
3. Simmer for about 20 minutes.
4. Stir in the beans and jalapeño pepper and simmer for about 30 minutes.
5. Serve hot with the topping of pita chips.

Per Serving:
Calories: 411| Fat: 6.4g| Carbs: 68.3g| Fiber: 19g| Protein: 23.4g

## BEANS & CORN CASSEROLE
**Prep Time: 20 mins.| Cook Time: 28 mins.| Serves: 6**

- ✓ Non-stick cooking spray
- ✓ 2 tsp. olive oil
- ✓ 2 bell peppers, seeded and chopped
- ✓ 1 red onion, minced
- ✓ 1 garlic clove, minced
- ✓ 1 tsp. ground cumin
- ✓ 1 tsp. red chili powder
- ✓ 1 (14-oz.) can black beans, drained and rinsed
- ✓ 2/3 C. canned sweet corn, drained and rinsed
- ✓ Salt, as required
- ✓ 1 chipotle pepper in adobo sauce
- ✓ 1/3 C. vegan mayonnaise
- ✓ 1½ C. tomato sauce
- ✓ 6 (8-inch) corn tortillas, cut into strips
- ✓ 1½ C. vegan cheese

1. Preheat your oven to 400 °F. Lightly grease a 9x9-inch baking dish with cooking spray.
2. In a large-sized skillet, heat the oil over medium heat and sauté the bell peppers, onion, garlic, cumin, and red chili powder for about 3-5 minutes.
3. Stir in the beans, corn, and salt and remove from the heat.
4. Set aside to cool slightly.
5. In a small-sized blender, add the chipotle pepper and pulse until finely minced.
6. Transfer the minced pepper into a bowl with mayonnaise and mix well.
7. In the bottom of the prepared baking dish, spread a thin layer of tomato sauce.
8. Arrange half of the tortilla strips on top of tomato sauce, overlapping.
9. Place half of the cooked onion mixture over tortilla strips evenly and drizzle with the mayonnaise mixture.
10. Spread half of the remaining tomato sauce on top evenly and sprinkle with half of the vegan cheese.
11. Repeat the layers of remaining tortilla strips, cooked onion mixture, tomato sauce, and remaining vegan cheese.
12. With a piece of foil, cover the baking dish and bake for approximately 15 minutes.
13. Remove the foil and bake for approximately 5-8 minutes.
14. Remove the baking dish from oven and set aside to cool for about 3-5 minutes before serving.

Per Serving:
Calories: 309| Fat: 11.5g| Carbs: 43.2g| Fiber: 12.1g| Protein: 11.5g

## BEANS PIE
**Prep Time: 15 mins.| Cook Time: 30 mins.| Serves: 6**

- ✓ Non-stick cooking spray
- ✓ 1 (15-oz.) can black beans, drained and rinsed
- ✓ 1 (15-oz.) can pinto beans, drained and rinsed
- ✓ 1 (16-oz.) can refried beans
- ✓ 1 (2-oz.) can sliced black olives
- ✓ ½ (15¼-oz.) can whole kernel corn, drained
- ✓ ½ C. chopped green bell pepper
- ✓ 1 jalapeño pepper, seeded and minced
- ✓ 1 tbsp. ground cumin
- ✓ 1 tbsp. red chili powder
- ✓ Salt and ground black pepper to taste
- ✓ 5 (10-inch) vegan whole-wheat tortillas
- ✓ 1½ C. vegan cheese, shredded

1. Preheat your oven to 350 °F. Lightly grease a 10-inch spring form pan with cooking spray.
2. Place the refried beans, pinto beans, black beans, corn, olives, bell pepper, jalapeño pepper, chili powder, cumin and black pepper in a pot over medium-high heat and cook for about 9-10 minutes.
3. In the bottom of the prepared pan, arrange 1 tortilla.
4. Place about 1/4 of the bean mixture over the tortilla, followed by ¼ C. of cheese.
5. Repeat the layers, ending with a tortilla, followed by the remaining r cheese.
6. Bake for approximately 20 minutes.
7. Serve warm.

Per Serving:
Calories: 433 | Fat: 9.2g | Carbs: 69.8g | Fiber: 21.6g | Protein: 21.5g

### CORN CASSEROLE
**Prep Time: 20 mins. | Cook Time: 55 mins. | Serves: 8**

- Non-stick cooking spray
- 2 (15-oz.) can whole kernel corn, divided
- 1½ C. soy milk, divided
- 2 tbsp. cornstarch, divided
- 2 C. veggie crumbles
- 4-5 tbsp. taco seasoning
- 1 (15-oz.) can diced tomatoes with juice
- 1 (4-oz.) can chopped green chiles
- 2 (8-oz.) packages vegan cornbread mix
- 1 tbsp. ground flaxseeds
- 1 tbsp. apple cider vinegar
- 1-2 tbsp. water
- 2 C. vegan cheese

1. Preheat your oven to 400 °F. Grease a 9x13-inch baking dish with cooking spray.
2. In a high-power blender, add 1 can of corn and pulse until chopped.
3. Add ½ C. of soy milk and 1 tbsp. of cornstarch and pulse until well combines.
4. Transfer the blended corn mixture into a saucepan over medium heat and bring to a gentle simmer, stirring occasionally.
5. Remove from the heat and set aside.
6. In a large-sized bowl, add the veggie crumbles and taco seasoning and stir to combine.
7. Add the tomatoes with juice and green chiles and stir to combine. Set aside.
8. For cornbread mixture: in a bowl, add the cornbread mix packages.
9. Make a well in the center of cornbread mix.
10. In the well, place the remaining cornstarch, soy milk, flaxseeds, and vinegar and mix until well combined.
11. Add half of the can of whole corn and half of the blended corn mixture and stir to combine.
12. In the bottom of the prepared baking dish, spread half of the cornbread mixture and top with veggie crumb mixture, followed by the remaining corn, blended corn mixture and 1 C. of vegan cheese.
13. Place the remaining cornbread mixture on top and sprinkle with the remaining vegan cheese.
14. Spray a sheet of foil with cooking spray lightly.
15. Arrange the piece of foil over the casserole, greased side down.
16. Bake for approximately 35-40 minutes.
17. Remove the foil and bake for approximately 10 minutes.
18. Remove the casserole from oven and set aside for about 10 minutes before serving.

Per Serving:
Calories: 566 | Fat: 20.4g | Carbs: 79.2g | Fiber: 10.6g | Protein: 21.5g

### RICE PAELLA
**Prep Time: 20 mins. | Cook Time: 20 mins. | Serves: 4**

- 1 C. brown rice
- Pinch of saffron
- 3 tbsp. warm water
- 6 C. vegetable broth
- 1 tbsp. olive oil
- 1 large yellow onion, chopped
- 1 medium green bell pepper, seeded and sliced
- 1 medium red bell pepper, seeded and sliced
- 1 C. carrot, peeled and slice thinly lengthwise
- 4 garlic cloves, sliced thinly
- ¾ C. fresh tomatoes, crushed
- 2 tbsp. tomato paste
- ½ tbsp. hot paprika
- 2 C. green beans, trimmed and halved
- 1 C. black olives, pitted
- ¼ C. fresh parsley, chopped
- Salt and ground black pepper, as required

1. In a large-sized pan of salted boiling water, add the rice and cook for about 20 minutes.
2. Drain the rice and set aside.
3. In a small-sized bowl, mix together the saffron threads and warm water. Set aside.
4. In a small-sized pan, add the broth and bring to a gentle simmer.
5. Adjust the heat to low to keep the broth warm.
6. Meanwhile, in a large-sized cast-iron skillet, heat the oil and sauté the onions for about 4-5 minutes.
7. Add the bell peppers, carrots and garlic slices and cook for about 7 minutes.

8. Stir in the saffron mixture, tomatoes, tomato paste, paprika, salt and black pepper and cook for about 2-3 minutes.
9. Add the green beans and stir to combine.
10. Stir in the cooked rice and broth and bring to a boil.
11. Simmer for about 20 minutes or until all the liquid is absorbed.
12. Stir in the olives and parsley and cover the pan.
13. Remove from the heat and set aside, covered for about 5-10 minutes before serving.

Per Serving:
Calories: 377| Fat: 11.1g| Carbs: 60.2g| Fiber: 9.2g| Protein: 13.7g

## RICE WITH SALSA
**Prep Time: 15 mins.| Cook Time: 30 mins.| Serves: 6**

- 2 garlic cloves, peeled and halved
- 2 tbsp. vegetable oil
- 1 C. long-grain white rice
- ¼ C. salsa
- ¼ C. frozen corn
- ¼ C. carrot, peeled and chopped
- 1 (14½-oz.) can vegetable broth

1. In a heavy-bottomed pan, heat the oil over high heat and sauté the garlic cloves for about 2-3 minutes.
2. With a slotted spoon, remove the garlic cloves and discard them.
3. In the pan, stir in the rice and immediately adjust the heat to medium-high.
4. Cook for about 2-3 minutes, stirring continuously.
5. Add the salsa, corn, carrots and broth and stir to combine.
6. Adjust the heat to low and cook, covered for about 18-20 minutes.
7. Remove from the heat and set aside, covered for about 5 minutes.
8. With a fork, fluff the rice and serve.

Per Serving:
Calories: 175| Fat: 5.2g| Carbs: 27.6g| Fiber: 0.9g| Protein: 4.1g

## RICE WITH TOMATO
**Prep Time: 15 mins.| Cook Time: 35 mins.| Serves: 4**

- 1½ C. vegetable broth
- 2 tsp. vegetable oil
- 1 C. medium-grain white rice
- 1 small onion, finely chopped
- 1 garlic clove, minced
- 1 medium tomato, pureed
- 1 jalapeño pepper, chopped
- ½ tsp. salt
- 2-3 tbsp. fresh cilantro, chopped

1. In a saucepan, add the broth over high heat and bring to a boil.
2. Adjust the heat to low to keep it hot.
3. In another large saucepan, heat the oil over medium heat and cook the rice and onion for about 8-10 minutes, stirring occasionally.
4. Stir in the garlic and cook for about 1-2 minutes.
5. Add the broth, pureed tomato, jalapeño pepper and salt and mix well.
6. Now adjust the heat to a medium-sized-low and cook, covered for about 18-20 minutes.
7. Remove from heat and stir in the cilantro.
8. Serve hot.

Per Serving:
Calories: 209| Fat: 2.9g| Carbs: 40.7g| Fiber: 1.9g| Protein: 5.4g

## TOMATO SALSA
**Prep Time: 15 mins.| Serves: 4**

- 3 large tomatoes, chopped
- 1 small red onion, chopped
- ¼ C. fresh cilantro leaves, chopped
- 1 jalapeño pepper, seeded and finely chopped
- 1 small garlic clove, minced finely
- 2 tbsp. fresh lime juice
- 1 tbsp. extra-virgin olive oil
- Salt and ground black pepper, as required

1. In a large-sized bowl, add all the ingredients and gently toss to coat well.
2. Serve immediately.

Per Serving:
Calories: 64| Fat: 3.8g| Carbs: 7.5g| Fiber: 2.2g| Protein: 15g

## MANGO & AVOCADO SALSA
**Prep Time: 15 mins.| Serves: 6**

- 1 avocado, peeled, pitted and cut into cubes
- 2 tbsp. fresh lime juice
- 1 mango, peeled, pitted and cubed
- 1 C. cherry tomatoes, halved
- 1 jalapeño pepper, seeded and chopped
- 1 tbsp. fresh cilantro, chopped
- Salt, as required

1. In a large-sized bowl, add and lime juice and mix well
2. Add the remaining ingredients and stir to combine.
3. Serve immediately.

Per Serving:
Calories: 108| Fat: 6.8g| Carbs: 12.6g| Fiber: 3.6g| Protein: 1.4g

## TOMATILLO SALSA
**Prep Time: 15 mins.| Serves: 8**

- 1 lb. tomatillo, quartered
- 1 C. fresh cilantro
- 1 habanero pepper, seeded
- 1 onion, roughly chopped
- 3 garlic cloves, peeled
- 1-2 chipotle peppers in adobo sauce
- 2 tbsp. fresh lime juice
- Salt and ground black pepper, as required

1. In a high-power blender, add all the ingredients and pulse until smooth.
2. Serve immediately.

Per Serving:
Calories: 30| Fat: 0.8g| Carbs: 5.7g| Fiber: 1.8g| Protein: 1g

## AVOCADO GUACAMOLE
**Prep Time: 10 mins.| Serves: 4**

- 2 medium ripe avocados, peeled, pitted, and chopped
- 1 small red onion, chopped
- 1 garlic clove, minced
- 1 Serrano pepper, seeded and chopped
- 1 tomato, seeded and chopped
- 2 tbsp. fresh cilantro leaves, chopped
- 1 tbsp. fresh lime juice
- Salt, as required

1. In a large-sized bowl, add avocado and mash it completely with a fork.
2. Add the remaining ingredients and gently stir to combine.
3. Serve immediately.

Per Serving:
Calories: 217| Fat: 19.7g| Carbs: 11.3g| Fiber: 7.4g| Protein: 2.3g

## SWEET BUNS
**Prep Time: 20 mins.| Cook Time: 20 mins.| Serves: 12**

**For Buns**
- 1 tbsp. ground flaxseeds
- 3 tbsp. water
- 3 tsp. active dry yeast
- ½ C. warm water
- ½ C. lukewarm unsweetened almond milk
- 1/3 C. granulated white sugar
- 1/3 C. coconut oil, softened
- 1 tsp. salt
- 3½-4 C. all-purpose flour
- Non-stick cooking spray

**For Topping**
- 1/3 C. granulated white sugar
- ¼ C. coconut oil, softened
- ½ C. all-purpose flour
- 1 tsp. ground cinnamon
- ¼ tsp. vanilla extract
- 1½ tsp. orange zest, grated

1. In a small-sized bowl, whisk together the ground flaxseeds and water. Set aside for about 10 minutes
2. In a bowl, add the warm water and yeast and mix until well combined.
3. Add the flaxseeds mixture, coconut oil, almond milk, 2 C. of the flour, sugar and salt and beat until well combined and smooth.
4. Add required amount from the remaining flour and mix until a dough is formed.
5. Place the dough onto a lightly floured surface and with your hands, knead until elastic.

6. In an oiled bowl, add the dough and turn to coat with the oil evenly.
7. With plastic wrap, cover the bowl and set aside in a warm place for at least 1½ hours.
8. Grease a large-sized baking sheet with cooking spray.
9. With your hands, punch down the dough.
10. Make 12 equal-sized balls from the dough and arrange onto the prepared baking sheet.
11. Meanwhile, for the topping: in a bowl, add the coconut oil and sugar and beat until creamy.
12. Add the flour and mix until a thick paste is formed.
13. Divide the paste into 3 portions.
14. Add the cinnamon, vanilla extract and orange peel into all 3 portions respectively.
15. Now, divide each part of dough into 4 equal portions.
16. With your hands, pat each portion into a 3-inch round.
17. Arrange 1 portion on top of each dough ball and press slightly to attach with the ball.
18. With a table knife, make about 5-6 cuts in a shell pattern.
19. With plastic wrap, cover the bowl and set aside in a warm place for at least 40 minutes.
20. Preheat your oven to 375 °F.
21. Bake for approximately 20 minutes.
22. Serve warm.

Per Serving:
Calories: 303| Fat: 12.1g| Carbs: 44.7g| Fiber: 1.7g| Protein: 4.8g

## WALNUT COOKIES

**Prep Time: 15 mins.| Cook Time: 12 mins.| Serves: 18**

- ✓ 2¼ C. all-purpose flour, sifted
- ✓ ¼ tsp. salt
- ✓ 1 C. coconut oil, softened
- ✓ ½ C. powdered sugar
- ✓ 1 tsp. vanilla extract
- ✓ ¾ C. walnuts, chopped
- ✓ Powdered sugar, as required

1. Preheat your oven to 400 °F. Line 2-3 cookie sheets with parchment papers.
2. In a bowl, add the flour and salt and mix well.
3. In another bowl, add the coconut oil and powdered sugar and beat until creamy.
4. Add the vanilla extract and stir to combine well.
5. Slowly add the flour mixture and mix until just combined.
6. Gently fold in the walnuts.
7. Make about 1¼-inch balls from the dough.
8. Arrange the dough balls onto the prepared cookie sheets about 2-inch apart and press each ball slightly.
9. Bake for approximately 10-12 minutes.
10. Remove the cookie sheets from oven and place onto a wire rack to cool for about 5-10 minutes.
11. Then invert the cookies onto the wire racks.
12. Coat the warm cookies with the extra powdered sugar evenly and place onto the wire racks to cool completely before serving.

Per Serving:
Calories: 207| Fat: 15.3g| Carbs: 15.8g| Fiber: 0.8g| Protein: 2.9g

## SOPAPILLA

**Prep Time: 15 mins.| Cook Time: 6 mins.| Serves: 5**

- ✓ 2 C. all-purpose flour plus more for dusting
- ✓ 2 tsp. baking powder
- ✓ 1 tsp. fine salt
- ✓ 2 tbsp. coconut oil, room temperature
- ✓ ¾ C. warm water
- ✓ Vegetable oil, for frying
- ✓ ½ C. granulated white sugar
- ✓ 1 tsp. ground cinnamon

1. For dough: in a large-sized bowl, blend the flour, baking powder and salt.
2. With a pastry cutter, cut in the coconut oil until well combined.
3. Slowly add in the warm water and with a wooden spoon, mix until dough just begins to form.
4. With your hands, knead the dough until smooth.
5. Shape the dough into a ball.
6. With a damp towel, cover the bowl of dough and set aside for about 20 minutes.
7. Now place the dough onto a floured surface and with a rolling pin, roll into ¼-inch thickness.
8. With a knife, cut the dough into 2-3-inch squares.
9. In a large-sized saucepan, heat oil over medium-high heat and fry the dough squares in 2-3 batches for about 30-60 seconds per side.
10. With a slotted spoon, transfer the sopapillas onto a paper-towel-lined baking sheet to drain.
11. In a small-sized bowl, blend the sugar and cinnamon.
12. Sprinkle the cooked sopapillas with cinnamon sugar and serve warm.

Per Serving:
Calories: 303| Fat: 5.9g| Carbs: 58.3g| Fiber: 1.4g| Protein: 5.2g

## APPLE CHIMICHANGAS
**Prep Time: 20 mins. | Cook Time: 21 mins. | Serves: 4**

**For Filling**
- 1 C. water
- 1/3 C. white sugar
- 2 tbsp. cornstarch
- ½ tsp. ground cinnamon
- 1/8 tsp. ground nutmeg
- Pinch of salt
- 1 tsp. fresh lemon juice
- ½ tsp. vanilla extract
- 2 Granny Smith apples, peeled, cored and cut into cubes

**For Chimichangas**
- 4 small vegan whole-wheat tortillas
- 2 tbsp. plus 4 tsp. caramel sauce, divided
- ¼ C. vegetable oil
- ¼ C. white sugar
- ½ tbsp. ground cinnamon

1. For filling: in a saucepan, add all ingredients except for apples and stir to combine.
2. Place the saucepan of mixture over medium heat and cook for about 3 minutes, stirring occasionally.
3. In add the apple cubes and cook for about 10 minutes, stirring occasionally.
4. Remove from heat and set aside to cool for 4-5 minutes.
5. Arrange tortillas onto a smooth surface.
6. Spread 1 tsp. of caramel sauce in the middle of each tortilla.
7. Place the apple filling over caramel sauce.
8. Close each tortilla on both sides and roll it in chimichanga.
9. Secure each with a toothpick.
10. In a skillet, heat oil over medium heat and fry the chimichangas for about 3-4 minutes or until golden brown form all sides.
11. With a slotted spoon, transfer the chimichangas onto a paper towel-lined plate to drain.
12. In a plate, blend the sugar and cinnamon.
13. Roll the warm chimichanga in cinnamon sugar and drizzle with the remaining caramel sauce.
14. Serve immediately.

Per Serving:
Calories: 394 | Fat: 14.6g | Carbs: 68.5g | Fiber: 4..5g | Protein: 1.9g

## CHOCOLATY SWEET POTATO PUDDING
**Prep Time: 15 mins. | Cook Time: 1 hr. | Serves: 3**

- 3 large orange sweet potatoes
- ½ C. plus 2 tbsp. lite coconut milk
- 1-2 tbsp. pure maple syrup
- 5 tbsp. unsweetened cocoa powder
- 3 tbsp. coconut sugar
- 1-1½ tsp. ground cinnamon
- 1/8 tsp. cayenne powder
- ¼ tsp. fine salt
- 1 tsp. vanilla extract

1. Preheat your oven to 400 °F. Line a baking sheet with parchment paper.
2. Arrange the sweet potatoes onto the prepared baking sheet.
3. Bake for approximately 45-60 minutes or until soft.
4. Remove the sweet potatoes from oven and set aside to cool.
5. Peel the sweet potatoes and place into a large-sized bowl.
6. With a fork, mash the sweet potatoes roughly.
7. In a food processor, add about 1½ C. of mashed sweet potatoes and pulse until smooth.
8. Add the remaining ingredients and pulse until smooth.
9. Transfer the pudding into a serving bowl and refrigerate to chill before serving.

Per Serving:
Calories: 294 | Fat: 4g | Carbs: 65.9g | Fiber: 9.6g | Protein: 4.7g

## RICE PUDDING
**Prep Time: 10 mins. | Cook Time: 40 mins. | Serves: 8**

- 3 C. water
- 1 C. long-grain rice
- 1 (2-inch) cinnamon stick
- 4 C. soy milk
- ½-1 C. white sugar
- ½ C. raisins

1. In a saucepan, add the water, rice and cinnamon stick over medium-high heat and bring to a boil.
2. Adjust the heat to medium and cook for about 15 minutes.
3. Add soy milk and simmer for about 10 more minutes.
4. Add in the sugar and simmer for about 10 minutes, stirring occasionally.
5. Remove from the heat and stir in the raisins.
6. Transfer the pudding into a serving bowl and set aside to cool slightly.
7. Serve warm.

Per Serving:
Calories: 160| Fat: 2.2g| Carbs: 32g| Fiber: 1.2g| Protein: 4.7g

## VANILLA FLAN
**Prep Time: 15 mins.| Cook Time: 15 mins.| Serves: 4**

**For Caramel**
- ¾ C. granulated white sugar

**For Flan Base**
- 1 can full-fat coconut milk
- 1¼ tsp. agar-agar powder
- 1 C. oat milk
- 1/3 C. white sugar
- 1 tsp. chickpea flour
- 1 tsp. vanilla extract

1. For caramel: in a medium-sized saucepan, add sugar over medium-low heat and cook for about 8-9 minutes, gently swirling the pan.
2. Immediately remove from the heat and pour caramel into 4 ramekins.
3. Gently tilt ramekins to coat the inside with caramel. Set aside.
4. For caramel base: in a medium-sized saucepan, add coconut milk and agar-agar and stir to combine.
5. In a high-power blender, add the oat milk, sugar, chickpea flour and vanilla extract and pulse until smooth.
6. Place the sugar mixture into the pan with the coconut milk mixture and stir to combine.
7. Place the saucepan over medium-low heat and cook for about 5 minutes, stirring frequently.
8. Remove from the heat and set aside to cool slightly.
9. Then place the base mixture into the ramekins.
10. Refrigerate the ramekins for 4 hours.
11. Just before serving, place bottom of each ramekin in a container of hot water for 1-2 minutes.
12. With a small-sized knife, carefully loosen the edges of each flan and invert onto serving plates.
13. Serve immediately.

Per Serving:
Calories: 522| Fat: 19g| Carbs: 88.4g| Fiber: 0.7g| Protein: 2.8g

## CHOCOLATE BROWNIES
**Prep Time: 15 mins.| Cook Time: 20 mins.| Serves: 16**

- 3 oz. unsweetened vegan chocolate, chopped
- ¾ C. canned black beans, rinsed and drained
- ¾ C. unsweetened applesauce
- ½ C. granulated white sugar
- ¼ C. unsweetened cocoa powder
- 2 tsp. pure vanilla extract
- ½ C. white whole-wheat flour
- ½ tsp. baking powder
- ¼ tsp. baking soda
- ½ tsp. ground cinnamon
- ¼ tsp. salt
- 1/8 tsp. cayenne powder
- 1 tsp. powdered sugar

1. Preheat your oven to 350 °F. Line a 9-inch square baking dish with a piece of foil.
2. In a food processor, add chocolate, beans and applesauce and pulse until smooth.
3. Add granulated white sugar, cocoa powder, and vanilla extract and pulse until well combined.
4. In a medium-sized-sized bowl, blend the flour, baking powder, baking soda, cinnamon, salt and cayenne powder.
5. Add the flour mixture into the chocolate mixture and pulse until just combined.
6. Place the mixture into the prepared baking dish and with your hands, press to smooth the surface.
7. Bake for approximately 20 minutes.
8. Remove from oven and place onto a wire rack to cool completely.
9. Sprinkle with powdered sugar evenly.
10. Cut into equal-sized brownies and serve.

Per Serving:

Calories: 102| Fat: 3.2g| Carbs: 18.3g| Fiber: 3.3g| Protein: 3.5g

### DULCE DE LECHE CREPE CAKE
**Prep Time: 20 mins.| Cook Time: 2 hrs.| Serves: 8**

**For Dulce de Leche**
- ✓ 1 (11¼-oz.) can sweetened condensed coconut milk

**For Crepes**
- ✓ 4 C. all-purpose flour
- ✓ 2 tsp. baking powder
- ✓ Pinch of ground cinnamon
- ✓ ¼ tsp. fine salt
- ✓ 4 2/3 C. almond milk
- ✓ ¼ C. plus 2 tsp. olive oil, divided

**For Whipped Cream**
- ✓ 1 (13½-oz.) can coconut whipping cream, refrigerated overnight
- ✓ ¼ C. powdered sugar
- ✓ ¼ tsp. vanilla extract

1. Preheat your oven to 450 °F.
2. In a 9-inch round pan, add the coconut milk and cover with a piece of foil tightly.
3. Place the pan in a large-sized pan.
4. In the large pan, add enough hot water halfway up the round pan.
5. Bake for 1½ hours.
6. Remove the pan from oven.
7. Carefully remove the foil from pan and set aside to cool.
8. For crepes: in a high-power blender, add the flour, baking powder, cinnamon and salt, and pulse until just combined.
9. Add almond milk and ¼ C. of oil and pulse until smooth.
10. Transfer the mixture into a bowl and refrigerate, covered for about 1 hour.
11. In a non-stick wok, heat remaining oil over medium heat.
12. Add about ¼ C. of the mixture and swirl the pan to coat the bottom evenly.
13. Cook for about 1-2 minutes per side.
14. Repeat with the remaining mixture.
15. For whipped cream: freezer a bowl for at least 10 minutes.
16. Pour the coconut whipping cream into the chilled bowl and, with a hand mixer, whisk at maximum speed for 3-4 minutes.
17. Add the powdered sugar and vanilla and whisk until well combined.
18. Arrange 1 crepe onto a plate.
19. Spread a thin layer of whipped coconut cream over the crepe and top with another crepe.
20. Repeat this process with remaining crepes and whipped coconut cream.
21. Top with dulce de leche and serve.

Per Serving:
Calories: 407| Fat: 18.4g| Carbs: 54.8g| Fiber: 2.3g| Protein: 7.8g

### CHOCOLATE CAKE
**Prep Time: 10 mins.| Cook Time: 30 mins.| Serves: 8**

- ✓ Non-stick cooking spray
- ✓ 1½ C. all-purpose flour
- ✓ 1 C. white sugar
- ✓ ¼ C. cocoa powder
- ✓ 1 tsp. baking soda
- ✓ 1½ tsp. ground cinnamon
- ✓ ¾ tsp. cayenne powder
- ✓ 1 C. cold water
- ✓ 5 tbsp. vegetable oil
- ✓ 1 tbsp. white vinegar
- ✓ 1 tsp. pure vanilla extract
- ✓ 2 tbsp. confectioners' sugar

1. Preheat your oven to 350 °F. Lightly grease a 9-inch round cake pan with cooking spray.
2. In a large-sized bowl, blend the flour, sugar, cocoa powder, baking soda, cinnamon, and cayenne powder.
3. Add the cold water, oil, and vanilla extract and stir until just combined.
4. Place the mixture into the prepared cake pan evenly.
5. Bake for approximately 30 minutes, or until a knife inserted in the center comes out clean.
6. Remove the cake pan from oven and place onto a wire rack for about 5-10 minutes.
7. Now invert the cake onto the wire rack to cool completely before serving.
8. Dust with confectioners' sugar and serve.

Per Serving:
Calories: 271| Fat: 9.1g| Carbs: 46.9g| Fiber: 1.7g| Protein: 3g

### CHURRO CINNAMON CHEESECAKE
**Prep Time: 20 mins.| Cook Time: 10 mins.| Serves: 8**

**For Crust**
- ✓ 1¾ C. cinnamon graham cracker crumbs
- ✓ 4-5 tbsp. coconut oil, melted

**For Filling**
- ✓ 1 C. raw cashews, soaked overnight and drained
- ✓ ¾ C. coconut cream
- ✓ ½ C. unsweetened almond milk
- ✓ 1/3 C. maple syrup
- ✓ 1 tsp. ground cinnamon
- ✓ 1 tsp. vanilla extract
- ✓ ¼ C. coconut oil, melted

1. For crust: preheat your oven to 375°F. Line the bottom of a 9-inch springform pan with parchment paper. Set aside.
2. In a bowl, add graham cracker crumbs and coconut oil and mix until well combined.
3. Place the crumb mixture into the prepared baking dish and with your hands, press evenly into bottom and partway up the sides.
4. Bake for approximately 10 minutes or until golden brown.
5. Remove the baking dish from oven and set aside to cool completely.
6. For filling: in a high-power blender, add the cashews, coconut cream, almond milk, maple syrup, vanilla extract and cinnamon and pulse until cashew are finely chopped.
7. Add the coconut oil and pulse until smooth.
8. Place the filling mixture over the crust evenly.
9. Cover the baking dish and refrigerate overnight before serving.

Per Serving:
Calories: 358| Fat: 25.5g| Carbs: 30.9g| Fiber: 1.9g| Protein: 4.1g

# ITALIAN RECIPES

### TOMATO SALAD
**Prep Time: 15 mins. | Serves: 4**

**For Dressing**
- ½ C. fresh basil, chopped
- 2 garlic cloves, minced
- 4 tbsp. extra-virgin olive oil
- 2 tbsp. balsamic vinegar
- Salt and ground black pepper, as required

**For Salad**
- 2 C. cherry tomatoes
- 2 C. fresh arugula
- 3 C. fresh salad greens

1. For dressing: in a small-sized blender, add all the ingredients and pulse until smooth.
2. For salad: in a large-sized bowl, add all the ingredients and mix.
3. Place the dressing over salad and toss to coat well.
4. Serve immediately.

Per Serving:
Calories: 153 | Fat: 14.5g | Carbs: 6.3g | Fiber: 2g | Protein: 1.9g

### MIXED VEGGIE SALAD
**Prep Time: 20 mins. | Serves: 6**

**For Salad**
- 2 large cucumbers, peeled and chopped
- 3 large Roma tomatoes, chopped
- ½ C. fresh Kalamata olives, pitted and sliced
- ½ C. fresh green olives, pitted and sliced
- 1 large avocado, peeled, pitted and chopped
- 6 C. fresh baby spinach leaves
- 1 tbsp. fresh lemon zest, grated finely

**For Dressing**
- ¼ C. olive oil
- 2 tbsp. fresh lemon juice
- 1 small garlic clove, minced finely
- ½ tsp. dried oregano, crushed
- ½ tsp. dried basil, crushed
- Salt and ground black pepper, as required

1. For salad: in a large-sized serving bowl, add all the ingredients and mix well.
2. For dressing: in a small-sized bowl, add all the ingredients and beat until well combined.
3. Place the dressing over the salad and gently toss to coat well.
4. Serve immediately.

Per Serving:
Calories: 143 | Fat: 12g | Carbs: 9.6g | Fiber: 3.3g | Protein: 2.5g

### VEGGIE NOODLES SALAD
**Prep Time: 20 mins. | Serves: 8**

**For Salad**
- 3 large zucchinis, spiralized with Blade C
- 2 large yellow squashes, spiralized with Blade C
- 2 carrots, peeled and spiralized with Blade C
- 2 C. grape tomatoes, halved
- 1/3 C. olive oil

**For Pesto**
- 2 C. fresh basil leaves
- 1 C. fresh parsley leaves
- ½ C. pine nuts
- 1 garlic clove, peeled
- ½ C. olive oil
- 1 tbsp. fresh lemon juice
- Salt and ground black pepper, as required

1. For salad: in a large-sized bowl, add vegetable noodles, tomatoes and oil, and toss to coat well.
2. For pesto: in a food processor, add all ingredients and pulse until smooth.
3. Place the pesto over salad and gently stir to combine.
4. Serve immediately.

Per Serving:
Calories: 258 | Fat: 25.1g | Carbs: 9g | Fiber: 3g | Protein: 3.6g

## BEANS SALAD
**Prep Time: 15 mins. | Serves: 2**

### For Salad
- 1 small cucumber, chopped
- 1 small tomato, chopped
- 2 C. fresh baby arugula
- 1 tsp. fresh parsley, minced
- 1 tsp. fresh mint, minced
- 1 (14-oz.) can white navy beans, rinsed and drained

### For Dressing
- 1/3 C. tahini
- Salt and ground black pepper, as required
- 2 tbsp. fresh lemon juice

1. For salad: place all ingredients in a salad bowl and mix.
2. For dressing: place all ingredients in n another bowl and beat until well combined.
3. Pour the dressing over salad and toss to coat well.
4. Serve immediately.

Per Serving:
Calories: 398 | Fat: 17.9g | Carbs: 43.5g | Fiber: 18.5g | Protein: 18.3g

## PASTA SALAD
**Prep Time: 20 mins. | Cook Time: 10 mins. | Serves: 6**

### For Salad
- 12 oz. vegan whole-wheat pasta
- 2 C. carrot, peeled and chopped
- 1 C. black olives, pitted and sliced
- 1 C. red bell pepper, seeded and chopped
- 1 C. yellow bell pepper, seeded and chopped
- 1 C. orange bell pepper, seeded and chopped
- ¾ C. fresh cilantro, chopped
- 1 jalapeño pepper, seeded and finely chopped
- 1 C. scallion, chopped

### For Vinaigrette
- 2 tbsp. balsamic vinegar
- 2 tbsp. extra-virgin olive oil
- 1 tbsp. fresh lemon juice
- 1 tsp. sesame oil
- 1½ tsp. red pepper flakes, crushed

1. In a pan of salted boiling water, add the pasta and cook for about 8-10 minutes or according to the package's directions.
2. Drain the pasta well and rinse under cold water.
3. Transfer the pasta into n a large-sized bowl.
4. Meanwhile, in another pan of salted boiling water, add the edamame and cook for about 5 minutes.
5. Drain the edamame well.
6. In the bowl of pasta, add the edamame and remaining salad ingredients except for the scallion and gently stir to combine.
7. For vinaigrette: in another bowl, add all the ingredients and beat until well combined.
8. Pour the vinaigrette over salad and gently stir to combine.
9. Serve immediately with the garnishing of scallion and sesame seeds.

Per Serving:
Calories: 333 | Fat: 9.4g | Carbs: 54.5g | Fiber: 5.5g | Protein: 10g

## STUFFED ZUCCHINI
**Prep Time: 15 mins. | Cook Time: 18 mins. | Serves: 8**

- Olive oil cooking spray
- 4 medium zucchinis, halved lengthwise
- 1 C. red bell pepper, seeded and minced
- ½ C. olives, pitted and minced
- ½ C. tomatoes, minced
- 1 tsp. garlic, minced
- 1 tbsp. dried oregano, crushed
- Salt and ground black pepper, as required
- ½ C. vegan cheese

1. Preheat your oven to 350 °F. Grease a large-sized baking sheet with cooking spray.
1. With a melon baller, scoop out the flesh of each zucchini half. Discard the flesh.
2. In a bowl, mix together bell pepper, olives, tomato, garlic, oregano and black pepper.
3. Stuff each zucchini half with veggie mixture evenly.
4. Arrange zucchini halves onto the prepared baking sheet and bake for approximately 15 minutes.
5. Now, set the oven to broiler on high.
6. Top each zucchini half with vegan cheese and broil for about 3 minutes.
7. Serve hot.

Per Serving:
Calories: 52| Fat: 2.5g| Carbs: 6.9g| Fiber: 2.4g| Protein: 2.1g

## BURGERS WITH MUSHROOM SAUCE
**Prep Time: 25 mins.| Cook Time: 20 mins.| Serves: 4**

**For Patties**
- ½ C. millet, rinsed
- 1 C. hot water
- 1 (14-oz.) can chickpeas, rinsed, drained and mashed roughly
- 1 carrot, peeled and grated finely
- ½ of red bell pepper, seeded and chopped
- ½ of yellow onion, chopped
- 1 garlic clove, minced
- ½ tbsp. fresh cilantro, chopped
- ½ tsp. curry powder
- Salt and ground black pepper, as required
- 4 tbsp. chickpea flour
- 2 tbsp. olive oil

**For Mushroom Sauce**
- 2 C. unsweetened soy milk
- 2 tbsp. arrowroot flour
- 1 tbsp. low-sodium soy sauce
- Pinch of ground black pepper
- 1 tsp. olive oil
- ¾ C. fresh button mushrooms, chopped
- 1 garlic clove, minced
- 2 tbsp. fresh chives, chopped

1. For patties: heat a small-sized non-stick pan over medium heat and toast the millet for about 5 minutes, stirring continuously.
2. Add the hot water and bring to a rolling boil.
3. Adjust the heat to low and simmer, covered for about 15 minutes.
4. Remove from the heat and set aside, covered for about 10 minutes.
5. Uncover the pan and let the millet cool completely.
6. After cooling, fluff the millet with a fork.
7. In a large-sized bowl, add the millet and remaining ingredients except for chickpea flour and oil and mix until well combined.
8. Slowly add the chickpea flour, 1 tbsp. at a time and mix well.
9. Make 4 equal-sized patties from the mixture.
10. In a non-stick frying pan, heat the oil over medium heat and cook the patties for about 3-4 minutes per side or until golden brown.
11. Meanwhile, for mushroom sauce: in a bowl, add the soy milk, flour, soy sauce and black pepper and beat until smooth. Set aside.
12. Heat the oil in a skillet over medium heat and sauté the mushrooms and garlic for about 3 minutes.
13. Stir in the soy milk mixture and cook for about 8 minutes, stirring frequently.
14. Stir in the chives and remove from the heat.
15. Place 2 patties onto each serving plate and top with mushroom sauce.
16. Serve immediately.

Per Serving:
Calories: 388| Fat: 11.9g| Carbs: 57.5g| Fiber: 9.1g| Protein: 14.4g

## BEET SOUP
**Prep Time: 10 mins.| Cook Time: 15 mins.| Serves: 2**

- 2 C. coconut yogurt
- 4 tsp. fresh lemon juice
- 2 C. beets, trimmed, peeled and chopped
- 2 tbsp. fresh dill
- Salt, as required
- 1 tbsp. pumpkin seeds
- 2 tbsp. coconut cream
- 1 tbsp. fresh chives, minced

1. In a high-power blender, add all ingredients and pulse until smooth.
2. Transfer the soup into a pan over medium heat and cook for about 3-5 minutes or until heated through.
3. Serve immediately with the garnishing of chives and coconut cream.

Per Serving:
Calories: 230 | Fat: 8g| Carbs: 33.5g| Fiber: 4.2g| Protein: 8g

## TOMATO BASIL SOUP
**Prep Time: 15 mins.| Cook Time: 15 mins.| Serves: 4**

- 2 tsp. olive oil
- 1 medium white onion, chopped
- 3 garlic cloves, minced
- 7 C. fresh plum tomatoes, chopped
- ½ C. fresh sweet basil, chopped
- Salt, as required
- ¼ tsp. cayenne powder

1. In a pan, heat the oil over medium heat and sauté the onion and garlic for about 5-6 minutes.
2. Add the tomatoes and cook for about 6-8 minutes, crushing with the back of spoon occasionally.
3. Stir in the basil, salt and cayenne powder and remove from the heat.
4. With a hand blender, puree the soup mixture until smooth.
5. Serve immediately.

Per Serving:
Calories: 75| Fat: 1g| Carbs: 15.8g| Fiber: 4.6g| Protein: 3.5g

## MUSHROOM SOUP

**Prep Time: 15 mins.| Cook Time: 25 mins.| Serves: 4**

- 2 tsp. avocado oil
- 1¼ C. fresh Portobello mushrooms, sliced
- 1¼ C. fresh button mushrooms, sliced
- ½ C. white onion, chopped
- 1 garlic clove, crushed
- ½ tsp. dried thyme
- Salt and ground black pepper, as require
- 1¾ C. unsweetened coconut milk
- 1½ C. water

1. In a soup pan, heat the avocado oil over medium-high heat and cook the mushrooms, onions, garlic, thyme, salt and black pepper for about 5-6 minutes.
2. Add in the coconut milk and water and bring to a boil.
3. Now, adjust the heat to medium-low and simmer for about 10-15 minutes, stirring occasionally.

4. Serve hot.

Per Serving:
Calories: 177| Fat: 14.9g| Carbs: 5.9g| Fiber: 0.9g| Protein: 2.9g

## ZUCCHINI SOUP

**Prep Time: 15 mins.| Cook Time: 25 mins.| Serves: 8**

- 2 tbsp. olive oil
- 2½ lb. zucchinis, chopped
- 1 C. yellow onion, chopped
- 4 garlic cloves, chopped
- 7 C. vegetable broth
- 1/3 C. fresh basil, chopped
- Salt and ground black pepper, as required

1. In a large-sized soup pan, heat the oil over medium-low heat and cook the zucchini and onion for about 4-5 minutes.
2. Add the garlic and cook for about 1 minute.
3. Stir in the broth and bring to a boil.
4. Adjust the heat to low and simmer for about 15 minutes.
5. Stir in the salt and black pepper and remove from the heat.
6. Remove from the heat and with an immersion blender, blend the soup until smooth.
7. Serve immediately.

Per Serving:
Calories: 99| Fat: 5.7g| Carbs: 7.5g| Fiber: 1.9g| Protein: 5.8g

## MIXED VEGGIE SOUP

**Prep Time: 20 mins.| Cook Time: 25 mins.| Serves: 8**

- 8 carrots, peeled and chopped
- 4 small zucchinis, chopped
- 4 small onions, chopped
- 2 (14-oz.) cans diced tomatoes with juice
- 1 leek, chopped
- 2 garlic cloves, minced
- 1 tsp. ground cumin
- ¼ tsp. cayenne powder
- ¼ tsp. paprika
- Salt and ground black pepper, as required
- 5 C. vegetable broth

1. In a large-sized soup pan, add all the ingredients except the croutons and bring to a boil.
2. Adjust the heat to low and simmer, partially covered for about 20 minutes.

61

3. Remove from the heat and set aside to cool slightly.
4. In a high-power blender, add the soup in batches and pulse until smooth.
5. Return the pureed mixture into the pan over medium heat and simmer for about 3-4 minutes.
6. Serve hot.

Per Serving:
Calories: 106| Fat: 1.4g| Carbs: 19g| Fiber: 4.8g| Protein: 6.36.3g

## LENTIL SOUP
**Prep Time: 15 mins.| Cook Time: 45 mins.| Serves: 4**

- ¼ C. extra-virgin olive oil
- 2 carrots, peeled and chopped
- 1 medium yellow onion, chopped
- 4 garlic cloves, minced
- ½ tsp. dried thyme
- 2 tsp. ground cumin
- 1 (28-oz.) can diced tomatoes, drained lightly
- 1 C. brown lentils, picked over and rinsed
- 4 C. vegetable broth
- 2 C. water
- Pinch of red pepper flakes
- Salt and ground black pepper, as required
- 1 C. fresh collard greens, tough ribs removed and chopped
- 1-2 tbsp. fresh lemon juice

1. In a large-sized Dutch oven, heat the oil over medium heat and cook the carrots and onion for about 5 minutes, stirring occasionally.
2. Add the garlic, thyme and spices and sauté for about 30 seconds.
3. Stir in the tomatoes and cook for about 2-3 minutes, stirring occasionally.
4. Add the lentils, broth, water, red pepper flakes salt and black pepper and stir to combine.
5. Adjust the heat to high and bring to a boil.
6. Adjust the heat to low and simmer, partially covered for about 25-30 minutes.
7. Remove from the heat and set aside to cool slightly.
8. In a high-power blender, add 2 C. of the soup and pulse until smooth.
9. Return the puréed soup into the pan with greens over medium heat and cook for about 5 minutes.
10. Remove from the heat and stir in the lemon juice.
11. Serve hot.

Per Serving:
Calories: 388| Fat: 15.3g| Carbs: 45.3g| Fiber: 19g| Protein: 20.2g

## BEANS & SPINACH SOUP
**Prep Time: 15 mins.| Cook Time: 25 mins.| Serves: 4**

- 1 tbsp. olive oil
- 1 celery stalk, chopped
- 1 onion, chopped
- 1 garlic clove, minced
- ¼ tsp. dried thyme, crushed
- 2 (16-oz.) cans white kidney beans, rinsed and drained
- 2 C. vegetable broth
- 2 C. water
- 3 C. fresh spinach, chopped
- Salt and ground black pepper, as required
- 1 tbsp. fresh lemon juice

1. In a large-sized soup pan, heat oil over medium heat and sauté the celery and onion for about 3-4 minutes.
2. Add the garlic and thyme sauté for about 1 minute.
3. Stir in beans, broth and water and bring to a boil.
4. Adjust the heat to low and simmer for about 15 minutes.
5. Remove from heat and with a slotted spoon, transfer about 2 C. of the beans mixture in a bowl.
6. Set aside to cool slightly.
7. In a high-power blender, add 2 C. of the bean mixture and pulse until smooth.
8. Return the pureed mixture in the soup and stir to combine.
9. Place the pan over medium heat and stir in spinach, salt and black pepper and cook for about 3-4 minutes.
10. Stir in lemon juice and serve hot.

Per Serving:
Calories: 259| Fat: 5.2g| Carbs: 39.6g| Fiber: 13.5g| Protein: 15.4g

## THREE BEANS SOUP
**Prep Time: 15 mins.| Cook Time: 30 mins.| Serves: 8**

- ¼ C. olive oil
- 1 onion, chopped
- 2 large potatoes, scrubbed and cubed
- 3 carrots, peeled and chopped
- 3 celery stalks, chopped
- 3 garlic cloves, minced
- 2 tsp. dried thyme, crushed
- 1 (4-oz.) can green chilies
- 1 tbsp. ground cumin

- ✓ 2 (15¼-oz.) cans red kidney beans, rinsed and drained
- ✓ 2 (16-oz.) cans Great Northern beans, rinsed and drained
- ✓ 1 (15-oz.) can black beans, rinsed and drained
- ✓ 15 oz. tomato-vegetable juice cocktail
- ✓ 5 C. vegetable broth
- ✓ 2 tbsp. brown sugar
- ✓ 1 C. red wine

1. In a large-sized soup pan, heat oil over medium heat and sauté the onion, potatoes, carrot and celery for about 3-4 minutes.
2. Add the garlic, thyme, green chilies, jalapeño peppers and cumin and sauté for about 1 minute.
3. Add the beans, juice cocktail, broth and brown sugar and bring to a boil over medium-high heat.
4. Adjust the heat to medium-low and cook, covered for about 25 minutes.
5. Stir in the red wine and remove from heat.
6. Serve hot.

Per Serving:
Calories: 542| Fat: 9.4g| Carbs: 88.2g| Fiber: 26.3g| Protein: 26.3g

## BEANS, FARRO & KALE STEW
**Prep Time: 15 mins.| Cook Time: 45 mins.| Serves: 6**

- ✓ 2 tbsp. olive oil
- ✓ 1 C. carrots, peeled and chopped
- ✓ 1 C. celery, chopped
- ✓ 1 C. yellow onion, chopped
- ✓ 4 garlic cloves, minced
- ✓ 1 (14½-oz.) can diced tomatoes
- ✓ 1 C. farro, rinsed
- ✓ ½ C. fresh parsley sprigs
- ✓ 1 bay leaf
- ✓ 1 tsp. dried oregano
- ✓ Salt, as required
- ✓ 5 C. vegetable broth
- ✓ 4 C. fresh kale, thick ribs removed and chopped
- ✓ 1 (15-oz.) can cannellini beans, drained and rinsed
- ✓ 1 tbsp. fresh lemon juice

1. In a large-sized pan, heat the oil over medium-high heat and sauté the carrots, celery and onion for about 3 minutes.
2. Add the garlic and sauté for about 30 seconds.
3. Stir in the tomatoes, farro, parsley sprigs, bay leaf, oregano, salt and broth and bring to a boil.
4. Adjust the heat to medium-low and simmer covered for about 20 minutes.
5. With a slotted spoon, remove the parsley sprigs and discard them.
6. Stir in the kale and cook for about 10-15 minutes or until desired doneness.
7. Stir in the cannellini beans and cook for about 1-2 minutes or until heated completely.
8. With a slotted spoon, remove the bay leaf and discard it. Stir in the lemon juice and serve hot.

Per Serving:
Calories: 286| Fat: 6.1g| Carbs: 45.8g| Fiber: 8.2g| Protein: 15.3g

## BARLEY & LENTIL STEW
**Prep Time: 15 mins.| Cook Time: 50 mins.| Serves: 8**

- ✓ 2 tbsp. olive oil
- ✓ 2 carrots, peeled and chopped
- ✓ 1 large red onion, chopped
- ✓ 2 celery stalks, chopped
- ✓ 2 garlic cloves, minced
- ✓ 1 tsp. ground coriander
- ✓ 2 tsp. ground cumin
- ✓ 1 tsp. cayenne powder
- ✓ 1 C. barley
- ✓ 1 C. red lentils
- ✓ 5 C. tomatoes, finely chopped
- ✓ 5-6 C. vegetable broth
- ✓ 6 C. fresh spinach, torn
- ✓ Salt and ground black pepper, as required
- ✓

1. In a large-sized pan, heat the oil over medium heat and sauté the carrots, onion, celery and celery for about 5 minutes.
2. Add the garlic and spices and sauté for about 1 minute.
3. Add the barley, lentils, tomatoes and broth and bring to a rolling boil.
4. Adjust the heat to low and simmer, covered for about 40 minutes.
5. Stir in the spinach, salt and black pepper and simmer for about 3-4 minutes.
6. Serve hot.

Per Serving:

Calories: 264| Fat: 5.8g| Carbs: 41.1g| Fiber: 14.1g| Protein: 14.3g

## ZOODLES WITH TOMATOES
**Prep Time: 15 mins.| Cook Time: 7 mins.| Serves: 3**

- 2 tbsp. avocado oil
- 2 medium zucchinis, spiralized with Blade C
- 1 garlic clove, minced
- 1 C. cherry tomatoes, sliced
- Salt, as required

1. In a skillet, heat avocado oil over medium heat and cook the zucchini for about 3 minutes.
2. Add the garlic and cook for about 1 minute.
3. Add the cherry tomatoes and salt and cook for about 2-3 minutes.
4. Serve hot.

Per Serving:
Calories: 46| Fat: 1.6g| Carbs: 7.6g| Fiber: 2.6g| Protein: 2.3g

## SQUASH WITH FRUIT
**Prep Time: 15 mins.| Cook Time: 40 mins.| Serves: 4**

- ¼ C. water
- 1 medium butternut squash, halved and seeded
- ½ tbsp. olive oil
- ½ tbsp. balsamic vinegar
- Salt and ground black pepper, as required
- 4 large dates, pitted and chopped
- 4 fresh figs, chopped
- 3 tbsp. pistachios, chopped
- 2 tbsp. pumpkin seeds

1. Preheat your oven to 375 °F.
2. Place the water in the bottom of a baking dish.
3. Arrange the squash halves in the baking dish, hollow side up and drizzle with oil and vinegar.
4. Sprinkle with salt and black pepper.
5. Spread the dates, figs and pistachios on top.
6. Bake for approximately 40 minutes or until squash becomes tender.
7. Serve hot with the garnishing of pumpkin seeds.

Per Serving:
Calories: 227| Fat: 5.5g| Carbs: 46.4g| Fiber: 7.5g| Protein: 5g

## LENTIL CASSEROLE
**Prep Time: 15 mins.| Cook Time: 30 mins.| Serves: 6**

- Non-stick cooking spray
- 1 zucchini, chopped
- 1 bell pepper, seeded and chopped
- 1 C. fresh button mushrooms, sliced
- 2½ C. cooked green lentils
- 2 C. marinara sauce
- 1½ C. vegan cheese

1. Preheat your oven to 350 °F.
2. Light grease an 8-inch casserole dish with cooking spray.
3. In a bowl, mix together the zucchini, bell pepper and mushrooms.
4. In the bottom of the prepared casserole dish, place the lentils and top with the veggie mixture, followed by tomato sauce and cheese.
5. Bake for approximately 20-30 minutes or until top becomes bubbly.
6. Remove from the oven and set aside for about 5 minutes before serving.

Per Serving:
Calories: 227| Fat: 5.5g| Carbs: 46.4g| Fiber: 7.5g| Protein: 5g

## BEANS & TOMATO BAKE
**Prep Time: 15 mins.| Cook Time: 1¼ hrs.| Serves: 4**

- 1 C. dried lima beans, soaked for 8 hours and drained
- 1 bay leaf
- 1 vegetable bouillon cube
- 2-3 tbsp. olive oil
- 2-3 garlic cloves, minced
- 1 small onion, finely chopped
- 1 small carrot, peeled and shredded
- 1 (15½-oz.) can diced tomatoes
- 1 tbsp. tomato paste
- 1-2 tsp. pure maple syrup
- 1 tsp. red wine vinegar
- 2 tsp. dried oregano

64

- 1 tsp. dried thyme
- Pinch of ground nutmeg
- Salt and ground black pepper, as required
- 3 tbsp. fresh parsley, chopped
- 3 tbsp. fresh mint, finely chopped

1. In a large-sized pan of water, add the beans and bay leaf over high heat and bring to a boil.
2. Adjust the heat to medium and simmer for about 30 minutes.
3. Drain the beans, reserving 1 C. of the cooking liquid.
4. Dissolve the bouillon cube in the reserved hot cooking liquid.
5. Preheat your oven to 375 °F.
6. In a Dutch oven, heat the oil over medium heat and sauté the onion and garlic for about 3-4 minutes.
7. Add the carrot and cook for about 1-2 minutes.
8. Add the tomatoes, bouillon cube mixture and remaining ingredients except for fresh herbs and bring to a boil.
9. Adjust the heat to low and cook for about 10-12 minutes.
10. Add the beans, parsley, and mint and stir to combine.
11. With a piece of foil, cover the pan and bake for approximately 30-40 minutes.
12. Remove the foil and bake for approximately 10-15 minutes.
13. Remove from the oven and set aside for 10 minutes before serving.

Per Serving:
Calories: 152| Fat: 7.8g| Carbs: 18.6g| Fiber: 4.9g| Protein: 4.5g

## BARLEY & MUSHROOM BAKE
**Prep Time: 16 mins.| Cook Time: 1 hr. 10 mins.| Serves: 4**

- 3 tbsp. olive oil
- 2 garlic cloves, minced
- 8 oz. fresh button mushrooms, cleaned, trimmed, and sliced
- 1 C. pearl barley
- 2 C. vegetable broth
- ½ tsp. dried thyme
- 3 tbsp. fresh parsley, chopped

1. Preheat your oven to 350 °F.
2. In a Dutch oven, heat oil over medium heat and cook the garlic for about 1-2 minutes, stirring continuously.
3. Add the mushrooms and cook for about 7-8 minutes, stirring frequently.
4. Add the barley, broth, and thyme. Stir to combine.
5. Cover the Dutch oven and transfer into the oven.
6. Bake for approximately 1 hour.
7. Remove the Dutch oven from oven and, with a fork, fluff the barley mixture.
8. Stir in the parsley and serve.

Per Serving:
Calories: 287| Fat: 10.1g| Carbs: 42g| Fiber: 8.5g| Protein: 9.4g

## ASPARAGUS RISOTTO
**Prep Time: 15 mins.| Cook Time: 45 mins.| Serves: 4**

- 15-20 fresh asparagus spears, trimmed and cut into 1½-inch pieces
- 2 tbsp. olive oil
- 1 C. yellow onion, chopped
- 1 garlic clove, minced
- 1 C. Arborio rice
- 1 tbsp. fresh lemon zest, grated finely
- 2 tbsp. fresh lemon juice
- 5½ C. hot vegetable broth
- 1 tbsp. fresh parsley, chopped
- ¼ C. nutritional yeast
- Salt and ground black pepper, as required

1. In a medium-sized pan of boiling water, cook the asparagus for about 3 minutes.
2. Drain the asparagus and rinse under cold running water.
3. Drain well and set aside.
4. In a large-sized pan, heat oil over medium heat and sauté the onion for about 5 minutes.
5. Add the garlic and sauté for about 1 minute.
6. Add the rice and stir fry for about 2 minutes.
7. Add the lemon zest, lemon juice, and ½ C. of broth and cook for about 3 minutes or until all the liquid is absorbed, stirring gently.
8. Add 1 C. of broth and cook until all the broth is absorbed, stirring occasionally.
9. Repeat this process by adding ¾ C. of broth until

all the broth is absorbed, stirring occasionally. (This procedure will take about 20-30 minutes.)
10. Stir in the cooked asparagus and remaining ingredients and cook for about 4 minutes.
11. Serve hot.

Per Serving:
Calories: 353| Fat: 9.9g| Carbs: 50.5g| Fiber: 6.5g| Protein: 16.9g

## BAKED RISOTTO
**Prep Time: 15 mins.| Cook Time: 25 mins.| Serves: 5**

- 2 tbsp. olive oil
- 1 lb. cremini mushrooms, cleaned, trimmed, and cut into ¼-inch slices
- 1 garlic clove, minced
- 5 fresh thyme sprigs
- 1 lb. frozen pearl onions
- Salt, as required
- 1½ C. Arborio rice
- ½ C. dry white wine
- 5 C. warm vegetable broth
- 1 C. frozen green peas
- 1 C. nutritional yeast
- Ground black pepper, as required
- 2 tbsp. fresh chives, chopped

1. Preheat your oven to 425 °F.
2. In a Dutch oven, melt the butter over medium-high heat and sauté the mushrooms, garlic, and thyme for about 5 minutes.
3. Add the onions and salt. Sauté for about 2 minutes.
4. Stir in the rice and wine and bring to a boil.
5. Cook for about 1-2 minutes
6. Adjust the heat to low.
7. Add 2 C. of warm broth and cook for about 5 minutes, stirring continuously.
8. Add the remaining broth and stir to combine.
9. Cover the Dutch oven and transfer into the oven.
10. Bake for approximately 15 minutes.
11. Remove the pan from oven and stir in the peas, nutritional yeast and black pepper.
12. Serve immediately.

Per Serving:
Calories: 525| Fat: 9.7g| Carbs: 78.5g| Fiber: 14.1g| Protein: 30.6g

## RICE & BEANS IN SAUCE
**Prep Time: 15 mins.| Cook Time: 15 mins.| Serves: 4**

- 1 (15-oz.) can cannellini beans, rinsed and drained
- 1 (15-oz.) can garbanzo beans, rinsed and drained
- ¾ C. uncooked instant rice
- 1 (14½-oz.) can stewed tomatoes, undrained
- 1 C. vegetable broth
- 1 tsp. Italian seasoning
- ¼ tsp. red pepper flakes, crushed
- 1 C. marinara sauce
- ¼ C. vegan cheese

1. In a large-sized skillet, add all ingredients except for marinara and vegan cheese and stir to combine.
1. Place the pan over medium-high heat and bring to a boil.
2. Adjust the heat to low and simmer, covered for about 7-9 minutes or until rice is tender.
3. Stir in the marinara sauce and cook for about 2-3 minutes or until heated through, stirring occasionally.
4. Top with cheese and serve.

Per Serving:
Calories: 430| Fat: 4.9g| Carbs: 91.8g| Fiber: 13.6g| Protein: 17.4g

## RICE & LENTIL CASSEROLE
**Prep Time: 20 mins.| Cook Time: 1 hr.| Serves: 6**

- 2½ C. water, divided
- 1 C. red lentils, rinsed
- ½ C. wild rice, rinsed
- 1 tsp. olive oil
- 1 small onion, chopped
- 3 garlic cloves, minced
- 1/3 C. zucchini, chopped
- 1/3 C. carrot, peeled and chopped
- 1/3 C. celery stalk, chopped
- 1 tomato, chopped
- 8 oz. tomato sauce
- 1 tsp. ground cumin,
- 1 tsp. dried oregano, crushed
- 1 tsp. dried basil, crushed
- Salt and ground black pepper, as required

1. In a pan, add 1 C. of the water and rice over medium-high heat and bring to a boil.
2. Adjust the heat to low and simmer, covered for about 20 minutes.
3. Meanwhile, in another pan, add the remaining water and lentils over medium heat and bring to a boil.
4. Adjust the heat to low and simmer, covered for about 15 minutes.
5. Transfer the cooked rice and lentils into a casserole dish and set aside.
6. Preheat your oven to 350 °F.

7. In a large-sized skillet, heat the oil over medium heat and sauté the onion and garlic for about 4-5 minutes.
8. Add the zucchini, carrot, celery, tomato and tomato paste and cook for about 4-5 minutes.
9. Stir in the cumin, herbs, salt and black pepper and remove from the heat.
10. Transfer the vegetable mixture into the casserole dish with rice and lentils and stir to combine.
11. Bake for approximately 30 minutes.
12. Remove from the heat and set aside for about 5 minutes.
13. Cut into equal-sized 6 pieces and serve.

Per Serving:
Calories: 192| Fat: 1.5g| Carbs: 34.5g| Fiber: 12g| Protein: 11.3g

## PASTA WITH TOMATOES
**Prep Time: 15 mins.| Cook Time: 15 mins.| Serves: 4**

- 1 (8-oz.) package vegan linguini pasta
- 2 tbsp. olive oil
- 1 tbsp. garlic, minced
- 1 tbsp. dried oregano, crushed
- 1 tbsp. dried basil, crushed
- 1 tsp. dried thyme, crushed
- 2 C. plum tomatoes, chopped

1. In a large-sized pan of lightly salted boiling water, add the pasta and cook for about 8-10 minutes or according to package's directions.
2. Drain the pasta well.
3. In a large-sized skillet, heat oil over medium heat and sauté the garlic for about 1 minute.
4. Stir in herbs and sauté for about 1 minute more.
5. Add the pasta and cook for about 2-3 minutes or until heated completely.
6. Fold in tomatoes and remove from heat.
7. Serve hot.

Per Serving:
Calories: 301| Fat: 8.9g| Carbs: 47.7g| Fiber: 6.7g| Protein: 8.5g

## PASTA WITH ASPARAGUS
**Prep Time: 15 mins.| Cook Time: 12 mins.| Serves: 4**

- ¼ C. olive oil
- 5 garlic cloves, minced
- ½ tsp. red pepper flakes, crushed
- 1/8 tsp. hot pepper sauce
- 1 lb. asparagus, trimmed and cut into 1½-inch pieces
- Salt and ground black pepper, as required
- ½ lb. cooked whole-wheat pasta, drained

1. In a large-sized cast-iron skillet, heat the oil over medium heat and cook the garlic, red pepper flakes and hot pepper sauce for about 1 minute.
2. Add the asparagus, salt and black pepper and cook for about 8-10 minutes, stirring occasionally.
3. Place the hot pasta and toss to coat well.
4. Serve immediately.

Per Serving:
Calories: 326| Fat: 13.8g| Carbs: 39g| Fiber: 8.5g| Protein: 11.9g

## PASTA WITH MUSHROOMS
**Prep Time: 15 mins.| Cook Time: 10 mins.| Serves: 4**

- 12 oz. vegan whole-wheat pasta
- 4 tbsp. avocado oil
- 1 lb. fresh white mushrooms, sliced
- 2 garlic clove, minced
- 2 C. walnut milk
- 2 tbsp. fresh parsley, chopped
- 1½ tbsp. fresh lime juice
- Salt, as required
- Pinch of cayenne powder

1. In a medium-sized saucepan, add salted water and bring to a rolling boil.
2. Add pasta and cook for about 8-10 minutes or according to the manufacturer's directions.
3. Meanwhile, in a large-sized skillet, heat 2 tbsp. of the oil over medium heat and sauté the mushroom and garlic for about 4-5 minutes.
4. With a slotted spoon, transfer the mushrooms onto a plate.
5. In the same skillet, heat the remaining oil over medium heat.
6. Slowly add the flour, beating continuously.

7. Cook for about 1 minute, stirring continuously.
8. Slowly add the milk, beating continuously until smooth.
9. Add the mushrooms, parsley, lime juice, salt and cayenne powder and cook for about 1-2 minutes.
10. Divide the pasta onto serving plates.
11. Top with mushroom sauce and serve.

Per Serving:
Calories: 381| Fat: 6.5g| Carbs: 67g| Fiber: 9.9g| Protein: 16.6g

## PASTA WITH VEGGIES
**Prep Time: 20 mins.| Cook Time: 20 mins.| Serves: 5**

- 2 tbsp. olive oil
- 5 C. broccoli, cut into 1-inch pieces
- 1½ C. onions, chopped
- ¾ C. carrots, peeled and julienne
- 3 C. fresh mushrooms, sliced
- 1¼ C. yellow squash, halved lengthwise and sliced thinly
- 1 tsp. vegetable broth
- ¼ C. oil-packed sun-dried tomatoes, minced
- 1¼ C. canned crushed tomatoes with juice
- 1 tbsp. fresh parsley, finely chopped
- ¼ tsp. dried oregano
- ¼ tsp. dried rosemary
- 1/8 tsp. red pepper flakes, crushed
- 1 lb. cooked vegan angel-hair pasta

1. In a Dutch oven, melt the butter oven over medium heat and sauté the broccoli, onions and carrots for about 5 minutes.
2. Add the mushrooms, squash and garlic and sauté for about 2 minutes.
3. Stir in the remaining ingredients except for pasta and cheese and bring to a gentle boil.
4. Simmer for about 8-10 minutes.
5. Divide the pasta onto serving plates and top with veggie mixture.
6. Serve with the garnishing of Parmesan cheese.

Per Serving:
Calories: 243| Fat: 7.2g| Carbs: 38.2g| Fiber: 4.9g| Protein: 10g

## PASTA WITH BOLOGNESE SAUCE
**Prep Time: 20 mins.| Cook Time: 2 hrs.| Serves: 6**

**Bolognese Sauce**
- 5 tbsp. olive oil, divided
- 3 celery stalks, finely chopped
- 1 medium carrot, peeled and finely chopped
- 1 medium onion, finely chopped
- ¾ C. quinoa, rinsed
- 3 C. fresh mushrooms, chopped
- 2 oz. raw walnuts, chopped
- 4 garlic cloves, chopped
- ¾ tsp. dried oregano
- ½ tsp. dried thyme
- ¼ tsp. dried rosemary
- ¼ tsp. dried sage
- 1/8 tsp. red pepper flakes
- 1½ C. vegetable broth
- 1 tbsp. soy sauce
- 1 tbsp. white miso
- 1 tsp. agar-agar
- 1½ tsp. paprika
- 1 (14-oz.) can crushed tomatoes
- 1 tbsp. balsamic vinegar
- 4 bay leaves
- 2 tbsp. nutritional yeast
- ¼ C. oat milk
- Salt and ground black pepper, as required
- ¼ C. fresh basil leaves

**For Pasta**
- ¾ lb. whole-wheat pasta (of your choice)

1. Preheat your oven to 300 °F.
2. Heat 3 tbsp. of the olive oil in a large-sized Dutch oven over medium heat and cook the celery, carrots and onion for about 10 minutes, stirring frequently.
3. Stir in the quinoa and cook for about 3 minutes.
4. Add the remaining oil, mushrooms and walnut and stir to combine.
5. Now, adjust the heat to medium-high and cook for about 5 minutes.
6. Add the garlic, dried herbs and red pepper flakes and cook for about 1-2 minutes.
7. Add the broth and cook for about 5 minutes.
8. Add the soy sauce, miso, agar-agar and paprika and stir to combine.
9. Add the tomatoes along with ½ a can of water, vinegar and bay leaves and bring to a boil.
10. Remove the Dutch oven from heat and transfer into the oven.
11. Bake, uncovered for about 1½ hours, stirring once after 1 hour.
12. Meanwhile, in a pan of the lightly salted boiling water, cook the pasta for about 8-10 minutes or according to package's instructions.
13. Drin the pasta well.
14. Remove the Dutch oven from oven and stir in the nutritional yeast and oat milk.
15. Divide the pasta onto serving plates and top with Bolognese sauce.
16. Garnish with basil leaves and serve.

Per Serving:
Calories: 534| Fat: 21g| Carbs: 29.8g| Fiber: 13.1g| Protein: 20.3g

### SPAGHETTI WITH BEANS BALLS
**Prep Time: 20 mins.| Cook Time: 35 mins.| Serves: 4**

**For Beans Balls**
- 1½ tbsp. ground flaxseeds
- 4 tbsp. water
- 1½ C. canned chickpeas, drained and rinsed
- ¼ C. vegan whole-wheat breadcrumbs
- 2 tbsp. nutritional yeast
- ½ tsp. Italian seasoning
- ½ tsp. onion powder
- ½ tsp. garlic powder
- Salt, as required

**For Spaghetti**
- ½ lb. vegan whole-wheat spaghetti
- 12 oz. spaghetti sauce

1. Preheat your oven to 425 °F.
2. Grease a large-sized baking sheet.
3. For beans balls: in a large-sized bowl, add the ground flax and water and mix well.
4. Set aside for about 5 minutes.
5. In a separate bowl, add the chickpeas and with a potato masher, mash well.
6. Add the flaxseeds mixture and remaining ingredients and mix well.
7. Make desired-sized balls from the mixture.
8. Arrange the balls onto the prepared baking sheet in a single layer.
9. Bake for approximately 30-35 minutes, flipping once halfway through.
10. Meanwhile, in a pan of lightly salted boiling water, cook the spaghetti for about 8-10 minutes or according to package's instructions.
11. Drain the spaghetti well.
12. Divide the spaghetti onto serving plates and top with balls and marinara sauce.
13. Serve immediately.

Per Serving:
Calories: 479| Fat: 6.2g| Carbs: 89.8g| Fiber: 5.3g| Protein: 19.4g

### PASTA & CHICKPEAS CURRY
**Prep Time: 15 mins.| Cook Time: 45 mins.| Serves: 6**

- 10 oz. vegan whole-grain pasta
- 1 tbsp. vegetable oil
- 1 medium white onion, chopped
- 3 garlic cloves, minced
- 1 tsp. dried basil, crushed
- 1 tbsp. curry powder
- ¼ tsp. red pepper flakes, crushed
- 2 lb. ripe tomatoes, chopped
- 4 C. cauliflower, cut into bite-sized pieces
- 1 medium red bell pepper, seeded and sliced thinly
- 1 (15-oz.) can chickpeas, drained and rinsed
- ½ C. black raisins
- 1 C. fresh baby spinach
- Salt and ground black pepper, as required
- ¼ C. fresh parsley, chopped

1. In a pan of salted boiling water, add the pasta and cook for about 8-10 minutes or according to package's directions.
2. Drain the pasta well and set aside.
3. In a large-sized skillet, heat the oil over medium heat and sauté the onion for about 4-5 minutes.
4. Add the garlic, basil, curry powder and red pepper flakes and sauté for about 1 minute.
5. Stir in the tomatoes, cauliflower and bell pepper and bring to a gentle boil.
6. Adjust the heat to medium-low and simmer, covered for about 15-20 minutes.
7. Stir in chickpeas and raisins and cook for about 5 minutes.
8. Stir in the spinach and cook for about 3-4 minutes.
9. Stir in the pasta, salt and black pepper and remove from the heat.
10. Serve hot with the garnishing of parsley.

Per Serving:
Calories: 326| Fat: 4.6g| Carbs: 62g| Fiber: 5.2g| Protein: 12.6g

### PASTA CASSEOLE
**Prep Time: 15 mins.| Cook Time: 1 hr. 10.| Serves: 6**

**For Sauce**
- ✓ 1 C. sunflower seeds, shelled, soaked for 30 minutes, drained and rinsed
- ✓ ¼ C. low-sodium soy sauce
- ✓ 1½ C. water
- ✓ Pinch of ground black pepper

**For Casserole**
- ✓ 1 (14-oz.) package whole-wheat fusilli pasta
- ✓ 2 tbsp. extra-virgin olive oil
- ✓ 3 C. Brussels sprout, trimmed and quartered
- ✓ Salt and ground black pepper, as required
- ✓ 1 C. water
- ✓ 1 (14-oz.) package frozen spinach, thawed

1. Preheat your oven to 400 °F. Grease a large-sized baking dish.
2. For sauce: in a high-power blender, add all the ingredients and pulse until smooth.
3. Transfer the sauce into a bowl and set aside.
4. In a pan of boiling water, add the pasta and cook for about 8-10 minutes.
5. Drain the pasta well and set aside.
6. Meanwhile, in a large-sized skillet, heat the oil over medium heat and cook the Brussels sprout and black pepper for about 3-4 minutes.
7. Add the water and cook for about 8-10 minutes.
8. Stir in the spinach and cook for about 1 minute.
9. Stir in the sauce and cook for about 1 minute.
10. Stir in the cooked pasta and remove from the heat.
11. Transfer the pasta mixture into prepared baking dish.
12. Bake for approximately 35 minutes.
13. Remove from the oven and set aside for about 5 minutes before serving.

Per Serving:
Calories: 371| Fat: 10.8g| Carbs: 57.91g| Fiber: 3.9g| Protein: 13.9g

## CIABATTA BREAD
**Prep Time: 20 mins.| Cook Time: 30 mins.| Serves: 16**

**For Sponge:**
- ✓ ½ C. water
- ✓ ½ tsp. active dry yeast
- ✓ 1 C. all-purpose flour

**For Bread:**
- ✓ 2 C. plus 2 tbsp. water
- ✓ 1 tsp. active dry yeas
- ✓ 4 C. all-purpose flour
- ✓ 1½ tsp. salt

1. For sponge: place water and yeast in a bowl and mix until dissolved. Let it rest for 5 minutes or until it begins to foam
2. In the bowl of yeast mixture, place flour and mix until well combined.
3. With a plastic wrap, cover the bowl and set aside at room temperature for at least 8 hours or up to overnight.
4. For bread: place water and yeast in a bowl and mix until dissolved. Let it rest for 5 minutes or until it begins to foam.
5. In the bowl of yeast mixture, add the sponge and with a spatula, break it into stringy blobs.
6. Add the flour and salt and mix until a wet and thick dough forms.
7. Set aside for 10-20 minutes
8. In the bowl of a stand electric mixer fitted with a dough hook, place the dough and mix over medium speed until smooth and elastic dough forms
9. With a kitchen towel, cover the dough and place in warm place for 2-3 hours or until doubled in size
10. Place the dough onto a generously floured surface and divide it in two portions.
11. With generously floured hands, place each dough portion onto parchment paper.
12. Press your fingertips into each dough portion about halfway to dimple the surface.
13. Then, with your hands, flatten each loaf slightly and set aside, uncovered for about 30-40 minutes.
14. Preheat your oven to 475 °F.
15. With the help of parchment paper, place each loaf onto a baking sheet.
16. Bake for approximately 20-30 minutes or until a toothpick inserted in the center comes out clean.
17. Remove the loaf pans from oven and place onto a wire rack to cool for about 10 minutes.
18. Now, invert each bread onto the wire rack and coat with melted butter
19. Cut each bread loaf into desired-sized slices and serve.

Per Serving:
Calories: 143| Fat: 0.4g| Carbs: 30g| Fiber: 1.1g| Protein: 4.2g

## FOCACCIA

**Prep Time: 20 mins. | Cook Time: 20 mins. | Serves: 8**

### For Bread
- ✓ 4 C. all-purpose flour plus more for dusting
- ✓ 2¼ tsp. instant dry yeast
- ✓ 2 tsp. white sugar
- ✓ 1½ tsp. salt
- ✓ 1 1/3 C. warm water
- ✓ 1 tbsp. plus 1 tsp. olive oil, divided
- ✓ Olive oil cooking spray

### For Topping
- ✓ ¼ C. cherry tomatoes, sliced
- ✓ ¼ C. olives, pitted and sliced
- ✓ 2 fresh rosemary sprigs
- ✓ 3 tbsp. olive oil,, divided
- ✓ 2 tsp. flaked salt
- ✓ Pinch of smoked paprika

1. In a large-sized bowl, blend the flour, yeast, sugar, and salt.
2. Add the water and 1 tbsp. of olive oil and mix until dough just comes together.
3. Grease a bowl with remaining oil.
4. Grease a baking sheet with cooking spray.
5. Place the dough onto a smooth surface.
6. With your hands, knead the dough until a smooth dough forms.
7. Shape the dough into a ball and place into the oiled bowl.
8. With a kitchen towel, cover the bowl and place in a warm place for about 45-60 minutes or until doubled in size.
9. Place the dough onto a lightly floured surface and roll into a ½-inch thick rectangle.
10. Arrange the dough rectangle into the prepared baking sheet.
11. With plastic wrap, cover the baking sheet and place in a warm place for about 20 minutes.
12. Preheat your oven to 400 °F.
13. With the back of a wooden spoon, press deep holes into the focaccia.
14. Press the cherry tomatoes, olives and rosemary into the focaccia.
15. Then drizzle with half of olive oil and sprinkle with salt and paprika.
16. Bake for approximately 20 minutes or until the dough is slightly golden.
17. Remove from the oven, and drizzle with remaining olive oil.
18. Serve warm.

Per Serving:
Calories: 27 | Fat: 8.1g | Carbs: 49.2g | Fiber: 1.9g | Protein: 6.6g

## HERBS BREAD

**Prep Time: 20 mins. | Cook Time: 45 mins. | Serves: 6**

- ✓ 3 C. all-purpose flour
- ✓ 1½ tbsp. fresh thyme, chopped
- ✓ ½ tsp. active dry yeast
- ✓ 1 tsp. salt
- ✓ 1¼ C. water
- ✓ ¼ C. olive oil

1. Place flour, fresh herbs, yeast and salt in a bowl and mix well.
2. Add water and oil and mix until a wet and shaggy dough forms.
3. With a spoon, mix until a dough comes together.
4. With a plastic wrap, cover the dough bowl and set aside in warm place for about 10-18 hours
5. Place the dough onto a lightly floured surface and toss with flour until dough is sticky.
6. Place the dough onto a lightly greased parchment paper.
7. With a damp kitchen towel, cover the dough and set aside at warm place for about 1-1½ hours.
8. Preheat your oven to 500°F.
9. Heat a Dutch oven with a lid in the oven for 30 minutes.
10. Place the dough onto a generously floured surface and shape into a ball.
11. With a floured sharp knife, cut an 'X' on top of the dough.
12. Remove the hot pan from oven and carefully place the dough alongside the parchment paper inside.
13. Cover the pan with lid and immediately set the temperature of oven to 425 °F.
14. Bake for approximately 30 minutes.
15. Remove the lid of the pan and bake for approximately 15 minutes or until a wooden skewer inserted in the center comes out clean.
16. Remove the loaf pan from oven and place onto a wire rack to cool for about 10 minutes.

17. Now, invert the bread onto the wire rack to cool completely before slicing.
18. cut the bread into desired-sized slices and serve.

Per Serving:
Calories: 302| Fat: 9.1g| Carbs: 48.3g| Fiber: 2g| Protein: 6.7g

## SUN-DRIED TOMATO BREAD
**Prep Time: 15 mins.| Cook Time: 45 mins.| Serves: 8**

- 12 oz. self-rising flour
- 1 tsp. white sugar
- 1 tsp. dried parsley
- 1 tsp. dried basil
- 1 tsp. dried oregano
- 1 C. unsweetened almond milk
- 1 tbsp. tomato puree
- 1 tbsp. sunflower oil
- 2 oz. sun-dried tomatoes, drained, pat dried and chopped

1. Preheat your oven to 375 °F.
2. Line the bottom of a greased loaf pan with parchment paper.
3. Place flour, sugar and dried herbs in a bowl and mix well.
4. In a separate bowl, place milk, tomato puree and oil and beat until well combined.
5. Add sun-dried tomatoes and stir to combine.
6. Add the milk mixture into the bowl of flour mixture and mix well.
7. Place the bread mixture into the prepared loaf pan evenly.
8. Bake for approximately 40-45 minutes or until a wooden skewer inserted in the center comes out clean.
9. Remove from the oven and place the loaf pan onto a wire rack to cool for about 10 minutes.
10. Now, invert the bread onto the wire rack.
11. Cut the bread loaf into desired-sized slices and serve warm.

Per Serving:
Calories: 204| Fat: 3.8g| Carbs: 36.4g| Fiber: 1.7g| Protein: 5.8g

## HERBED FLATBREAD
**Prep Time: 15 mins.| Cook Time: 36 mins.| Serves: 6**

- 2 C. spelt flour
- 2 tsp. dried oregano, crushed
- 2 tsp. dried basil, crushed
- 1 tbsp. salt
- ¼ tsp. cayenne powder
- 2 tbsp. olive oil
- ¾ C. water

1. In a bowl, add the flour, herbs and spices and mix well.
2. Add the oil and ½ C. of water and mix until well combined.
3. Slowly add the remaining water and mix until a dough ball forms.
4. Place the dough onto a lightly floured surface and with your hands, gently knead the dough for about 5 minutes.
5. Divide the dough in 6 portions.
6. Place 1 dough portion onto a floured surface and roll into a 4-inch circle.
7. Sprinkle the top of bread with a Pinch of salt.
8. Heat a non-stick crepe pan over medium-high heat and cook the flatbread for about 5-6 minutes, flipping occasionally.
9. Repeat with remaining dough portions.
10. Serve immediately.

Per Serving:
Calories: 215| Fat5.9g| Carbs: 33.7g| Fiber: 5.6| Protein: 5.4g

## LEMON SORBET
**Prep Time: 10 mins.| Serves: 4**

- 2 tbsp. fresh lemon zest, grated
- ½ C. pure maple syrup
- 2 C. water
- 1½ C. fresh lemon juice

1. Freeze an ice cream maker tub for about 24 hours before making this sorbet.
2. Add all of the ingredients except the lemon juice in a pan and simmer them over medium heat for about 1 minute or until the sugar dissolves, stirring continuously.
3. Remove the pan from the heat and stir in the lemon juice.
4. Transfer the mixture into an airtight container and refrigerate for about 2 hours.
5. Transfer the mixture into an ice cream maker and process it according to the manufacturer's directions.
6. Return the ice cream to the airtight container and freeze for about 2 hours.

Per Serving:
Calories: 127| Fat: 0.8g| Carbs: 29g| Fiber: 0.6g| Protein: 0.8g

## BERRIES GRANITA
**Prep Time: 15 mins. | Serves: 6**

- ½ C. fresh strawberries, hulled and sliced
- ½ C. fresh raspberries
- ½ C. fresh blueberries
- ½ C. fresh blackberries
- 1 tbsp. maple syrup
- 1 tbsp. fresh lemon juice
- 1 C. ice cubes, crushed
- ¼ C. coconut cream
- 2-3 drop liquid stevia
- 1 tsp. fresh mint leaves

1. In a high-power blender, add the berries, maple syrup, lemon juice and ice cubes and pulse on high speed until smooth.
2. Transfer the berries mixture into an 8x8-inch baking dish evenly and freeze for at least 30 minutes.
3. Remove from the freezer and with a fork, stir the granita completely.
4. Freeze for about 2-3 hours, scraping after every 30 minutes with the help of a fork.
5. Meanwhile, in a bowl, add the coconut cream and stevia and beat until soft peaks form.
6. Place the granita into the serving glasses and top each with whipped coconut cream.
7. Garnish with mint leaves and serve immediately.

Per Serving:
Calories: 54 | Fat: 2.6g | Carbs: 7.9g | Fiber: 2.1g | Protein: 0.7g

## COFFEE GRANITA
**Prep Time: 10 mins. | Serves: 8**

- 4 C. hot brewed extra strong coffee
- 2 tsp. ground cinnamon
- ½ C. white sugar

1. In a large-sized bowl, add coffee, cinnamon and sugar and stir until sugar is completely dissolved.
2. Add ¼ C. of cream and beat until well combined.
3. Refrigerate for about 30 minutes.
4. Remove from refrigerator and transfer the mixture into a shallow baking dish.
5. Freeze for about 3 hours, scraping after every 30 minutes with the help of a fork.
6. With a piece of foil, cover tightly and freeze before serving.
7. While serving, in a bowl, add remaining cream and beat until soft peaks form.
8. Place the granita into serving glasses.

Per Serving:
Calories: 50 | Fat: 0g | Carbs: 13g | Fiber: 0.3g | Protein: 0.2g

## ALMOND BRITTLE
**Prep Time: 15 mins. | Cook Time: 10 mins. | Serves: 8**

- 1 C. almonds
- ¼ C. coconut oil
- ½ C. white sugar
- 2 tsp. vanilla extract
- ¼ tsp. salt
- 1/8 tsp. coarse salt

1. Line a 9x9-inch cake pan with parchment paper.
2. Add the coconut oil, sugar, vanilla and ¼ tsp. of salt in an 8-inch non-stick wok over medium heat and cook until well combined, stirring continuously.
3. Stir in the almonds and bring to a boil, stirring continuously.
4. Cook for about 2-3 minutes, stirring continuously.
5. Remove the wok from heat and place mixture into the prepared pan evenly.
6. With the back of a spoon, stir to spread the almonds and sprinkle with salt.
7. Set aside for about 1 hour or until cooled completely.
8. Break into pieces and serve.

Per Serving:
Calories: 177 | Fat: 12.8g | Carbs: 15.2g | Fiber: 1.5g | Protein: 2.5g

## COCONUT MACAROONS
**Prep Time: 15 mins. | Cook Time: 16 mins. | Serves: 12**

- 1¼ C. unsweetened coconut, shredded finely
- ¼ C. blanched almond flour
- ¼ C. maple syrup
- 3 tbsp. coconut oil

73

1. Preheat your oven to 350 °F. Line a baking sheet with parchment paper.
2. In a food processor, add all the ingredients and pulse until a thick, sticky mixture forms.
3. With a scooper, place the balls onto the prepared baking sheet about 1 inch apart.
4. Bake for 12-16 minutes until golden.
5. Remove from the oven and immediately transfer the macaroons onto a wire rack to cool completely before serving.

Per Serving:
Calories: 90| Fat: 7.3g| Carbs: 6.2g| Fiber: 1g| Protein: 0.8g

## TIRAMISU
**Prep Time: 15 mins.| Serves: 4**

- 10½ oz. silken tofu, pressed and drained
- ½ C. coconut cream
- 4 tbsp. white sugar
- 7 oz. plain graham crackers
- 1 C. very strong brewed coffee
- 1 tsp. unsweetened cocoa powder

1. In a high-power blender, add tofu, coconut cream and sugar and pulse until smooth.
2. Soak the crackers in coffee and arrange into the bottom of 4 tiramisu dishes.
3. Place a layer of the cream mixture over the biscuits.
4. Repeat the layers and then dust with cocoa powder.
5. Refrigerate for at least 8 hours before serving.

Per Serving:
Calories: 370| Fat: 14g| Carbs: 55.7g| Fiber: 2.5g| Protein: 9.2g

## VANILLA PANNA COTTA
**Prep Time: 20 mins.| Cook Time: 17 mins.| Serves: 4**

**For Panna Cotta**

- 2 tbsp. cornstarch
- 1 tsp. agar-agar powder
- 1 C. unsweetened soy milk, divided
- ¼ C. caster sugar
- 7 oz. coconut cream
- 1 tbsp. vanilla bean paste
- Pinch of salt

**For Strawberry Coulis**
- 8¾ oz. fresh strawberries, hulled and roughly chopped
- 2 tbsp. caster sugar
- 1 tbsp. cornstarch
- 3 tbsp. water
- 1 tbsp. fresh lime juice

6. For panna cotta: n a small-sized bowl, blend the cornstarch and agar-agar powder.
7. Add 4 tbsp. of the soya milk and stir to combine.
8. In a saucepan, add the remaining soy milk and caster sugar over medium heat and cook for about 2 minutes, stirring continuously.
9. Add the coconut cream, vanilla bean paste and salt and cook for about 3-5 minutes, stirring continuously.
10. Add the cornstarch paste and simmer for about 3-5 minutes, stirring continuously.
11. Remove the pan from heat and through a sieve, strain the mixture.
12. Divide the strained mixture into 4 silicone molds evenly.
13. Set aside for about 15 minutes.
14. Then refrigerate the molds for about 2 hours.
15. Meanwhile, for strawberry coulis: in a high-power blender, add all ingredients and pulse until smooth.
16. Transfer the strawberry mixture into a saucepan over medium heat and cook for 4-5 minutes, stirring continuously.
17. Remove from the heat and set aside to cool for 30 minutes.
18. Serve the panna cotta with the topping of strawberry coulis.

Per Serving:
Calories: 341| Fat: 13.1g| Carbs: 55.7g| Fiber: 2.8g| Protein: 3.7g

## CHOCOLATE PANNA COTTA
**Prep Time: 15 mins.| Cook Time: 5 mins.| Serves: 4**

- 1½ C. unsweetened almond milk, divided
- 1 tbsp. vegan powdered gelatin
- 1 C. unsweetened coconut milk
- 1/3 C. white sugar
- 3 tbsp. cacao powder

- ✓ 2 tsp. instant coffee granules
- ✓ 6 drops liquid stevia

1. In a large-sized bowl, add ½ C. of almond milk and sprinkle evenly with gelatin.
2. Set aside until soaked.
3. In a pan, add the remaining almond milk, coconut milk, Swerve, cacao powder, coffee granules, and stevia and bring to a gentle boil, stirring continuously.
4. Remove from the heat.
5. In a high-power blender, add the gelatin mixture and hot milk mixture and pulse until smooth.
6. Transfer the mixture into serving glasses and set aside to cool completely.
7. With plastic wrap, cover each glass and refrigerate for about 3-4 hours before serving.

Per Serving:
Calories: 136| Fat: 12.1g| Carbs: 5.8g| Fiber: 1.5g| Protein: 4.4g

## FIG CAKE
**Prep Time: 15 mins.| Cook Time: 55 mins.| Serves: 8**

- ✓ Olive oil cooking spray
- ✓ 1½ C. unbleached all-purpose flour plus more for dusting
- ✓ 2 tbsp. ground flaxseeds
- ✓ 6 tbsp. water
- ✓ ¾ tsp. baking powder
- ✓ Pinch of salt
- ✓ 1 tsp. fresh lemon zest, grated finely
- ✓ 2/3 C. sugar
- ✓ 1/3 C. unsweetened almond milk
- ✓ ¼ C. extra-virgin olive oil
- ✓ 4 tbsp. vegan butter, melted
- ✓ ½ tsp. vanilla extract
- ✓ 10 oz. fresh figs, chopped

1. Preheat your oven to 350 °F. Arrange a rack in the center portion of the oven.
2. Grease a 9-inch springform pan with cooking spray and then dust with flour lightly.
3. In a bowl, blend the flaxseed and water. Set aside for about 5 minutes.
4. In a large-sized bowl, sift together the flour, baking powder and salt.
5. Add the lemon zest and mix well.
6. In another bowl, add the sugar and flaxseeds mixture and with a hand mixer, beat until thick and pale yellow.
7. Add the almond milk, oil, vegan butter and vanilla extract and beat until well combined.
8. Add the flour mixture and with a wooden spoon, mix until well combined.
9. Set aside for about 10 minutes.
10. In the bowl of the flour mixture, add about ¾ of the figs and gently stir to combine.
11. Place the mixture into the prepared pan evenly and bake for approximately 15 minutes.
12. Remove from the oven and top the cake with the remaining figs evenly.
13. Bake for approximately 35-40 minutes or until top becomes golden brown.
14. Remove from the oven and place the pan onto a wire rack for about 10 minutes.
15. Carefully remove the cake from the pan and place onto the wire rack to cool completely.
16. Cut into desired-sized slices and serve.

Per Serving:
Calories: 362| Fat: 14.4g| Carbs: 58.1g| Fiber: 4.7g| Protein: 4g

## BANANA CAKE
**Prep Time: 15 mins.| Cook Time: 30 mins.| Serves: 12**

- ✓ Olive oil cooking spray
- ✓ 1¾ C. all-purpose flour
- ✓ 1 tsp. baking soda
- ✓ 2 tsp. baking powder
- ✓ ¼ tsp. salt
- ✓ 1 C. granulated white sugar
- ✓ ½ C. olive oil
- ✓ ½ C. applesauce
- ✓ 1 large ripe banana, peeled and mashed
- ✓ ½ C. fresh lemon juice
- ✓ 3 tsp. fresh lemon zest, grated
- ✓ 2 tsp. vanilla extract

1. Preheat your oven to 350 °F. Grease a 9-inch cake pan with cooking spray.
2. In a medium-sized bowl, blend the flour, baking soda, baking powder, and salt.
3. In a large-sized bowl, add the sugar, olive oil, and

applesauce and with a hand mixer, mix on high speed for 2 minutes.
4. Add in the mashed banana and whisk to combine.
5. Add in the lemon juice, lemon zest, and vanilla extract and mix until just combined.
6. Slowly add the flour mixture and stir until just combined.
7. Place the mixture into the prepared cake pan evenly.
8. Bake for approximately 35 minutes or until top becomes golden brown.
9. Remove from the oven and place the pan onto a wire rack for about 10 minutes.
10. Carefully remove the cake from the pan and place onto the wire rack to cool completely.
11. Cut into desired-sized slices and serve.

Per Serving:
Calories: 221| Fat: 8.7g| Carbs: 35.1g| Fiber: 1g| Protein: 2.1g

## MAPLE BAKED PEAR
**Prep Time: 10 mins.| Cook Time: 25 mins.| Serves: 4**

- ✓ 4 Anjou pears, halved and cored
- ✓ ¼ tsp. ground cinnamon
- ✓ ½ C. pure maple syrup
- ✓ 1 tsp. pure vanilla extract

1. Preheat your oven to 375 °F. Line a baking sheet with parchment paper.
2. Carefully cut a small-sized sliver off the underside of each pear half.
3. Arrange the pear halves onto the prepared baking sheet, cut side upwards and sprinkle with cinnamon.
4. In a small-sized bowl, add the maple syrup and vanilla extract and beat well.
5. Reserve about 2 tbsp. of the maple syrup mixture.
6. Place the remaining maple syrup mixture over the pears and bake for approximately 25 minutes or until lightly browned.
7. Remove from the oven and immediately drizzle with the reserved maple syrup mixture.
8. Serve warm.

Per Serving:
Calories: 227| Fat: 0.4g| Carbs: 58.5g| Fiber: 6.6g| Protein: 0.8g

# CHINESE RECIPES

### DRAGON FRUIT SALAD
**Prep Time: 15 mins.| Serves: 2**

**For Dressing**
- 2 tbsp. rice wine vinegar
- 2 tbsp. soy sauce
- 2 tsp. olive oil
- 2 tsp. sesame oil
- 2 tsp. maple syrup
- Salt and ground black pepper, as required

**For Salad**
- 1 C. dragon fruit, cubed
- 3 C. fresh baby spinach
- ½ C. tomato, sliced
- 2 tsp. pickled ginger, sliced

1. For dressing: in a small-sized bowl, add all the ingredients and beat until well combined.
2. For salad: in a large-sized serving bowl, add all the ingredients and mix well.
3. Pour the dressing and toss to coat well.
4. Serve immediately.

Per Serving:
Calories: 172| Fat: 9.8g| Carbs: 18.2g| Fiber: 3.1g| Protein: 3.2g

### PAPAYA & CARROT SALAD
**Prep Time: 15 mins.| Serves: 4**

**For Salad**
- 2 large green papayas, peeled, seeded and julienned
- 2 large carrots, peeled and julienned
- 2 tbsp. cilantro leaves, minced
- 2 tbsp. fresh mint leaves, minced
- ½ C. peanuts, finely chopped

**For Dressing**
- ¼ C. shallot, chopped
- 2 garlic cloves, chopped
- 2 Serrano peppers, seeded and chopped
- 2-3 tbsp. fresh lime juice
- 2 tbsp. soy sauce
- Dash of hot sauce
- 2 tbsp. white sugar

1. For salad: in a large-sized salad bowl, add all ingredients except for peanuts and mix.
2. For dressing: in a food processor, add all ingredients and pulse until well combined and smooth.
3. Pour dressing over salad and gently toss to coat well.
4. Serve immediately with the garnishing of peanuts.

Per Serving:
Calories: 223| Fat: 9.5g| Carbs: 32.4g| Fiber: 5.4g| Protein: 6.7g

### SAUTEED GREEN BEANS
**Prep Time: 15 mins.| Cook Time: 13 mins.| Serves: 4**

- 2 tbsp. peanut oil
- 2 scallions, chopped
- 1 garlic clove, minced
- 1 tbsp. fresh ginger, grated
- 1 lb. green beans, trimmed
- 1 tbsp. dark soy sauce
- ½ tsp. chili sauce
- ½ tsp. white sugar
- ¼ tsp. salt
- ¼ tsp. ground white pepper

1. In a large-sized skillet, heat oil over medium heat and sauté scallions, garlic and ginger for about 2-3 minutes.
2. Add green beans and sauté for about 6-7 minutes.
3. Add soy sauce, chili sauce, sugar, salt and white pepper and cook for about 2-3 minutes.
4. Serve hot.

Per Serving:
Calories: 107| Fat: 7g| Carbs: 10.4g| Fiber: 4.3g| Protein: 2.6g

## GARLICKY BROCCOLI

**Prep Time: 10 mins. | Cook Time: 8 mins. | Serves: 2**

- 1 tbsp. extra-virgin olive oil
- 3-4 garlic cloves, minced
- 2 C. broccoli florets
- 2 tbsp. soy sauce

1. In a large-sized skillet, heat the oil over medium heat and sauté the garlic for about 1 minute.
2. Add the broccoli and stir fry for about 2 minutes.
3. Stir in the soy sauce and stir fry for about 4-5 minutes or until desired doneness.
4. Serve hot.

Per Serving:
Calories: 109 | Fat: 7.3g | Carbs: 8.5g | Fiber: 2.6g | Protein: 4.7g

## GENERAL TSO CAULIFLOWER

**Prep Time: 15 mins. | Cook Time: 25 mins. | Serves: 4**

**For Cauliflower**
- ¾ C. all-purpose flour
- ¾ C. unsweetened almond milk
- Salt and ground black pepper, as required
- ¾ C. vegan panko breadcrumbs
- 1 head cauliflower, cut into bite-sized florets

**For Sauce**
- 2 tbsp. cornstarch
- 2 tbsp. water
- 1 tbsp. sesame oil
- 2 garlic cloves, chopped
- 1 tsp. fresh ginger, chopped
- ¼ C. brown sugar
- 2 tbsp. tomato paste
- ½ C. vegetable broth
- ¼ C. soy sauce
- ¼ C. rice vinegar
- Salt and ground black pepper, as required

**For Garnishing**
- 2 tbsp. sesame seeds
- 2 scallions, sliced

1. Preheat your oven to 350 °F. Line a baking sheet with parchment paper.
2. For cauliflower: in a shallow bowl, add the flour, almond milk, salt and black pepper and mix well.
3. In a separate shallow bowl, place the breadcrumbs.
4. Dip the cauliflower florets into flour mixture and then coat with the breadcrumbs.
5. Arrange the cauliflower florets onto the prepared baking sheet in a single layer.
6. Bake for approximately 25 minutes.
7. Meanwhile, for sauce: in a small-sized bowl, blend the cornstarch and water and mix well. Set aside.
8. In a small-sized saucepan, heat the sesame oil over medium heat and sauté the garlic for about 40-60 seconds.
9. Add the ginger, brown sugar, and tomato paste and cook for about 1 minute.
10. Add the cornstarch mixture and remaining ingredients and cook for about 5 minutes, stirring frequently.
11. Remove the cauliflower florets from oven and place onto a platter.
12. Place the sauces on to and mix well.
13. Garnish with scallions and sesame seeds and serve immediately.

Per Serving:
Calories: 296 | Fat: 6g | Carbs: 41.1g | Fiber: 3.2g | Protein: 6.6g

## EGGPLANT IN SAUCE

**Prep Time: 15 mins. | Cook Time: 14 mins. | Serves: 4**

**For Eggplant**
- 2 (10-oz.) small Chinese long eggplants, cut into bite-sized pieces
- 1 tsp. salt
- 1 tbsp. cornstarch

**For Sauce**
- 1 tbsp. light soy sauce
- ½ tsp. dark soy sauce
- 1 tbsp. water
- 2 tsp. white sugar
- 1 tsp. cornstarch

**For Cooking**
- 2½ tbsp. peanut oil
- 3 garlic cloves, chopped
- 1 tsp. fresh ginger, minced

1. For eggplant: in a large-sized bowl of water, add the salt and stir to combine well.
2. Place the eggplant pieces and set aside, covered for about 15 minutes.
3. Drain the eggplant pieces and pat dry them with paper towels.
4. Then sprinkle the eggplant pieces with cornstarch evenly.
5. For the sauce: in a small-sized bowl, add all ingredients and mix well. Set aside.
6. In a large-sized non-stick skillet, heat 2 tbsp. of oil over medium-high heat.
7. Place the eggplant pieces in the bottom of skillet without overlapping and cook for about 4-5 minutes per side.
8. Transfer the eggplants pieces onto a plate.
9. In the same skillet, heat the remaining oil over medium heat and sauté the garlic and ginger for about 30 seconds.
10. Stir in the eggplant pieces and sauce and cook for about 2-3 minutes.
11. Serve hot.

Per Serving:
Calories: 133| Fat: 8.7g| Carbs: 13.6g| Fiber: 5.2g| Protein: 1.9g

## VEGGIES IN SAUCE
**Prep Time: 20 mins.| Cook Time: 20 mins.| Serves: 2**

**For Veggies**
- 1 large Chinese eggplant, cut into bite-sized pieces
- Salt, as required
- 2 tsp. cornstarch
- ¼ C. peanut oil
- 1 small russet potato, cut into ¼-inch pieces
- 1 bell pepper, seeded and chopped
- 2 scallions, chopped
- 2 garlic cloves, minced
- 2 tsp. sesame seeds

**For Sauce**
- ¼ C. vegetable broth
- 1 tbsp. dry sherry
- 1 tbsp. soy sauce
- ½ tbsp. dark soy sauce
- ½ tbsp. white sugar
- 1 tsp. cornstarch
- Salt, as required

1. In a large-sized bowl of the water, add the eggplant and 2 tsp. of the salt and mx well
2. Place a plate over the eggplant pieces to submerge them in the water.
3. Set aside for about 15-20 minutes.
4. Drain the eggplant pieces and with paper towels, pat dry them completely.
5. In a bowl, place the eggplant pieces and cornstarch and gently toss to coat. Set aside.
6. For sauce: in a bowl, add all the ingredients and mix until well combined. Set aside.
7. In a large-sized skillet, heat the peanut oil over medium-high heat.
8. In the skillet, place the eggplant pieces without overlapping and cook for about 2-3 minutes, without moving.
9. Adjust the heat to medium heat and flip the eggplant pieces.
10. Cook for about 2-3 minutes or until golden brown.
11. With a slotted spoon, transfer the eggplant pieces onto a large-sized plate.
12. Now, in the skillet, place the potato pieces and cook for about 2-3 minutes, without moving.
13. Flip and cook for about 2-3 minutes, without moving.
14. With a slotted spoon, transfer the potato pieces onto the plate with the eggplant.
15. Remove some of the oil from the skillet, leaving about 1 tsp. inside.
16. In the same skillet, add the scallions and garlic and sauté for about 1 minute.
17. Add the sauce, stirring continuously until well combined.
18. Stir in the bell pepper, cooked eggplant and potato and cook for about 1-2 minutes, stirring continuously.
19. Garnish with sesame seeds and serve immediately.

Per Serving:
Calories: 218| Fat: 3.4g| Carbs: 43.1g| Fiber: 11.5g| Protein: 6.7g

## VEGGIES STIR FRY
**Prep Time: 15 mins.| Cook Time: 5 mins.| Serves: 4**

- 1 tbsp. canola oil
- 1½ C. broccoli florets
- 1 tbsp. water
- 1½ C. snow peas, ends trimmed
- ¾ C. carrot, peeled and julienned
- ½ C. sliced water chestnuts, drained
- 6 fresh shiitake mushrooms, sliced thinly
- ½ tsp. fresh ginger, minced
- 1 garlic clove, minced
- 3 tbsp. vegetable broth
- 3 tbsp. low-sodium soy sauce
- 1 tsp. cornstarch

1. In a large-sized non-stick wok, heat oil over medium-high heat and stir fry the broccoli and water for about 1 minute.
2. Add snow peas, carrots, water chestnuts, mushrooms, ginger and garlic and ginger and stir fry for about 2-3 minutes.
3. Meanwhile, in a small-sized bowl, blend the broth, soy sauce, and cornstarch.
4. Add the cornstarch mixture into the wok and stir fry for about 1 minute.
5. Serve hot.

Per Serving:
Calories: 136| Fat: 4.2g| Carbs: 19.5g| Fiber: 6g| Protein: 7.8g

## GENERAL TSO TOFU

**Prep Time: 15 mins.| Cook Time: 12 mins.| Serves: 3**

### For Tofu
- 10 oz. firm tofu, pressed, drained and cubed
- 2 tbsp. soy sauce
- 1 tbsp. rice vinegar
- 6 tbsp. cornstarch
- 2 tbsp. extra-virgin olive oil
- 2 garlic cloves, minced
- 1 tbsp. sesame seeds

### For Sauce
- 3 tbsp. vegetable broth
- 3 tbsp. rice vinegar
- 3 tbsp. soy sauce
- 3 tbsp. brown sugar
- 1 tbsp. cornstarch
- 1/8 tsp. red pepper flakes, crushed

1. For tofu: in a bowl, add the tofu cubes, soy sauce and vinegar and toss to coat well.
2. Refrigerate overnight.
3. Remove the tofu cubes from the bowl and discard the marinade.
4. In a bowl, add the tofu cubes and cornstarch and toss to coat.
5. In a skillet, heat the oil over medium-high heat and cook the tofu cubes for about 3-5 minutes or until golden brown.
6. With a slotted spoon, transfer the tofu cubes onto a plate and set aside.
7. In the same skillet, add the garlic and cook for about 1-2 minutes, stirring frequently.
8. Meanwhile, for the sauce: in a bowl, add all ingredients and mix well.
9. In the skillet, add the sauce and cook for about 2-3 minutes or until desired thickness, stirring frequently.
10. Stir in the tofu cubes and cook for about 1-2 minutes.
11. Serve hot with the garnishing of sesame seeds.

Per Serving:
Calories: 268| Fat: 14.5g| Carbs: 22.1g| Fiber: 1.6g| Protein: 10.4g

## GLAZED TOFU

**Prep Time: 15 mins.| Cook Time: 20 mins.| Serves: 3**

4 tbsp. sake
3 tbsp. low-sodium soy sauce
1 tbsp. coconut sugar
¼ tbsp. chili powder
1 tbsp. olive oil
1 onion, cut into thin slices
1 (14-oz.) block firm tofu, pressed, drained and cut into 16 square
1 red chili, sliced
1 scallion, cut into thin slices

1. For sauce: in a bowl, add the sake, soy sauce, coconut sugar and chili powder and beat until well combined. Set aside.
2. In a non-stick skillet, heat the oil over medium heat and cook the onion for about 4-5 minutes.
3. Add the tofu, red chili and sauce and stir to combine.
4. Adjust the heat to high and bring to a boil.
5. Adjust the heat to medium-high and cook, covered for about 5 minutes, basting the tofu with sauce 2-3 times.
6. Adjust the heat to high and cook, uncovered for about 2-3 minutes or until desired thickness of the sauce.
7. Stir in the scallion and remove from the heat.
8. Serve immediately.

Per Serving:
Calories: 203| Fat: 5.8g| Carbs: 26.6g| Fiber: 2.7g| Protein: 12.5g

80

## TOFU WITH BROCCOLI

**Prep Time: 20 mins. | Cook Time: 25 mins. | Serves: 3**

**For Tofu**
- 14 oz. firm tofu, drained, pressed and cut into 1-inch slices
- 1/3 C. cornstarch, divided
- 1/3 C. olive oil
- 1 tsp. fresh ginger, grated
- 1 medium onion, sliced thinly
- 3 tbsp. low-sodium soy sauce
- 2 tbsp. balsamic vinegar
- 1 tbsp. maple syrup
- 1 tsp. sesame oil
- ½ C. water

**For Broccoli**
- 2 C. broccoli florets

1. In a shallow bowl, place tofu cubes and ¼ C. of the cornstarch and toss to coat well.
2. In a cast iron skillet, heat the olive oil over medium heat and cook the tofu cubes for about 8-10 minutes or until golden from all sides.
3. With a slotted spoon, transfer the tofu cubes onto a plate. Set aside.
4. In the same skillet, add the ginger and sauté for about 1 minute.
5. Add the onions and sauté for about 2-3 minutes.
6. Add the soy sauce, vinegar, maple syrup and sesame oil and bring to a gentle simmer.
7. In the meantime, in a small-sized bowl, dissolve the remaining cornstarch in water.
8. Slowly add the cornstarch mixture into the sauce, stirring continuously.
9. Stir in the cooked tofu and cook for about 1 minute.
10. Meanwhile, in a large-sized pan of water, arrange a steamer basket and bring to a boil.
11. Place the broccoli florets in the steamer basket and steam, covered for about 5-6 minutes.
12. Drain the broccoli and transfer into the skillet of tofu and stir to combine.
13. Serve hot.

Per Serving:
Calories: 414 | Fat: 29.7g | Carbs: 28.7g | Fiber: 3.8g | Protein: 14g

## TOFU WITH MUSHROOMS

**Prep Time: 15 mins. | Cook Time: 25 mins. | Serves: 4**

**For Tofu**
- 16 oz. extra-firm tofu, pressed, drained and cut into ½-inch cubes
- 1 garlic clove, minced
- 3 tbsp. rice vinegar
- 3 tbsp. low-sodium soy sauce
- 3 tbsp. cornstarch
- 2 tbsp. sesame oil
- 1 tbsp. brown sugar
- 1 tsp. red pepper flakes
- 2 tbsp. coconut oil

**For Mushrooms**
- ¼ C. water
- 1 small yellow onion, minced
- 3 large garlic cloves, minced
- 1 tsp. fresh ginger, grated
- 2 C. fresh mushrooms, sliced
- 3 tbsp. red curry paste
- 13 oz. light coconut milk
- 1 tbsp. low-sodium soy sauce
- 1 tbsp. samba oelek
- 2 tbsp. fresh lime juice
- 1 tsp. lime zest, grated
- 8 fresh basil leaves, chopped

1. For tofu: in a resealable bag, place all ingredients.
2. Seal the bag and shake to coat well.
3. Refrigerate to marinate for 2-4 hours.
4. In a large-sized skillet, melt the coconut oil over medium heat and stir fry the tofu cubes for about 4-5 minutes or until golden brown completely.
5. With a slotted spoon, transfer the tofu cubes into a bowl.
6. For curry: in a large-sized pan, add the water over medium heat and ring to a simmer.
7. Add the minced onion, garlic and ginger and cook for about 5 minutes.
8. Add the mushrooms and curry paste and stir to combine well.
9. Stir in the remaining ingredients except for basil and simmer for about 10 minutes.
10. Stir in the tofu and simmer for about 5 minutes.
11. Garnish with basil and serve.

81

Per Serving:
Calories: 556| Fat: 47.1g| Carbs: 24.8g| Fiber: 4.1g| Protein: 14.6g

### TOFU WITH GREEN PEAS
**Prep Time: 15 mins.| Cook Time: 15 mins.| Serves: 6**

- 1 tbsp. chile garlic sauce
- 3 tbsp. soy sauce
- 2 tbsp. canola oil, divided
- 1 (16-oz.) package extra-firm tofu, pressed, drained and cubed
- 1 C. onion, chopped
- 1 tbsp. fresh ginger, minced
- 2 garlic cloves, minced
- 1 C. frozen peas, thawed
- 2½ C. snow peas, trimmed
- 2½ C. sugar snap peas, trimmed
- 1 tsp. sesame seeds

1. For sauce: in a bowl, add the chile garlic sauce and soy sauce and mix until well combined.
2. In a large-sized skillet, heat 1 tbsp. of the oil over medium-high heat and cook the tofu for about 4-5 minutes or until browned completely, stirring occasionally.
3. Transfer the tofu into a bowl
4. In the same skillet, heat the remaining oil over medium heat and sauté the onion for about 3-4 minutes.
5. Add the ginger and garlic and sauté for about 1 minute.
6. Stir in all three peas and cook for about 2-3 minutes.
7. Stir in the sauce mixture and tofu and cook for about 1-2 minutes.
8. Serve hot with the garnishing of sesame seeds.

Per Serving:
Calories: 187| Fat: 9.4g| Carbs: 15.5g| Fiber: 5g| Protein: 12.6g

### TOFU WITH VEGGIES
**Prep Time: 20 mins.| Cook Time: 42 mins.| Serves: 4**

- 1 (14-oz.) package extra-firm tofu, pressed, drained and cut into small cubes
- 2 tbsp. sesame oil, divided
- 4 tbsp. low-sodium soy sauce
- 3 tbsp. maple syrup
- 2 tbsp. peanut butter
- 2 tbsp. fresh lime juice
- 1-2 tsp. chili garlic sauce
- 1 lb. green beans, trimmed
- 2-3 small red bell peppers, seeded and cubed
- 2 scallion greens, chopped

1. Preheat your oven to 400 °F. Line a baking sheet with parchment paper.
2. Arrange the tofu cubes onto the prepared baking sheet in a single layer.
3. Bake for approximately 25-30 minutes.
4. Meanwhile, in a small-sized bowl, add 1 tbsp. of the sesame oil, soy sauce, maple syrup, peanut butter, lime juice, and chili garlic sauce and beat until well combined. Set aside.
5. Remove from the oven and place the tofu cubes into the bowl of sauce.
6. Stir the mixture well and set aside for about 10 minutes, stirring occasionally.
7. With a slotted spoon, remove the tofu cubes from bowl, reserving the sauce
8. Heat a large-sized cast-iron skillet over medium heat and cook the tofu cubes for about 5 minutes, stirring occasionally.
9. With a slotted spoon, transfer the tofu cubes onto a plate. Set aside.
10. In the same skillet, add the remaining sesame oil, green beans, bell peppers and 2-3 tbsp. of reserved sauce and cook, covered for about 4-5 minutes.
11. Adjust the heat to medium-high, and stir in the cooked tofu remaining reserved sauce.
12. Cook for about 1-2 minutes, stirring frequently.
13. Stir in the scallion greens and remove from the heat.
14. Serve hot.

Per Serving:
Calories: 347| Fat: 19.9g| Carbs: 32.1g| Fiber: 6.6g| Protein: 17.2g

### TOFU & RICE SALAD
**Prep Time: 15 mins.| Serves: 4**

**For Salad**
- 1 (12-oz.) package firm tofu, pressed, drained and sliced
- 1½ C. cooked brown rice
- 3 large tomatoes, peeled, chopped
- ¼ C. fresh basil leaves

**For Dressing**
- 3 scallions, chopped
- 2 tbsp. black sesame seeds, toasted
- 2 tbsp. low-sodium soy sauce
- ½ tsp. sesame oil, toasted
- Drop of hot pepper sauce
- 1 tbsp. maple syrup

- ¼ tsp. red chili powder

1. In a large-sized salad bowl, place all the ingredients and toss to coat well.
2. Serve immediately.

Per Serving:
Calories: 393| Fat: 8.6g| Carbs: 66.9g| Fiber: 5.7g| Protein: 15.1g

## TOFU CHOW MEIN
**Prep Time: 15 mins.| Cook Time: 25 mins.| Serves: 4**

- 8 oz. uncooked Chinese wheat noodles
- 3 tbsp. sesame oil, divided
- 1 (16-oz.) package extra-firm tofu, drained, pressed and cut into ½-inch cubes
- 2 C. fresh mushrooms, sliced
- 1 medium bell pepper, seeded and julienned
- ¼ C. low-sodium soy sauce
- 3 scallions, sliced thinly

1. In a large-sized pan of lightly salted boiling water, add the noodles and cook for about 8-10 minutes or according to package's directions.
2. Drain the noodles well.
3. In a bowl, add the pasta and 1 tbsp. of oil and toss to coat well.
4. Now, arrange the pasta onto a large-sized baking sheet and set aside for about 1 hour.
5. In a large-sized cast iron skillet, heat 1 tbsp. of oil over medium heat.
6. In the skillet, place the noodles in an even layer and cook for about 5 minutes.
7. Transfer the noodles onto a plate.
8. In the same skillet, heat the remaining oil over medium-high heat and stir fry the tofu, mushrooms and bell pepper for about 3-4 minutes, stirring occasionally.
9. Add the noodles and soy sauce and cook for about 2-3 minutes, tossing occasionally.
10. Serve hot with the garnishing of scallion.

Per Serving:
Calories: 427| Fat: 19.8g| Carbs: 45.8g| Fiber: 5.5g| Protein: 21.8g

## TOFU & VEGGIE HOT POT
**Prep Time: 15 mins.| Cook Time: 25 mins.| Serves: 5**

- 5¼ C. vegetable broth
- 2 garlic cloves, crushed
- 4 (¼-inch-thick) slices fresh ginger, peeled
- 2 tsp. canola oil
- 1¾ C. shiitake mushrooms, sliced
- ¼ tsp. red pepper flakes, crushed
- 1 small bok choy head, cut into ½-inch pieces (stems and leaves separated)
- 3½ oz. Chinese wheat noodles
- 1 (14-oz.) package firm tofu, pressed, drained and cut into ½-inch cubes
- 1 C. carrots, peeled and grated
- 4-6 tsp. rice vinegar
- 2 tsp. low-sodium soy sauce
- 1 tsp. sesame oil, toasted
- ¼ C. scallions, chopped

1. In a Dutch oven, add broth, ginger and garlic and bring to a boil
2. Adjust the heat to medium-low and simmer, partially covered for about 15 minutes.
3. Meanwhile, in a large-sized non-stick skillet, heat oil over medium-high heat and cook the mushrooms and red pepper flakes for about 3-5 minutes, stirring occasionally.
4. Add bok choy stems and cook for about 3-4 minutes, stirring occasionally.
5. Discard the ginger and garlic from broth.
6. Transfer the mushroom mixture to the broth and immediately Adjust the heat to medium-low.
7. Add in the noodles and simmer for about 3 minutes.
8. Add bok choy greens and tofu and simmer for about 2 minutes.
9. Stir in carrots, vinegar, soy sauce and sesame oil and remove from the heat.
10. Serve with the garnishing of scallions.

Per Serving:
Calories: 344| Fat: 14.6g| Carbs: 32.2g| Fiber: 5.3g| Protein: 18.5g

## TOFU & BAMBOO SHOOT SOUP
**Prep Time: 15 mins.| Cook Time: 20 mins.| Serves: 4**

- ½ C. dried mushrooms
- 12 dried lily buds
- 3 tbsp. cold water
- 2 tbsp. cornflour
- 4 C. low-sodium vegetable broth
- 2 tbsp. dark soy sauce
- 2 tbsp. white vinegar
- ½ tsp. salt
- 1 C. spiced tofu, shredded
- 1 C. bamboo shoots, shredded
- 1½ tsp. ground white pepper
- 1 tbsp. sesame oil
- ¼ C. scallion, chopped

1. In a bowl of boiling water, soak the dried mushrooms for about 25-30 minutes or until tender.
2. In another bowl of boiling water, soak the dried lily buds for about 10-15 minutes or until tender.
3. Then drain the lily buds and cut off the hard tough tips. Set aside.
4. In a small-sized bowl, add the water and cornflour and mix until smooth. Set aside.
5. In a large-sized soup pan, add the broth over medium heat and bring to a boil.
6. Add the soy sauce, vinegar and salt and stir to combine.
7. Add the mushrooms, lily buds, tofu, bamboo shoots and white pepper and cook for about 4-5 minutes, stirring occasionally.
8. Adjust the heat to low and add in the cornflour mixture, stirring continuously.
9. Cook for about 5-8 minutes or until slightly thickened, stirring frequently.
10. Divide the soup into serving bowls and drizzle with sesame oil.
11. Serve hot with the garnishing of scallion.

Per Serving:
Calories: 124| Fat: 6.4g| Carbs: 8.8g| Fiber: 2.2g| Protein: 9.4g

## TOFU & GREENS SOUP
**Prep Time: 15 mins.| Cook Time: 55 mins.| Serves: 4**

- ✓ 8 oz. frozen shepherd's purse
- ✓ 4 C. chicken broth
- ✓ 1 tsp. sesame oil
- ✓ Salt, as required
- ✓ ¼ tsp. ground white pepper
- ✓ ¼ C. cornstarch
- ✓ ¼ C. water
- ✓ 7 oz. silken tofu, pressed, drained and cut into ½-inch cubes

1. Through a colander, rinse the shepherd's purse completely.
2. With your hands, gently squeeze the water from the shepherd's purse.
3. Then chop the leaves into small pieces. Set aside.
4. In a medium-sized pan, add the chicken broth, sesame oil, salt and white pepper and bring to a gentle simmer.
5. Meanwhile, dissolve the cornstarch in water.
6. In the soup pan, add the cornstarch mixture, stirring continuously.
7. Simmer for about 1 minute, tiring continuously.
8. Add the shepherd's purse and gently stir to combine.

9. Add the tofu cubes and gently stir to combine.
10. Simmer for about 2-4 minutes.
11. Serve hot.

Per Serving:
Calories: 141| Fat: 4.1g| Carbs: 13.7g| Fiber: 2g| Protein: 11.9g

## SWEET & SOUR TEMPEH
**Prep Time: 15 mins.| Cook Time: 20 mins.| Serves: 2**

- ✓ 1/3 C. apple cider vinegar
- ✓ ¼ C. ketchup
- ✓ 2 tbsp. low-sodium soy sauce
- ✓ ¼ C. coconut sugar
- ✓ 1 tsp. garlic powder
- ✓ 1 tbsp. avocado oil
- ✓ 1 (8-oz.) package tempeh, cut into 1-inch cubes
- ✓ 1 tbsp. scallion, chopped
- ✓ 1 tsp. white sesame seeds

1. In a saucepan, add the vinegar, ketchup, soy sauce, coconut sugar and garlic powder over medium heat and bring to a gentle simmer, stirring continuously.
2. Adjust the heat to low and cook for about 10-15 minutes or until the sauce is reduced by half.
3. Meanwhile, in a large-sized skillet, heat the oil over medium heat.
4. Place the tempeh cubes in a single layer and cook for about 5 minutes per side or until browned.
5. Add the tempeh cubes in the pan of sauce and toss to coat well.
6. Remove from the heat and serve hot with the topping of scallion and sesame seeds.

Per Serving:
Calories: 375| Fat: 14g| Carbs: 45.6g| Fiber: 0.8g| Protein: 23.2g

## TEMPEH WITH VEGGIES

**Prep Time: 15 mins. | Cook Time: 17 mins. | Serves: 3**

### For Sauce
- 3 tbsp. tahini
- 2 tbsp. low-sodium soy sauce
- 1 tbsp. sesame oil
- 1 tbsp. chili garlic sauce
- 1 tbsp. maple syrup

### For Tempeh & Veggies
- 3 tbsp. olive oil, divided
- 8 oz. tempeh, cut into a 1x2-inch rectangular strip
- 8 oz. fresh button mushrooms, sliced thinly
- 8 oz. fresh spinach
- 1 tbsp. fresh ginger, minced
- 1 tbsp. garlic, minced

1. For sauce: in a bowl, add all ingredients and beat until well combined.
2. In a large-sized skillet, heat the oil over medium-high heat and cook the tempeh for about 4-5 minutes or until browned.
3. With a slotted spoon, transfer the tempeh into a bowl and set aside.
4. In the same skillet, heat the remaining oil over medium-high heat and cook the mushrooms for about 6-7 minutes, stirring frequently.
5. With a slotted spoon, transfer the mushrooms into a bowl and set aside.
6. In the same skillet, add the spinach, ginger and garlic and cook for about 2-3 minutes.
7. Stir in the cooked tempeh, mushrooms and sauce and cook for about 1-2 minutes, stirring continuously.
8. Serve hot.

Per Serving:
Calories: 473 | Fat: 35.4g | Carbs: 25.2g | Fiber: 4.5g | Protein: 22.7g

## CRISPY FRIED NOODLES

**Prep Time: 15 mins. | Cook Time: 20 mins. | Serves: 4**

- 1 tbsp. plus 2 tsp. vegetable oil, divided
- 1 C. carrot, peeled and shredded
- ½ C. white onion, sliced thinly
- ½ C. scallion, sliced thinly
- 2 tsp. garlic, minced
- 12 oz. cooked Hong Kong noodles
- ¼ C. low-sodium soy sauce
- 2 tbsp. cold water
- 1 tbsp. hoisin sauce
- 1 tbsp. sesame oil, toasted
- 2 tsp. cornstarch
- 1 C. bean sprouts

1. In a large-sized skillet, heat 2 tsp. of vegetable oil over medium-high heat and sauté the carrots and white onions for about 3-5 minutes.
2. Add the scallion and garlic and sauté for about 30-60 seconds.
3. Transfer the carrot mixture onto a plate and cover with a piece of foil to keep warm.
4. In the same skillet, heat the remaining vegetable oil over medium-low heat.
5. Place the noodles in an even layer and cook for about 3-4 minutes per side or until browned and crispy on the edges.
6. Meanwhile, for the sauce: in a small-sized bowl, add the soy sauce, water, sesame oil and cornstarch and beat until well combined.
7. In the skillet, add the cooked vegetables and bean sprouts and stir to combine.
8. Stir in the sauce and bring to a gentle simmer.
9. Cook for about 2-3 minutes.
10. Serve hot.

Per Serving:
Calories: 240 | Fat: 10.5g | Carbs: 31.2g | Fiber: 2.4g | Protein: 7.5g

## SESAME NOODLES

**Prep Time: 10 mins. | Cook Time: 10 mins. | Serves: 4**

- 1 lb. uncooked Chinese noodles
- ¼ C. low-sodium soy sauce
- 2 tbsp. rice vinegar
- 1 tbsp. sesame oil, toasted
- ½ tsp. chili garlic sauce
- 1 tsp. ground ginger
- ½ tsp. garlic powder
- ¼ tsp. freshly ground black pepper
- ½ C. scallions, sliced
- 1 tsp. sesame seeds, toasted

1. In a large-sized pan of salted boiling water, cook the noodles for about 8-10 minutes.
2. Meanwhile, in a bowl, add the soy sauce, vinegar, sesame oil, chili garlic sauce, ground ginger, garlic powder and black pepper and beat until well combined.
3. Drain the noodles and rinse under cold running water.
4. Again, drain the noodles and transfer into a bowl.
5. Add the vinegar mixture and scallions toss to coat well.
6. Garnish with sesame seeds and serve.

Per Serving:
Calories: 378| Fat: 6.4g| Carbs: 64.8g| Fiber: 0.5g| Protein: 14.3g

## NOODLES & VEGGIE SOUP
**Prep Time: 15 mins.| Cook Time: 12 mins.| Serves: 4**

- ✓ 4 oz. Chinese wheat noodles
- ✓ 1 tbsp. canola oil
- ✓ 1½ tbsp. garlic, minced
- ✓ 1 tbsp. fresh ginger, minced
- ✓ 1 Serrano pepper, seeded and minced
- ✓ 1 (32 fluid oz.) container vegetable broth
- ✓ 1 tbsp. plus 1 tsp. low-sodium soy sauce, divided
- ✓ 1 tbsp. rice wine
- ✓ 2 C. fresh mushrooms, sliced
- ✓ 2 C. broccoli florets
- ✓ ½ C. warm water
- ✓ 2 tsp. white miso
- ✓ 1 (14-oz.) package extra-firm tofu, pressed, drained and cubed
- ✓ ½ C. scallions, sliced thinly
- ✓ 4 tsp. sesame oil, toasted and divided

1. In a large-sized pan of salted boiling water, cook the noodles for about 8-10 minutes or according to package's directions.
2. Drain the noodles completely and set aside.
3. Meanwhile, in a large-sized pan, heat the oil over medium heat and sauté the garlic, ginger and Serrano pepper for about 1 minute.
4. Add broth, 1 tbsp. of soy sauce and wine and bring to a gentle simmer.
5. Stir in the mushrooms and broccoli and simmer for about 5-7 minutes.
6. Meanwhile, in a small-sized bowl, add the warm water and miso and beat until smooth.
7. Add the miso mixture into the pan and stir to combine well.
8. Stir in the tofu and cook for about 1-2 minutes.
9. Stir in the scallions and remove from the heat
10. Divide the noodles into 4 serving bowls and top with the hot soup.
11. Drizzle each bowl with sesame oil and remaining soy sauce and serve.

Per Serving:
Calories: 320| Fat: 15.1g| Carbs: 31g| Fiber: 4.2g| Protein: 19.3g

## RICE NOODLES WITH SNOW PEAS
**Prep Time: 20 mins.| Cook Time: 10 mins.| Serves: 2**

**For Sauce**
- ✓ 2 garlic cloves, minced
- ✓ 1 tbsp. coconut sugar
- ✓ ½ tsp. red pepper flakes, crushed
- ✓ 2 tbsp. fresh lime juice
- ✓ 2 tbsp. soy sauce

**For Noodles**
- ✓ 6 oz. thin rice noodles
- ✓ 2 tbsp. sesame oil, toasted and divided
- ✓ 1 small red bell pepper, seeded and sliced thinly
- ✓ ¼ of yellow onion, sliced thinly
- ✓ 12 snow peas
- ✓ 4 tsp. curry powder, divided
- ✓ 1 tbsp. soy sauce

**For Topping**
- ✓ 2 scallions, sliced thinly
- ✓ 1 tsp. sesame seeds

1. For sauce: in a bowl, add all the ingredients and beat until well combined. Set aside.
2. In a large-sized bowl of very hot water, add the noodles and set aside, covered for about 5-10 minutes or prepare according to package's directions.
3. Drain the noodles and then cut into 3-inch pieces. Set aside.
4. In a large-sized cast iron skillet, heat 1 tbsp. of peanut oil over medium-high heat and sauté the bell pepper and onion for about 4 minutes
5. Add the snow peas, 2 tsp. of curry powder and soy sauce and sauté for about 2-3 minutes.
6. Transfer the vegetable mixture into a large-sized bowl.
7. In the same, skillet, heat the remaining oil over medium heat and cook the noodles, sauce and remaining curry powder for about 1 minute.
8. Return the vegetable mixture in the skillet with noodles and cook for about 1-2 minutes, tossing occasionally.
9. Divide the noodle mixture onto serving plates and top with scallion and sesame seeds.

10. Serve immediately.

Per Serving:
Calories: 306| Fat: 14.7g| Carbs: 41g| Fiber: 4.6g| Protein: 4.7g

## NOODLES WITH TOFU

**Prep Time: 15 mins.| Cook Time: 17 mins.| Serves: 6**

**For Sauce**
- ✓ 3 garlic cloves, minced
- ✓ 3 tbsp. brown sugar
- ✓ 2 tbsp. Sriracha
- ✓ 2 tbsp. fresh lime juice
- ✓ ¼ C. soy sauce
- ✓ 2 tbsp. water

**For Tofu & Noodles**
- ✓ 3 tbsp. vegetable oil, divided
- ✓ 12-oz. extra-firm tofu, drained and cubed into ¾-inch size
- ✓ Salt and ground black pepper, as required
- ✓ 2 medium carrots, peeled and thinly sliced diagonally
- ✓ 1 lb. cooked noodles
- ✓ 6 scallions (separated white and green parts), sliced
- ✓ 2 C. cabbage, sliced thinly

1. For sauce: in a bowl, add all ingredients and mix until well combined. Set aside.
2. In a large-sized skillet, heat 1 tbsp. of oil over medium-high heat and cook the tofu with salt and black pepper for about 4-5 minutes, stirring occasionally.
3. Transfer the tofu into a large-sized bowl.
4. In the same skillet, heat 1 tbsp. of oil over medium heat and cook for about 4-5 minutes, stirring occasionally.
5. Transfer the carrots into the bowl with tofu.
6. In the same skillet, heat remaining oil over medium heat and cook the noodles with white part of scallions for about 2-3 minutes, stirring occasionally.
7. Stir in the sauce and cook for about 2 minutes, stirring occasionally.
8. Stir in tofu mixture, cabbage and green part of scallions and cook or about 1-2 minutes.
9. Serve hot.

Per Serving:
Calories: 265| Fat: 11.7g| Carbs: 31.4g| Fiber: 2.7g| Protein: 10.6g

## PINEAPPLE & CORN HOT POT

**Prep Time: 15 mins.| Cook Time: 30 mins.| Serves: 3**

- ✓ 1 tbsp. vegetable oil
- ✓ 2 lemongrass stalks, halve
- ✓ 1 scallion, thinly slice
- ✓ 3 small chilies, sliced
- ✓ 1 (1-inch) piece fresh ginger, sliced
- ✓ 2 medium tomatoes, finely chopped
- ✓ 1 C. pineapple, chopped
- ✓ 4 C. water
- ✓ ½ ear of corn, cut into 2-inch slices
- ✓ 1 tsp. soy sauce
- ✓ 1 tbsp. coconut sugar
- ✓ 1½ tsp. salt
- ✓ 5 oz. Chinese noodles
- ✓ 1 (14-oz.) block tofu, pressed, drained and chopped
- ✓ 3 C. fresh mushrooms, sliced
- ✓ 1-2 C. fresh spinach, torn

1. In a large-sized pan, heat the oil over medium heat and sauté the lemongrass stalks, scallion, chilies and ginger for about 5 minutes.
2. Add the tomatoes and pineapple and cook for about 5 minutes.
3. Add the water, corn, soy sauce, coconut sugar and salt and simmer for about 20 minutes.
4. Meanwhile, in a pan of lightly salted boiling water, cook the noodles for about 8-10 minutes.
5. Transfer the broth into a serving hot pot.
6. Serve alongside the noodles, tofu, mushrooms and spinach.

Per Serving:
Calories: 361| Fat: 11.2g| Carbs: 51.1g| Fiber: 6g| Protein: 20.3g

## VEGGIE CHOW MEIN

**Prep Time: 15 mins.| Cook Time: 23 mins.| Serves: 4**

- ✓ 10½ oz. Chinese wheat noodles
- ✓ 1 tbsp. vegetable oil
- ✓ 2 C. mushrooms, sliced thinly
- ✓ 1 red bell pepper, seeded and sliced thinly
- ✓ 3 scallions, finely chopped
- ✓ 2 tsp. fresh ginger, minced
- ✓ 3 garlic cloves, finely chopped
- ✓ 10 baby corn, halved lengthwise
- ✓ 2 C. broccolini, halved lengthwise
- ✓ 1 C. white sugar snap peas, halved lengthwise
- ✓ 2 C. fresh baby spinach
- ✓ 2-3 tbsp. soy sauce

- ✓ 2 tbsp. vegan oyster sauce
- ✓ 1 tsp. sesame oil
- ✓ 1 tbsp. fresh lemon juice

1. In a large-sized pan of salted boiling water, cook the noodles for about 8-10 minutes.
2. Drain the noodles and set aside.
3. In a skillet, heat the vegetable oil over medium heat and stir fry the mushrooms, bell peppers, scallions, ginger and garlic for about 5 minutes.
4. Add the corn, broccolini and sugar snaps and stir fry for about 5 minutes.
5. Add the spinach, soy, oyster sauce and sesame oil and stir fry for about 2 minutes.
6. Add the cooked noodles and lemon juice and toss to combine.
7. Serve hot.

Per Serving:
Calories: 214| Fat: 6.7g| Carbs: 32.9g| Fiber: 4.6g| Protein: 8.3g

## VEGGIE LO MEIN

**Prep Time: 15 mins.| Cook Time: 18 mins.| Serves: 4**

- ✓ **For Sauce**
- ✓ 2 tbsp. dark soy sauce
- ✓ 1 tbsp. light soy sauce
- ✓ 1 tsp. sesame oil
- ✓ 1 tsp. white sugar

**For Lo Mein**
- ✓ 4-6 oz. uncooked Chinese noodles
- ✓ 1 tbsp. sesame oil
- ✓ 2-3 C. mixed veggies (carrots, bell pepper, cabbage, bok choy, mushrooms, or broccoli), julienned
- ✓ 3 scallions (separate green and white parts), chopped
- ✓ 1-2 tbsp. rice wine

1. For sauce: in a bowl, add all ingredients and whisk until smooth. Set aside.
2. In a large-sized pan of salted boiling water, cook the noodles for about 8-10 minutes.
3. Drain the noodles and set aside.
4. In a large-sized wok, heat the sesame oil over medium heat and stir fry the veggies and white part of scallions for about 5 minutes.
5. Add the rice wine and cook for about 1-2 minutes, stirring continuously.
6. Add the cooked noodles and sauce and toss to coat well.
7. Serve hot with the garnishing of scallion greens.

Per Serving:
Calories: 180| Fat: 5g| Carbs: 28.9g| Fiber: 5.8g| Protein: 5.6g

## VEGGIE FRIED RICE

**Prep Time: 10 mins.| Cook Time: 6 mins.| Serves: 4**

- ✓ 3 tbsp. vegetable oil
- ✓ ½ C. onion, cut into 1-inch cubes
- ✓ 2 tsp. garlic, chopped
- ✓ ¼ C. carrots, peeled and chopped
- ✓ ¼ C. green peas, shelled
- ✓ 2-3 tbsp. frozen corn
- ✓ 4 C. cooked white rice
- ✓ 1 tbsp. sesame oil, toasted
- ✓ 1 tbsp. soy sauce
- ✓ Salt, as required
- ✓ ½ tsp. ground white pepper

1. In a skillet, heat oil over medium heat and stir fry the onion and garlic for about 1 minute.
2. Add carrots and peas and stir fry for about 2-3 minutes.
3. Add the cooked rice, salt, white pepper powder, soy sauce and sesame oil and cook for about 1-2 minutes, tossing frequently.
4. Serve hot.

Per Serving:
Calories: 323| Fat: 14.1g| Carbs: 43.7g| Fiber: 1.7g| Protein: 4.9g

## TOFU FRIED RICE

**Prep Time: 15 mins.| Cook Time: 16 mins.| Serves: 4**

- ✓ 2 tbsp. extra-virgin olive oil
- ✓ ½ C. white onion, chopped
- ✓ ½ C. carrot, peeled and cut into small pieces
- ✓ 4 oz. tofu, pressed, drained and crumbled
- ✓ 1 tsp. garlic powder

- ½ tsp. ground turmeric
- ½ tsp. salt
- 1/8 tsp. ground black pepper
- 2 C. cooked white rice
- ½ C. fresh green peas, shelled
- 2 tbsp. tamari
- ½ tsp. sesame oil

1. In a wok, heat 1 tbsp. of the olive oil over medium-high heat and cook the onions and carrots for about 5 minutes, stirring frequently.
2. With a slotted spoon, transfer the carrot mixture into a bowl.
3. In the same wok, heat the remaining oil over medium-high heat and cook the tofu, turmeric, garlic powder, salt and black pepper for about 5 minutes, stirring frequently.
4. Add the cooked rice, carrot mixture and peas and cook for about 1 minute.
5. Add the tamari and sesame oil and cook for about 5 minutes, stirring frequently.
6. Serve hot.

Per Serving:
Calories: 457| Fat: 9.5g| Carbs: 81g| Fiber: 3.3g| Protein: 11.3g

## STICKY RICE BALLS
**Prep Time: 20 mins.| Cook Time: 5 mins.| Serves: 10**

- 2¾ oz. black sesame seeds, toasted
- 2½ tbsp. white sugar
- 1 oz. vegan butter, softened
- 3 tbsp. boiling water
- 4½ oz. glutinous rice flour
- 4 tbsp. cold water

1. In a food processor, add the sesame seeds and sugar and pulse until smooth.
2. Add the butter and pulse until well combined.
3. Transfer the mixture into a bowl and refrigerate to firm slightly.
4. Make 20 equal-sized balls from the mixture and refrigerate until using.
5. In a bowl, add the hot water and glutinous rice and stir to combine.
6. Slowly add the cold water and with your hands, knead until a smooth and soft dough forms
7. Make 20 equal-sized balls from the dough.
8. With your fingers, flatten a dough ball into a round wrapper.
9. Place a ball of filling in the center of wrapper.
10. Gently push the wrapper upwards to seal completely.
11. In a large-sized pan of boiling water, add the balls in 2 batches and with the back of a spoon, gently push them around.
12. Cook for about 1 minute.
13. Transfer the balls into a large-sized serving bowl alongside some cooking liquid and serve warm.

Per Serving:
Calories: 112| Fat: 4.2g| Carbs: 17g| Fiber: 1.5g| Protein: 2.4g

## FRIED SESAME BALLS
**Prep Time: 20 mins.| Cook Time: 26 mins.| Serves: 8**

- 1½ C. glutinous rice flour, divided
- 1/3 C. granulated white sugar
- ¼ C. boiling water
- ¼ C. plus 1 tbsp. cold water (room temperature)
- 7 oz. red bean paste
- ¼ C. sesame seeds, toasted
- 2 C. vegetable oil

1. For dough: in a bowl, add ½ C. of glutinous rice flour and sugar and mix well.
2. Add the boiling water and with a rubber spatula, mix until smooth.
3. Set aside for about 5 minutes.
4. Add the remaining glutinous flour and cold water and mix until a dough forms
5. Place the dough in a silicone bag and set aside for about 30 minutes.
6. Roll the red pen paste into 8 small balls and set aside.
7. Make 8 balls from the dough.
8. With your hands, flatten each dough ball into a 3-inch disk.
9. Arrange 1 red bean paste ball in the center of each dough ball.
10. Then wrap the dough around the paste ball to cover completely.
11. With your hands, shape the dough into a ball.
12. Through a strainer, rinse the sesame seeds completely and drain well.

13. With kitchen towels, pat dry the sesame seeds slightly.
14. In a shallow dish, place the moistened sesame seeds
15. Coat each ball with sesame seeds evenly.
16. Then roll the ball in your hands to press the sesame seeds into the dough.
17. In a deep pan, heat the oil to 320 °F.
18. Add 4 sesame balls into the oil and cook for about 10 minutes, frequently stirring in a circular motion with a slotted spoon.
19. After 10 minutes of cooking, cook for about 3 minutes, stirring and gently pressing the balls occasionally.
20. Adjust the heat slightly and fry for about 5 minutes more, stirring occasionally.
21. With a slotted spoon, transfer the balls onto a paper towel-lined wire rack to drain.
22. Repeat with the remaining balls.
23. Serve warm.

Per Serving:
Calories: 674 | Fat: 572g | Carbs: 37.8g | Fiber: 1.2g | Protein: 3.8g

## BANANA FRITTERS

**Prep Time: 15 mins. | Cook Time: 16 mins. | Serves: 8**

- ½ C. water
- ½ C. all-purpose flour
- ½ C. cornstarch
- 2 tbsp. unsweetened almond milk
- 1 tbsp. coconut oil, melted
- 1 tbsp. granulated white sugar
- 4 large ripe bananas, peeled and cut into 1-inch chunks
- 1½ C. vegetable oil
- 1 tbsp. powdered sugar

1. In a bowl, add the water, flour, cornstarch, milk, butter, white sugar and mix until well combined.
2. Add the banana chunks and coat with the mixture evenly.
3. In a deep skillet, heat oil over medium-high heat and fry the banana chunks in 4 batches for about 2-4 minutes or until golden brown.
4. With a slotted spoon, transfer the banana chunks onto a wire rack to drain.
5. Set aside to cool down slightly.
6. Serve with a sprinkling of powdered sugar.

Per Serving:
Calories: 497 | Fat: 42.7g | Carbs: 29.4g | Fiber: 1.8g | Protein: 1.6g

## TAPIOCA PUDDING

**Prep Time: 10 mins. | Cook Time: 35 mins. | Serves: 6**

- 6 C. water, divided
- 1½ lb. taro, peeled and cut into ½ inch pieces
- ½ C. tapioca pearls
- 1 (13.7-oz.) can coconut milk
- 1 C. white sugar

1. In a medium-sized pan, add 4 C. of water and taro over high heat and bring to a boil.
2. Adjust the heat to medium and cook for about 20 minutes.
3. Remove from the heat and drain the water.
4. With a fork, mash the taro pieces slightly
5. Meanwhile, in a small-sized pan, add remaining water and bring to a boil.
6. Stir in the tapioca and cook for about 6 minutes.
7. Remove from the heat and set the pan aside, covered for about 10-15 minutes, or until the pearls are translucent.
8. Through a colander, strain the tapioca and rinse under cold running water.
9. Return the tapioca into the pan with coconut, taro and sugar and mix well.
10. Place the pan over medium heat and cook for about 2-3 minutes or until sugar dissolves completely, stirring continuously.
11. Remove from the heat and set aside to cool slightly.
12. Serve either warm.

Per Serving:
Calories: 465 | Fat: 15.6g | Carbs: 83.7g | Fiber: 7.2g | Protein: 2.1g

## SOY PUDDING

**Prep Time: 10 mins. | Cook Time: 15 mins. | Serves: 6**

**For Pudding**
- 4 C. soy milk

- ✓ 1 tbsp. agar-agar powder
- ✓ ½ C. water
- ✓ 2 tsp. vanilla extract

**For Syrup**
- ✓ ¾ C. water
- ✓ ½ C. white sugar
- ✓ 1 (1-inch) piece fresh ginger, smashed

1. For pudding: in a medium-sized saucepan, add soy milk over medium heat and cook for about 2-3 minutes or until warmed.
2. In another pan, add ½ C. of water over medium heat and ring to a boil.
3. Add agar-agar powder and stir until dissolved.
4. Stir in the warm soy milk and vanilla extract and bring t a gentle boil, stirring continuously.
5. Remove from the heat and through a strainer, strain the mixture into a large-sized pan.
6. With a clean kitchen towel, warp the lid tightly.
7. Then cover the pan with lid and set aside to cool slightly.
8. Refrigerate the pan for about 2 hours.
9. For syrup: in a small-sized pan, add all ingredients over medium heat and cook for about 3-5 minutes or until sugar is dissolved, stirring continuously.
10. Remove from the heat and discard the ginger.
11. Remove the pan of pudding from the refrigerator and with a flat spatula, cut into thin slices.
12. Top with sugar syrup and serve.

Per Serving:
Calories: 162 | Fat: 2.9g| Carbs: 28.8g| Fiber: 1.3g| Protein: 5.5g

## MANGO PUDDING
**Prep Time: 15 mins.| Serves: 4**

- ✓ ½ C. hot water
- ✓ 3 tsp. vegan gelatin
- ✓ 1/3 C. white sugar
- ✓ 2 large ripe mangoes, peeled, pitted and sliced
- ✓ 1 C. coconut milk

1. In a bowl, add the boiling water and gelatin and beat vigorously until dissolved.
2. Add the sugar and stir until dissolved.
3. In a food processor, add the mango and pulse until smooth.
4. Add the gelatin mixture and coconut milk and pulse until well combined.
5. Transfer the pudding into serving bowls and refrigerate for about 4-6 hours before serving.

Per Serving:
Calories: 310 | Fat: 14.9g| Carbs: 45.2g| Fiber: 4g| Protein: 5g

## ALMOND JELLY
**Prep Time: 10 mins.| Serves: 4**

- ✓ 1 2/3 C. boiling water
- ✓ 2 (¼-oz.) envelopes vegan gelatin
- ✓ ½ C. granulated white sugar
- ✓ 4 tsp. pure almond extract
- ✓ ½ C. cold coconut milk

1. In a bowl, add the boiling water and gelatin and beat vigorously until dissolved.
2. Add sugar and gently beat until dissolved.
3. Add almond extract and beat until well combined.
4. Add milk and beat until well combined.
5. Place the mixture into an 8x8-inch baking dish and refrigerate to chill for about 2-3 hours or until set completely.
6. Remove from the refrigerator and cut into squares.
7. Serve immediately.

Per Serving:
Calories: 136 | Fat: 1g| Carbs: 26.9g| Fiber: 0g| Protein: 4g

## MANGO ICE CREAM
**Prep Time: 15 mins.| Cook Time: 5 mins.| Serves: 6**

- ✓ 2 C. mango, peeled, pitted and cubed
- ✓ ½ plus 1/3 C. granulated white sugar, divided
- ✓ 2-2½ tbsp. fresh lime juice
- ✓ 1¾ C. coconut cream
- ✓ 1¼ C. coconut milk

1. In a large-sized bowl, add the mango cubes and 1/3 C. of sugar and mix well.
2. Cover the bowl and refrigerate overnight.
3. In a pan, add mango mixture over medium-low heat and cook for about 5 minutes, stirring occasionally.
4. Remove from the heat and set aside to cool.

5. In a high-power blender, add the mango mixture and pulse until smooth.
6. Add the lime juice and pulse until combined.
7. Transfer the mango puree into a bowl and refrigerate, covered for about 1 hour.
8. In a large-sized bowl, add coconut cream, coconut milk and remaining sugar and beat until well combined and sugar dissolves completely.
9. Add the mango puree and gently stir to combine.
10. Transfer the mango mixture into a freezer-safe container and freeze for at least 6 hours, stirring occasionally.

Per Serving:
Calories: 325| Fat: 19.4g| Carbs: 40.6g| Fiber: 2.4g| Protein: 2.4g

# INDIAN RECIPES

### CILANTRO CREPES

**Prep Time: 15 mins. | Cook Time: 3 mins. | Serves: 8**

- 1 1/3 C. chickpea flour
- ½ tsp. red chili powder
- Salt, as required
- 1 (1-inch piece) fresh ginger, grated finely
- 1 C. fresh cilantro leaves, chopped
- 1 green chili, seeded and finely chopped
- 1 C. water
- Non-stick cooking spray

1. In a large-sized bowl, mix together the flour, chili powder and salt.
2. Add the ginger, cilantro and chili and mix well.
3. Add the water and mix until a smooth mixture forms.
4. Set aside, covered for about 1½ hours.
5. Lightly, grease a large-sized non-stick skillet with cooking spray and heat over medium-high heat.
6. Add the desired amount of the mixture and tilt the pan to spread it evenly.
7. Cook for about 15 seconds per side.
8. Repeat with the remaining mixture.
9. Serve warm.

Per Serving:
Calories: 123| Fat: 2.1g| Carbs: 20.5g| Fiber: 6g| Protein: 6.5g

### SAVORY PANCAKES

**Prep Time: 15 mins. | Cook Time: 12 mins. | Serves: 2**

- 1 C. water
- 1 C. chickpea flour
- 1 tsp. ground turmeric
- ½ tsp. red pepper flakes, crushed
- Salt and ground black pepper, as required
- 1 green bell pepper, seeded and finely chopped
- 3 scallions, finely chopped
- 1 tbsp. olive oil

1. In a food processor, add the water, flour, turmeric, red pepper flakes, salt and black pepper and pulse until well combined.
2. Transfer the mixture into a bowl and set aside for about 3-5 minutes.
3. Add the bell pepper and scallion and mix well.
4. In a skillet, heat the oil over medium heat.
5. Add half of the mixture and spread in an even layer.
6. Cook for about 5-6 minutes, flipping once after 3 minutes.
7. Repeat with the remaining mixture.
8. Serve warm.

Per Serving:
Calories: 224| Fat: 6.7g| Carbs: 33g| Fiber: 9.7g| Protein: 10.2g

### TOMATO OMELET

**Prep Time: 15 mins. | Cook Time: 24 mins. | Serves: 4**

- 1 C. chickpea flour
- ¼ tsp. cayenne powder
- Pinch of ground cumin
- Salt, as required
- 1½-2 C. water
- 1 medium onion, finely chopped
- 2 medium plum tomatoes, finely chopped
- 2 tbsp. fresh cilantro, chopped
- 2 tbsp. avocado oil, divided

1. In a bowl, add the flour, spices, and salt and mix well.
2. Slowly add the water and mix until well combined.
3. Fold in the onion, tomatoes, green chili, and cilantro.
4. In a large-sized non-stick frying pan, heat ½ tbsp. of the oil over medium heat.
5. Add ½ of the tomato mixture and tilt the pan to spread it.
6. Cook for about 5-7 minutes.
7. Place the remaining oil over the omelet and carefully flip it over.
8. Cook for about 4-5 minutes or until golden brown.
9. Repeat with the remaining mixture.

93

Per Serving:
Calories: 121| Fat: 2.6g| Carbs: 18.8g| Fiber: 4.2g| Protein: 6.1g

## TOMATO & CUCUMBER SALAD
**Prep Time: 15 mins.| Cook Time: 1 min.| Serves: 4**

- ½ tsp. cumin seeds
- 4 tbsp. olive oil
- 2 tbsp. fresh lemon juice
- 2 garlic cloves, minced
- 1 C. onion, thinly sliced
- 4 medium ripe tomatoes, sliced
- 1 small cucumber, thinly sliced
- Salt and ground black pepper, as required
- ½ tsp. fresh mint leaves, finely chopped

1. Heat a non-stick frying over medium heat and sauté the cumin seeds for about 30-50 seconds.
2. Remove from the heat and place the cumin seeds onto a plate to cool completely.
3. Add the oil and lemon juice in a bowl and beat until well combined.
4. In a salad bowl, place the cucumber, tomatoes, onion, garlic, salt and black pepper.
5. Add the oi mixture, mint and cumin and gently toss to coat well.
6. Serve immediately.

Per Serving:
Calories: 170| Fat: 14.5g| Carbs: 11g| Fiber: 2.6g| Protein: 2.1g

## WARM CHICKPEAS SALAD
**Prep Time: 10 mins.| Cook Time: 10 mins.| Serves: 4**

- 4 tbsp. olive oil
- 1 large red onion, finely chopped
- 2 garlic cloves, minced
- 2 (15-oz.) cans chickpeas, rinsed and drained
- Pinch of red pepper flakes, crushed
- ½ tsp. ground ginger
- 1 tbsp. fresh lemon juice
- Salt and ground black pepper, as required
- ¼ tsp. paprika
- ½ tsp. ground cumin
- 2 tbsp. fresh cilantro, chopped

1. In a skillet, heat 1 tbsp. of oil over medium-low heat and sauté the onion and garlic for about 5-7 minutes
2. Add chickpeas, red pepper flakes and ground ginger and cook for about 1 minute.
3. Add lemon juice and cook for about 1-2 minutes or until all the liquid is absorbed.
4. Transfer the chickpea mixture into a serving bowl.
5. Add remaining oil, paprika and cumin and gently stir to combine.
6. Serve warm with the garnishing of cilantro.

Per Serving:
Calories: 394| Fat: 16.6g| Carbs: 52.6g| Fiber: 10.4g| Protein: 11.2g

## VEGGIE BURGERS
**Prep Time: 15 mins.| Cook Time: 15 mins.| Serves: 2**

- 5 oz. green beans, trimmed and sliced
- 2 medium carrots, peeled and grated
- 1 vegan whole-wheat bread slice, crumbled
- 4 oz. boiled potatoes
- ½ tsp. fresh ginger, grated
- ½ tsp. mango powder
- ½ tsp. garam masala powder
- ¼ tsp. red chili powder
- 4 tbsp. fresh cilantro, chopped
- Salt, as required
- 1 tbsp. vegetable oil

1. In a pan of lightly salted boiling water, add the carrots and green beans and cook, covered for about 8-10 minutes.
2. Drain the carrots and green beans well.
3. In a food processor, add the boiled potatoes, cilantro, breadcrumbs, ginger, mango powder, garam masala, chili powder and salt and pulse until well combined.
4. Make about ¾-inch sized patties from the mixture.
5. Refrigerate the patties for about 5-10 minutes.
6. In a skillet, heat the oil over medium heat and cook the patties for about 2-3 minutes.
7. Flip and cook for about 1-2 minutes.
8. Serve hot.

Per Serving:

Calories: 177| Fat: 7.7g| Carbs: 25.8g| Fiber: 6.3g| Protein: 4.5g

## VEGGIES & CASHEWS BURGERS
**Prep Time: 20 mins.| Cook Time: 20 mins.| Serves: 4**

- 2 C. fresh spinach leaves
- 4 tbsp. chickpeas flour
- 1 green chili, chopped
- 1 (1½-inch) piece fresh ginger, roughly chopped
- 2 boiled medium potatoes
- ½ C. boiled green peas
- 1 tsp. dry mango powder
- 1 tsp. chaat masala powder
- ¼ tsp. garam masala powder
- Salt, as required
- 8 cashew halves
- 2-3 tbsp. canola oil

1. Soak the spinach in hot water in a heatproof bowl for about 2 minutes.
2. Drain the spinach and immediately place into a bowl of cold water for 1 minute.
3. Through a colander, drain the spinach completely.
4. With your hands, squeeze the spinach lightly to remove extra water.
5. Then chop the spinach finely and set aside.
6. Heat a small-sized non-stick frying pan over medium-low heat and cook the chickpea flour for about 1-2miutes, stirring continuously.
7. Transfer the toasted chickpea flour into a large-sized bowl.
8. With a mortar and pestle, crush the ginger and green chili into a paste.
9. Transfer the ginger paste into the bowl with the toasted chickpea flour.
10. Add the spinach, potatoes, green peas, spices and salt and with a potato masher, mash until well combined.
11. Make 8 small patties from the mixture.
12. Press 1 cashew half into each patty.
13. In a skillet, heat oil over medium heat and cook the patties in 2 batches for about 3-5 minutes per side.
14. Serve hot.

Per Serving:
Calories: 230| Fat: 11.7g| Carbs: 27g| Fiber: 4.9g| Protein: 5.9g

## LENTIL BURGERS
**Prep Time: 15 mins.| Cook Time: 10 mins.| Serves: 3**

- 1 C. chickpea lentils
- 1 C. onion, finely chopped
- 2 green chilies, finely chopped
- 1 tsp. garlic paste
- 1 tsp. ginger paste
- Pinch of ground turmeric
- Salt, as required
- ¼ C. olive oil

1. In a bowl of water, soak the chickpea lentil for at least 3-4 hours.
2. Drain the lentils and rinse under cold running water.
3. Through a strainer, strain the lentils completely.
4. In the bowl of a food processor, place lentils and pulse until a coarse paste is formed.
5. Transfer the lentils into a bowl.
6. Add the onion, green chilies, garlic paste, ginger paste, turmeric and salt and mix until well combined.
7. Make small equal-sized patties from the mixture.
8. In a skillet, heat olive oil over medium heat and cook half of the patties for 5 minutes, flipping occasionally.
9. Serve immediately.

Per Serving:
Calories: 258| Fat: 17.8g| Carbs: 22.5g| Fiber: 4.5g| Protein: 4.5g

## SPICED POTATOES
**Prep Time: 15 mins.| Cook Time: 10 mins.| Serves: 4**

- 2 tbsp. vegetable oil
- ¼ tsp. caraway seeds
- ¼ tsp. cumin seeds
- ¼ tsp. ground coriander
- ½ C. red onion, finely chopped
- 1 green chili pepper, seeded and finely chopped
- 3 garlic cloves, minced
- 1 tsp. fresh ginger, minced
- 1 tsp. ground turmeric
- 1 tsp. cayenne powder

- ✓ 2 C. cooked potatoes, hopped
- ✓ 1-2 tbsp. fresh lemon juice
- ✓ Salt and ground black pepper, as required
- ✓ 2 tbsp. fresh cilantro, chopped
- ✓ 2 tbsp. fresh mint, chopped

1. In a large-sized wok, heat the oil over medium heat and sauté the caraway seeds, cumin seeds and ground coriander for about 20-30 seconds.
2. Add the onion and sauté for about 4-5 minutes.
3. Add in the chili pepper, garlic, ginger, cayenne powder and turmeric and sauté for about 1 minute.
4. Stir in the potatoes, lemon juice, salt and black pepper and cook for about 2-3 minutes.
5. Serve hot with the garnishing of cilantro and mint leaves.

Per Serving:
Calories: 129| Fat: 7.2g| Carbs: 15.3g| Fiber: 2.8g| Protein: 1.9g

## COCONUT SPINACH
**Prep Time: 15 mins.| Cook Time: 18 mins.|
Serves: 4**

- ✓ 3 tbsp. coconut oil
- ✓ 1½ tbsp. brown sugar
- ✓ ½ tsp. cumin seeds
- ✓ 1 tbsp. black mustard seeds
- ✓ ¼ tsp. fenugreek seeds
- ✓ 2 lb. fresh spinach, trimmed
- ✓ 1 tbsp. green chili, minced
- ✓ ½ tbsp. fresh ginger, grated
- ✓ 2/3 C. almonds, soaked in warm water for 4 hours and drained
- ✓ 1/3 C. unsweetened coconut, shredded
- ✓ Salt and ground black pepper, as required
- ✓ 2 tbsp. water
- ✓ 1/8 tsp. ground nutmeg

1. In a large-sized skillet, melt coconut oil over medium heat and sauté the brown sugar, cumin seeds, mustard seeds and fenugreek seeds for about 1 minute.
2. Add the spinach, green chili, ginger, almonds, coconut, salt and black pepper and stir to combine.
3. Adjust the heat to low and simmer, covered for about 10 minutes.
4. Uncover and stir in water and simmer for about 3-4 minutes.
5. Stir in the nutmeg and simmer for about 1-2 minutes more.

Per Serving:

Calories: 287| Fat: 22.2g| Carbs: 17.9g| Fiber: 8.2g| Protein: 10.9g

## SPICED OKRA
**Prep Time: 10 mins.| Cook Time: 15 mins.|
Serves: 3**

- ✓ 1 tbsp. vegetable oil
- ✓ ½ tsp. cumin seeds
- ✓ ¾ lb. okra pods, trimmed and cut into 2-inch pieces
- ✓ ½ tsp. garam masala powder
- ✓ ½ tsp. red chili powder
- ✓ 1 tsp. ground coriander
- ✓ Salt and ground black pepper, as required

1. In a large-sized skillet, heat the oil over medium heat and sauté the cumin seeds for about 30 seconds.
2. Add the okra and stir fry for about 1-1½ minutes.
3. Adjust the heat to low and cook covered for about 6-8 minutes, stirring occasionally.
4. Add the curry powder, red chili, and coriander and stir to combine.
5. Adjust the heat to medium and cook uncovered for about 2-3 minutes more.
6. Season with salt and pepper and remove from the heat.
7. Serve hot.

Per Serving:
Calories: 89| Fat: 5.1g| Carbs: 9g| Fiber: 3.9g| Protein: 2.3g

## OKRA & TOMATO CURRY
**Prep Time: 15 mins.| Cook Time: 23 mins.|
Serves: 3**

- ✓ ¼ C. vegetable oil
- ✓ 1 tsp. mustard seeds
- ✓ 1 tsp. cumin seeds
- ✓ 2 medium onions, chopped

- ✓ 1 medium green chili pepper, chopped
- ✓ ¾ lb. okra pods, trimmed and cut into 2-inch pieces
- ✓ 1¼ tbsp. ground coriander
- ✓ ½ tsp. ground turmeric
- ✓ ½ tsp. red chili powder
- ✓ 2 medium tomatoes, chopped
- ✓ ¾ tsp. salt

1. In a skillet, heat 2 tbsp. of oil over medium heat and stir fry the mustard seeds and cumin seeds for about 30-60 seconds.
2. Stir in the onion and green chili and sauté for about 4-5 minutes,
3. With a slotted spoon, transfer the onion mixture into a bowl.
4. In the same skillet, heat remaining oil over medium heat and cook the okra for about 2-3 minutes or until lightly browned, stirring frequently.
5. Stir in the cooked onion mixture and cook for about 1-2 minutes.
6. Stir in the coriander, turmeric ad chili powder and cook for about 4-5 minutes.
7. Stir in the tomatoes and cook, covered for 6-7 minutes.
8. Stir in the salt and cook, uncovered for about 1-2 minutes.
9. Serve hot.

Per Serving:
Calories: 261| Fat: 19.2g| Carbs: 19.7g| Fiber: 6.7g| Protein: 4.2g

## BANANA CURRY
**Prep Time: 15 mins.| Cook Time: 15 mins.| Serves: 4**

- ✓ ¼ C. sunflower oil
- ✓ 2 onions, chopped
- ✓ 8 garlic cloves, minced
- ✓ ½ C. curry powder
- ✓ 1 tsp. white sugar
- ✓ 1 tbsp. ground ginger
- ✓ 1 tbsp. ground cumin
- ✓ 1 tsp. ground turmeric
- ✓ 1 tsp. ground cinnamon
- ✓ 1 tsp. red chili powder
- ✓ Salt and ground black pepper, as required
- ✓ 2/3 C. soy yogurt
- ✓ 1 (10-oz.) can tomato sauce
- ✓ 2 bananas, peeled and sliced
- ✓ 3 tomatoes, finely chopped
- ✓ ¼ C. unsweetened coconut flakes

1. In a large-sized pan, heat the oil over medium heat and sauté the onion for about 4-5 minutes.
2. Add the garlic, curry powder, sugar and spices and sauté for about 1 minute.
3. Add the soy yogurt and tomato sauce and bring to a gentle boil.
4. Stir in the bananas and simmer for about 3 minutes
5. Stir in the tomatoes and simmer for about 1-2 minutes.
6. Stir in the coconut flakes and immediately remove from the heat.
7. Serve hot.

Per Serving:
Calories: 345| Fat: 19g| Carbs: 44g| Fiber: 10.8g| Protein: 7.4g

## EGGPLANT CURRY
**Prep Time: 10 mins.| Cook Time: 35 mins.| Serves: 3**

- ✓ 1 tbsp. olive oil
- ✓ ½ of small yellow onion, finely chopped
- ✓ 2 small garlic cloves, mince
- ✓ ½ tsp. fresh ginger root, minced
- ✓ 1 small Serrano pepper, seeded and minced
- ✓ 1 tsp. curry powder
- ✓ ¼ tsp. cayenne powder
- ✓ 1 medium plum tomato, chopped fine
- ✓ 1 large eggplant, cubed
- ✓ Salt, as required
- ✓ ¾ C. unsweetened coconut milk
- ✓ 1 tbsp. fresh cilantro, chopped

1. In a large-sized skillet, heat the oil over medium heat and sauté the onion for about 6 minutes.
2. Add the garlic, ginger, Serrano pepper and spices and sauté for about 1 minute.
3. Add the tomato and cook for about 3 minutes, crushing with the back of a spoon.
4. Add the eggplant and salt and cook for about 1 minute, stirring occasionally.

5. Stir in the coconut milk and bring to a gentle boil.
6. Adjust the heat to medium-low and simmer, covered for about 20 minutes or until done completely.
7. Serve with the garnishing of cilantro.

Per Serving:
Calories: 184| Fat: 13.4g| Carbs: 13g| Fiber: 6.3g| Protein: 2.9g

## SWISS CHARD CURRY
**Prep Time: 15 mins.| Cook Time: 35 mins.| Serves: 2**

- 1 bunch Swiss chard, stems removed and finely chopped
- 3 tbsp. vegetable oil
- 1 medium onion, finely chopped
- 2 tbsp. curry paste
- ½ C. water
- 2 garlic cloves, minced
- 1 (2-inch) piece fresh ginger, minced

1. In a skillet, heat the oil over medium-high heat and sauté the onion for about 4-5 minutes.
2. Stir in the Swiss chard and cook for about 3-4 minutes.
3. Add the curry paste and stir to combine.
4. Now adjust the heat to low and cook, covered for about 15-20 minutes, mixing as required.
5. Stir in the ginger and garlic and cook for about 5 minutes.
6. Serve hot.

Per Serving:
Calories: 255| Fat: 21g| Carbs: 15.5g| Fiber: 4.1g| Protein: 3.9g

## SPINACH & POTATO CURRY
**Prep Time: 15 mins.| Cook Time: 25 mins.| Serves: 4**

- 3 tbsp. olive oil
- 1 tsp. cumin seeds
- 1 medium yellow onion, chopped
- 3 dried whole red chilies
- 8 garlic cloves, roughly chopped
- 1 tsp. fresh ginger, grated
- 3 medium tomatoes, chopped
- 1½ tbsp. red chili powder
- 1½ tbsp. ground coriander
- ½ tsp. ground cumin
- ½ tsp. ground turmeric
- Salt, as required
- 3 medium Yukon gold potatoes, peeled and cut into about ½-inch cubes
- 3-4 tbsp. water
- 1 lb. baby spinach, roughly chopped

1. In a large-sized saucepan, heat the oil over medium heat and sauté the cumin seeds for about 30-60 seconds.
2. Add the onions and dried red chilies and sauté for about 4-5 minutes.
3. Add garlic and ginger and sauté for about 1 minute.
4. Add in the tomatoes, spices, and salt and cook for about 2-3 minutes, stirring frequently.
5. Add in the potatoes and water and stir to combine.
6. Adjust the heat to low and simmer, covered for about 7-9 minutes.
7. Add in the spinach and simmer, covered for about 1 minute.
8. Uncover the pan and Adjust the heat to medium.
9. Cook for about 3-5 minutes, stirring occasionally.
10. Serve hot.

Per Serving:
Calories: 276| Fat: 12g| Carbs: 39.6g| Fiber: 9.3g| Protein: 7.9g

## CABBAGE WITH POTATOES
**Prep Time: 15 mins.| Cook Time: 25 mins.| Serves: 6**

- 2 tbsp. vegetable oil
- ¾ tsp. cumin seeds
- ¾ tsp. mustard seeds
- 1 medium cabbage head, cored and shredded
- 2-3 medium potatoes, chopped
- 1 medium onion, sliced finely
- ½ tsp. ground turmeric
- ½ tsp. ground coriander
- Salt and ground black pepper, as required
- 2-4 tbsp. desiccated coconut, shredded
- ¼ C. water
- 3 tbsp. fresh cilantro, chopped

1. In a skillet, heat the oil over medium heat and sauté the mustard and cumin seeds and stir fry for about 30 seconds.
2. Add the onion and sauté for about 4-6 minutes.
3. Add the shredded cabbage, potato, coriander, turmeric, salt and black pepper and stir to combine.
4. Adjust the heat to medium-low and cook, covered for about 8-10 minutes.
5. Add the coconut and water and stir to combine.
6. Cook for about 3-5 minutes.
7. Serve hot with the garnishing of cilantro.

Per Serving:
Calories: 140| Fat: 5.6g| Carbs: 21.1g| Fiber: 5.3g| Protein: 3.1g

## CAULIFLOWER WITH GREEN PEAS
**Prep Time: 15 mins.| Cook Time: 15 mins.| Serves: 3**

- 2 medium tomatoes, chopped
- ¼ C. water
- 2 tbsp. olive oil
- 3 garlic cloves, minced
- ½ tbsp. fresh ginger, minced
- 1 tsp. ground cumin
- 2 tsp. ground coriander
- 1 tsp. cayenne powder
- ¼ tsp. ground turmeric
- 2 C. cauliflower, chopped
- 1 C. fresh green peas, shelled
- Salt and ground black pepper, as required
- ½ C. warm water

1. In a high-power blender, add tomato and ¼ C. of water and pulse until a smooth puree form. Set aside.
2. In a large-sized skillet, heat the oil over medium heat and sauté the garlic, ginger, green chilies and spices for about 1 minute.
3. Add the cauliflower, peas and tomato puree and cook, stirring for about 3-4 minutes.
4. Add the warm water and bring to a boil.
5. Adjust the heat to medium-low and cook, covered for about 8-10 minutes or until vegetables are done completely.
6. Serve hot.

Per Serving:
Calories: 163| Fat: 10.1g| Carbs: 16.1g| Fiber: 5.6g| Protein: 6g

## POTATOES WITH CAULIFLOWER
**Prep Time: 15 mins.| Cook Time: 30 mins.| Serves: 4**

- 4 tbsp. canola oil, divided
- 1 medium cauliflower head, cut into small florets
- 3 large potatoes, cubed
- ½ tsp. cumin seeds
- 1 medium onion, chopped
- ¾ tsp. ginger paste
- ¾ tsp. garlic paste
- 4 medium tomatoes, chopped
- 1 tsp. ground coriander
- 1 tsp. ground turmeric
- ½ tsp. dry mango powder
- ½ tsp. red chili powder
- ½ tsp. garam masala powder
- 2 tbsp. fresh cilantro, chopped
- Salt, as required

1. Heat 2 tbsp. of oil in a large-sized saucepan over medium-low heat and stir fry the cauliflower florets for about 2-3 minutes.
2. Add in the potatoes and stir fry for about 6-7 minutes.
3. Transfer the potato mixture onto a plate and set aside.
4. In the same pan, heat remaining oil over medium heat and sauté cumin seeds for about 30-40 seconds.
5. Add the onions and sauté for about 2-3 minutes.
6. Add the ginger and garlic paste and sauté for about 1 minute.
7. Add the tomatoes and cook for about 2 minutes, crushing with the back of spoon.
8. Stir in the coriander, turmeric, mango powder and red chili powder and cook, covered for about 2-3 minutes.
9. Add the potatoes, cauliflower and garam masala powder and stir to combine.
10. Adjust the heat to medium-low and cook for about 2-3 minutes.
11. Add in the cilantro and salt and stir to combine.
12. Adjust the heat to low and cook, covered for about 6-7 minutes. (If you feel the masala is sticking, you may add some water).

13. Serve hot.

Per Serving:
Calories: 370| Fat: 14.8g| Carbs: 55.4g| Fiber: 10.7g| Protein: 7.5g

## THREE VEGGIES CURRY
**Prep Time: 15 mins.| Cook Time: 30 mins.| Serves: 4**

- 2 tbsp. vegetable oil
- 2 garlic cloves, minced
- 1 tsp. fresh ginger, minced
- 1½ tsp. ground cumin
- 1 tsp. ground coriander
- ¾ tsp. ground turmeric
- ½ tsp. red chili powder
- 2 onions, chopped
- 4 tomatoes, chopped
- 3 carrots, peeled and sliced
- 2 potatoes, cut into 1-inch pieces
- 1 C. green peas, shelled
- Salt, as required
- ¾ C. water
- 2-3 tbsp. fresh cilantro, chopped

1. In a large-sized skillet, heat the vegetable oil over medium heat and sauté the garlic, ginger and spices for about 1 minute.
2. Add the onions and sauté for about 3 minutes.
3. Add the tomatoes and cook for about 2-3 minutes, stirring frequently.
4. Stir in the carrots, potatoes and peas and cook for about 2-3 minutes, stirring frequently.
5. Stir in salt and water and cook, covered for about 20 minutes, stirring occasionally.
6. Serve hot with the garnishing of cilantro.

Per Serving:
Calories: 243| Fat: 8.2g| Carbs: 38.9g| Fiber: 8.8g| Protein: 6.5g

## MIXED VEGGIE COMBO
**Prep Time: 15 mins.| Cook Time: 30 mins.| Serves: 6**

- 2 tbsp. canola oil
- 2 C. onions, chopped
- 1 fresh green chili pepper, minced
- 3 garlic cloves, minced
- 1 tbsp. fresh ginger root, grated
- Pinch of saffron, crumbled
- 1 tsp. ground cumin
- 1 tsp. ground coriander
- ½ tsp. ground turmeric
- ½ tsp. ground cinnamon
- ¼ tsp. ground cardamom
- 1 tsp. salt
- 5 C. eggplants, cubed
- 1 C. fresh orange juice
- 4 C. zucchini, cubed
- 1½ C. bell peppers, seeded and chopped
- 3 C. fresh tomatoes, chopped
- ¼ C. fresh cilantro, chopped

1. In a large-sized skillet, heat the oil over medium heat and cook the onion for about 8-9 minutes, stirring frequently.
2. Add the green chili, ginger, garlic, saffron, spices and salt and sauté for about 1 minute.
3. Stir in the eggplant and orange juice and cook, covered for about 12-15 minutes.
4. Stir in the zucchini, bell peppers, tomatoes, and cilantro and cook, covered for about 12-15 minutes.
5. Serve hot.

Per Serving:
Calories: 136| Fat: 5.4g| Carbs: 21.3g| Fiber: 5.9g| Protein: 3.6g

## VEGETARIAN BALLS IN GRAVY
**Prep Time: 20 mins.| Cook Time: 28 mins.| Serves: 6**

**For Balls**
- 1 C. cooked chickpeas
- 1 C. cooked red kidney beans
- ½ C. cooked quinoa
- Salt and ground black pepper, as required
- 2 tbsp. black bean flour
- 1 medium yellow onion, peeled and chopped
- 2 garlic cloves, chopped
- ¼ C. fresh cilantro, chopped
- 1 tsp. cumin seeds
- Pinch of baking soda
- 1 tbsp. fresh lemon juice
- 2 tsp. olive oil

**For Gravy**
- 1 tsp. olive oil
- 1 tsp. cumin seeds
- 1 medium yellow onion, peeled and finely chopped
- 1 (1-inch) piece fresh ginger, peeled and grated finely
- 2 tomatoes, finely chopped
- 2 green chilies, finely chopped
- ½ tsp. garam masala powder
- ½ tsp. ground turmeric
- ½ tsp. red chili powder
- Salt, as require
- 2 C. water
- ¼ C. fresh cilantro, chopped

1. For balls: in a food processor, add all ingredients, except for oil, and pulse until a coarse meal forms.
2. Transfer the mixture into a bowl.
3. Cover the bowl with a piece of foil and refrigerate for at least 1 hour.
4. Remove the mixture from the refrigerator and make equal-sized balls.
5. In a non-stick skillet, heat oil over medium heat and cook the balls for about 2-3 minutes or until golden brown from all sides.
6. For gravy: in a large-sized Dutch oven, heat oil over medium heat and sauté cumin seeds for about 1 minute.
7. Add onion and sauté for about 6-7 minutes.
8. Stir in ginger, tomatoes, green chilies, and spices. Cook for about 1-2 minutes.
9. Add water and bring to a boil.
10. Adjust the heat to low and simmer, covered, for about 10 minutes.
11. Carefully place the balls in the gravy and cook, covered, for about 3-5 minutes.
12. Serve hot with the garnishing of cilantro.

Per Serving:
Calories: 183| Fat: 4g| Carbs: 30.6g| Fiber: 6.6g| Protein: 7.5g

## LENTIL CURRY
**Prep Time: 15 mins.| Cook Time: 35 mins.| Serves: 4**

- 1 tbsp. canola oil
- 1-2 Serrano peppers, chopped
- 4 garlic cloves, minced
- 1 (2-inch) piece fresh ginger, grated
- 1 tsp. ground turmeric
- 1 tsp. ground cumin
- ½ tsp. ground coriander
- ½ tsp. red chili powder
- 2 tsp. curry powder
- 1 tsp. garam masala powder
- Salt and ground black pepper, as required
- 2 C. vegetable broth
- 1 C. red lentils, rinsed
- 1 (14-oz.) can crushed tomatoes
- ¼ C. water
- 1 (13½-oz.) can full-fat coconut milk
- 3 tbsp. unsweetened creamy almond butter
- 1 tbsp. fresh lemon juice
- ½ C. fresh cilantro, roughly chopped

1. In a large-sized saucepan, melt the coconut oil over medium-high heat and sauté the Serrano peppers, garlic and ginger for about 2 minutes.
2. Add the spices, salt and black pepper and sauté for about 30-60 seconds.
3. Add in the broth and stir to combine well.
4. Add in the lentils and tomatoes and stir to combine well.
5. Adjust the heat to low and simmer, covered for about 20-25 minutes.
6. Add in water and simmer, covered for about 5 minutes.
7. Stir in the coconut milk, almond butter, salt and black pepper and cook, uncovered for about 5-8 minutes, stirring occasionally.

Per Serving:
Calories: 493| Fat: 29.9g| Carbs: 41.2g| Fiber: 7.7g| Protein: 18.4g

## CHICKPEAS CURRY
**Prep Time: 15 mins.| Cook Time: 20 mins.| Serves: 4**

- 1 (18-oz.) cans chickpeas
- 1 onion, chopped
- 1 tomatoes, chopped
- 1 green chili pepper, chopped
- 4-5 garlic cloves, chopped
- 1 (1-inch) piece fresh ginger root, chopped
- 3 tbsp. olive oil
- 2-3 bay leaves
- 1 tsp. red chili powder
- ½ tsp. ground turmeric
- 1 tsp. ground coriander
- 1 tsp. garam masala powder
- ½ C. water
- 2 tbsp. fresh cilantro, chopped

1. In a food processor, add the tomato, onion, garlic, ginger and green chili and pulse until smooth.
2. In a pan, heat the oil over medium heat and sauté the bay leaves and stir fry for about 30 seconds.
3. Add the pureed mixture and stir fry for about 3-4 minutes.

4. Stir in the garam masala, coriander powder, turmeric, red chili powder and salt and stir fry for 2-3 minutes.
5. Add water and bring to a boil.
6. Stir in the chickpeas and cook for about 5-7 minutes.
7. Serve hot with the garnishing of cilantro.

Per Serving:
Calories: 267| Fat: 12.2g| Carbs: 34.3g| Fiber: 7g| Protein: 7.2g

## CHICKPEAS WITH POTATO
**Prep Time: 15 mins.| Cook Time: 30 mins.| Serves: 4**

- 2 tbsp. olive oil
- 1 bay leaf
- 1 tsp. cumin seeds
- 3 green cardamom pods
- 2 whole cloves
- 1 large onion, finely chopped
- 3-4 garlic cloves, finely chopped
- 1 (1-inch) piece fresh ginger, finely chopped
- 1 (14½-oz.) can diced tomatoes
- 1 tsp. ground coriander
- ½ tsp. ground turmeric
- ½ tsp. garam masala powder
- ½ tsp. ground cumin
- ½ tsp. smoked paprika
- ¼ tsp. cayenne powder
- Salt, as required
- 1 (20-oz.) can chickpeas
- 1 large potato, cut into ½-inch cubes
- 1½-2 C. water
- 2 tbsp. fresh cilantro, chopped

1. In a Dutch oven, heat oil over medium heat and sauté the bay leaf, cumin seeds cardamom pods and cloves for about 30-50 seconds.
2. Add the onion, garlic and ginger and sauté for about 4-6 minutes.
3. Add in the tomatoes and spices and cook for about 3-4 minutes, stirring frequently.
4. Add in the chickpeas and potatoes and cook for about 2-3 minutes, stirring continuously.
5. Add in the water and cook, covered for about 12-15 minutes.
6. Stir in the cilantro and lime juice and serve hot.

Per Serving:
Calories: 342| Fat: 9.2g| Carbs: 57.3g| Fiber: 10.7g| Protein: 0.5g

## RED KIDNEY BEANS CURRY
**Prep Time: 15 mins.| Cook Time: 1 hr. 40 mins.| Serves: 6**

**For Kidney Beans**
- 1¼ C. red kidney beans, soaked overnight and drained
- 1 black cardamom
- 1 tsp. salt
- 4-5 C. water

**For Gravy**
- 2 tbsp. canola oil
- 1 tsp. cumin seeds
- 2 small bay leaves
- 1 medium onion, finely chopped
- 1-2 green chilies, finely chopped
- 1 tbsp. ginger paste
- 1 tbsp. garlic paste
- 1 C. tomato puree
- 1 tbsp. tomato paste
- ¼ tsp. ground turmeric
- 1 tsp. red chili powder
- 1 tbsp. ground coriander
- ½-1 tsp. garam masala powder
- Salt and ground black pepper, as required
- ¼-½ C. coconut cream
- 1 tbsp. dry fenugreek leaves, crushed
- ¼ C. fresh cilantro, finely chopped

1. In a large-sized saucepan, add the beans, cardamom, salt and 4-5 C. water over high heat and bring to a boil.
2. Adjust the heat to medium and cook, covered for about 50-60 minutes.
3. Remove from the hat and set aside.
4. In a heavy-bottomed saucepan, heat oil over medium heat and sauté the cumin seeds and bay leaves for about 30-40 seconds.
5. Add in the onions and sauté for about 4-5 minutes.
6. Stir in the green chilies, ginger and garlic paste and sauté for about 1 minute.

7. Add the tomato puree and cook for about 2-3 minutes, stirring occasionally.
8. Stir in the tomato paste and cook for about 1-2 minutes, stirring occasionally.
9. Add in the spices, salt and black pepper, and cook for about 1 minute, stirring continuously.
10. Add the cooked beans along with the cooked liquid and stir to combine.
11. Adjust the heat to medium-high and bring to a boil.
12. Adjust the heat to low and with the back of spoon, mash some beans.
13. Stir in the coconut cream and fenugreek leaves and simmer, covered for about 10-15 mins, stirring occasionally.
14. Serve hot with the garnishing of cilantro.

Per Serving:
Calories: 203| Fat: 7.9g| Carbs: 24.6g| Fiber: 10.6g| Protein: 10.3g

## MIXED BEANS CURRY

**Prep Time: 15 mins.| Cook Time: 30 mins.| Serves: 4**

- ✓ 1 tbsp. vegetable oil
- ✓ ½ tsp. cumin seeds
- ✓ 1 medium red onion, chopped
- ✓ 1 green chili, chopped
- ✓ 1 tsp. fresh ginger, grated
- ✓ 1 tsp. garlic, grated
- ✓ 1 (14-oz.) can fire-roasted diced tomatoes
- ✓ 1 tsp. curry powder
- ✓ ½ tsp. ground cumin
- ✓ ¼ tsp. ground turmeric
- ✓ ¼ tsp. garam masala powder
- ✓ Salt, as required
- ✓ 1 C. canned black beans, rinsed and drained
- ✓ ½ C. canned white beans, rinsed and drained
- ✓ ½ C. canned red kidney beans, rinsed and drained
- ✓ 1-1½ C. water
- ✓ ½ C. coconut milk
- ✓ 2 tbsp. fresh cilantro, chopped
- ✓ 1 tbsp. fresh lemon juice

1. In a large-sized saucepan, heat the oil over medium heat and sauté the cumin seeds for about 30-50 seconds.
2. Add the onions and sauté for about 3-4 minutes.
3. Add green chili, ginger and garlic and sauté for about 1 minute.
4. Add in the tomatoes and cook for about 4-5 minutes.
5. Add in the spices and salt and cook for about 3-4 minutes.
6. Stir in the beans and cook, covered for about 5 minutes.
7. Stir in the water and coconut milk and simmer for about 5 minutes.
8. Stir in the cilantro and lemon juice and serve hot.

Per Serving:
Calories: 250| Fat: 11.5g| Carbs: 30.3g| Fiber: 10.6g| Protein: 9.5g

## TOMATO RICE

**Prep Time: 15 mins.| Cook Time: 30 mins.| Serves: 4**

- ✓ 1 tbsp. vegetable oil
- ✓ ½ tsp. black mustard seeds
- ✓ 2-3 black peppercorns
- ✓ 2 whole cloves
- ✓ 1 medium-sized onion, thinly sliced
- ✓ ¼ tbsp. ginger paste
- ✓ ¼ tbsp. garlic paste
- ✓ 3-4 curry leaves
- ✓ 1 bay leaf
- ✓ 1 tsp. ground coriander
- ✓ ½ tsp. red chili powder
- ✓ ½ tsp. garam masala powder
- ✓ 2 medium-sized tomatoes, finely chopped
- ✓ 1 green chili pepper, chopped
- ✓ Salt and ground black pepper, as required
- ✓ 1 C. long-grain basmati rice, rinsed
- ✓ 2 C. water
- ✓ ¼ C. fresh cilantro, roughly chopped

1. In a large-sized saucepan, heat oil over medium heat and sauté the mustard seeds, black peppercorns and whole cloves for about 40-60 seconds.
2. Add the onion and sauté for about 4-5 minutes.
3. Add in ginger, garlic, curry leaves, bay leaf and spices and sauté for about 1 minute.
4. Add tomatoes, green chili peppers, salt, and black pepper and cook for about 5-6 minutes, stirring frequently.
5. Add in the rice and cook for about 1-2 minutes, stirring continuously.
6. Stir in the water and cilantro and cook, covered for about 15 minutes.
7. Turn off the heat but keep the pan, covered for about 5 minutes before serving.
8. Remove the lid and with a fork, fluff the rice.
9. Serve hot.

Per Serving:
Calories: 227| Fat: 4.1g| Carbs: 42.8g| Fiber: 2.2g| Protein: 4.4g

## RICE WITH PEAS
**Prep Time: 15 mins.| Cook Time: 30 mins.| Serves: 4**

- ✓ 2 tbsp. canola oil
- ✓ 1 tsp. cumin seeds
- ✓ 1 (1-inch) cinnamon stick
- ✓ 6 whole cloves
- ✓ 3 cardamom pods
- ✓ 1 bay leaf
- ✓ ½ onion, sliced
- ✓ 2 green chilies, chopped
- ✓ ½ tsp. ginger paste
- ✓ ½ tsp. garlic paste
- ✓ 1½ C. green peas, shelled
- ✓ 2 C. water
- ✓ 2 tsp. fresh lemon juice
- ✓ 1 tsp. salt
- ✓ 1 C. basmati rice, soaked for 20 minutes and drained

1. In a large-sized saucepan, heat oil over medium heat and sauté cumin seeds, cinnamon stick, whole cloves, cardamom pods and bay leaf for about 30-60 seconds.
2. Add onion, chillies, ginger and garlic paste and sauté for about 3-4 minutes.
3. Add green peas, water, lemon juice and salt and bring to a boil.
4. Add in rice and again, bring to a boil.
5. Cover the pan and simmer for about 20 minutes.
6. Turn off the heat but keep the pan, covered for about 15 minutes before serving.

Per Serving:
Calories: 284| Fat: 7.7g| Carbs: 46.7g| Fiber: 3.8g| Protein: 6.6g

## RICE WITH CARROTS
**Prep Time: 15 mins.| Cook Time: 25 mins.| Serves: 4**

- ✓ 1 C. long-grain white rice
- ✓ 2 C. water
- ✓ ¼ C. roasted peanuts
- ✓ 1 tbsp. olive oil
- ✓ 1 onion, sliced thinly
- ✓ 1 tsp. fresh ginger root, minced
- ✓ ¾ C. carrot, peeled and grated
- ✓ Salt and ground black pepper, as required

1. In a saucepan, add the water and rice over high heat and bring to a boil.
2. Adjust the heat to low and simmer, covered for about 20 minutes.
3. Meanwhile, in a food processor, add the peanuts and pulse until powdered.
4. In a wok, heat the oil over medium-high heat and sauté the onion for about 4-6 minutes.
5. Add the carrots, ginger and salt and stir to combine.
6. Now adjust the heat to low and simmer, covered for about 5 minutes.
7. Add the peanuts and black pepper and stir to combine.
8. Transfer the cooked rice into the wok with the vegetable mixture and gently mix.
9. Serve hot.

Per Serving:
Calories: 270| Fat: 8.4g| Carbs: 43.1g| Fiber: 2.5g| Protein: 6.1g

## RICE WITH VEGGIES
**Prep Time: 15 mins.| Cook Time: 45 mins.| Serves: 6**

- ✓ 1 tbsp. canola oil
- ✓ 2 large onions, sliced
- ✓ 2-3 green chilies, chopped
- ✓ 2-3 garlic cloves, minced
- ✓ 1 tsp. cumin seeds
- ✓ 2 medium carrots, cut into 1-inch pieces
- ✓ 2 C. cauliflower, cut into 1-inch pieces florets
- ✓ 1 C. green beans
- ✓ 2 C. basmati rice, rinsed, soaked for 20 minutes and drained
- ✓ 1 C. fresh green peas, shelled
- ✓ ½ C. coconut yogurt
- ✓ 1 tbsp. fresh lemon juice
- ✓ 2 tbsp. biryani masala
- ✓ Salt, as required
- ✓ 4 C. water
- ✓ 1/3 C. fresh cilantro, chopped
- ✓ 1/3 C. fresh mint, chopped

1. In a large-sized heavy-bottomed saucepan, heat oil over medium-high heat and cook the onions for about 8-10 minutes, stirring occasionally.

2. Add in the green chilies, garlic and cumin seeds and sauté for about 1 minute.
3. Add carrots, cauliflower and french beans and cook for about 6-8 minutes, stirring occasionally.
4. Add in the rice, green peas, yogurt, lemon juice, biryani masala and salt and gently stir to combine.
5. Add in the water and bring to a boil.
6. Add the cilantro and mint and gently stir to combine.
7. Adjust the heat to low and simmer for about 18-20 minutes.
8. Serve hot.

Per Serving:
Calories: 328| Fat: 4g| Carbs: 64.5g| Fiber: 5.5g| Protein: 8.8g

## NAAN
**Prep Time: 15 mins.| Cook Time: 20 mins.| Serves: 4**

- ✓ 1 C. warm water
- ✓ 2¼ tsp. active dry yeast
- ✓ 1 tsp. agave nectar
- ✓ 1¼ C. brown rice flour
- ✓ ½ C. potato starch
- ✓ ¼ C. tapioca starch
- ✓ 2 tbsp. psyllium husk powder
- ✓ ½ tsp. salt
- ✓ ¼ C. plain almond yogurt
- ✓ Non-stock cooking spray

1. In a bowl, add the warm water, yeast and agave nectar and gently stir to combine.
2. Set aside for about 5 minutes.
3. In another large bowl, mix together the flour, potato starch, tapioca starch, psyllium husk and salt.
4. Add the yeast mixture and almond yogurt and with your hands, mix until a dough ball forms.
5. Place the dough ball onto a clean and smooth surface and with your hands, knead for about 3-4 minutes

6. Transfer the dough into the same bowl.
7. With a cloth, cover the bowl and set aside in a warm place for about 1 hour.
8. Divide the dough into four equal-sized pieces.
9. Roll each dough piece into a 1/8-inch thick circle.
10. Lightly grease a large-sized skillet with cooking spray and heat over high heat.
11. Place 1 dough circle into the skillet and cook for about 2-2½ minutes per side.
12. Remove from the heat and place in a dishcloth to keep warm and moist.
13. Repeat with remaining dough pieces.
14. Serve warm.

Per Serving:
Calories: 331| Fat: 2g| Carbs: 73.6g| Fiber: 6.5g| Protein: 4.7g

## CHAPATI (FLATBREAD)
**Prep Time: 20 mins.| Cook Time: 18 mins.| Serves: 12**

- ✓ 2 C. buckwheat flour
- ✓ ½ tsp. salt
- ✓ 2/3 C. water
- ✓ 4½ tsp. olive oil, divided

1. In a bowl, mix together the flour and salt.
2. Make a well in the center of flour mixture.
3. Add the water and 4 tsp. of oil in the well and mix until a crumbly dough forms.
4. With your hands, knead until dough ball forms.
5. Coat the dough with remaining oil and set aside for about 1 hour.
6. Divide the dough into 12 equal-sized portions and shape each into a ball.
7. Place each dough ball onto a floured surface and with a rolling pin, roll into a ¼-inch thin circle.
8. Heat a non-stick skillet over medium heat.
9. Carefully place 1 chapati in the skillet and cook for about 30-45 minutes per side or until brown spots appear on both sides, pressing with a flat spatula gently and occasionally.
10. Remove from the skillet and place the chapatti in a dishcloth to keep warm and moist.
11. Repeat with remaining chapatis.
12. Serve warm.

Per Serving:
Calories: 82| Fat: 2.4g| Carbs: 14.1g| Fiber: 2g| Protein: 2.5g

## SEMOLINA HALWA
**Prep Time: 10 mins.| Cook Time: 12 mins.| Serves: 8**

**For Sugar Syrup**
- 2 C. granulated white sugar
- 3 C. water
- 2 drops of orange food color

**For Halwa Base**
- ½ C. vegan butter
- 4 green cardamom pods, crushed
- 1 C. semolina
- ¼ C. raisins
- ¼ C. mixed nuts, chopped

1. For sugar syrup: in a medium-sized-sized saucepan, add all ingredients over medium-low heat and cook for about 3-5 minutes, stirring continuously.
2. Remove from the heat and set aside.
3. For halwa base: in a large-sized heavy-bottomed skillet, melt the vegan butter over medium heat and stir in the crushed cardamom pods.
4. Add the semolina and cook for about 2-3 minutes, stirring continuously.
5. Add in the sugar syrup and cook for about 2-3 minutes, stirring frequently.
6. Stir in the raisins and cover the skillet.
7. Immediately remove from the heat and set aside, covered for about 10 minutes.
8. Garnish with nuts and serve warm.

Per Serving:
Calories: 392| Fat: 13.1g| Carbs: 67.8g| Fiber: 1.2g| Protein: 3.4g

## CARROT HALWA
**Prep Time: 15 mins.| Cook Time: 35 mins.| Serves: 12**

- 3 C. water
- 1 C. raw cashews
- 2 tbsp. vegetable oil, divided
- ½ C. almonds, sliced
- 4 C. carrots, peeled and roughly grated
- 1 tsp. ground cardamom
- 1 C. white sugar

1. In a high-power blender, add water and cashews and pulse until smooth and creamy.
2. Heat 1 tbsp. of oil in a large-sized non-stick skillet and cook the almonds for about 1-2 minutes, stirring continuously.
3. Add the carrots and cardamom and cook for about 2 minutes, stirring continuously.
4. Add the cashew mixture and stir to combine.
5. Adjust the heat to medium-low and cook for about 15-20 minutes or until most of the liquid is absorbed, stirring occasionally.
6. Add the sugar and the remaining oil and cook for about 5-10 minutes or until all the liquid is absorbed, stirring frequently.
7. Serve warm with the garnishing of almond slices before serving.

Per Serving:
Calories: 187| Fat: 9.6g| Carbs: 25g| Fiber: 1.8g| Protein: 2.9g

## NUTTY MILK PUDDING
**Prep Time: 15 mins.| Cook Time: 10 mins.| Serves: 4**

- 1¼-2 C. water
- ½ C. oat milk
- ½ C. coconut milk
- ¼ C. raw cashews, soaked in warm water for 15 minutes and drained
- 2 tbsp. raw pistachios
- 7-8 saffron strands
- 1 green cardamom pod, seeds removed
- ¼ C. white sugar
- 2 tbsp. almond flour
- Pinch of salt
- 2 tbsp. mixed nuts, chopped

1. In a high-power blender, add the water, oat milk, coconut milk, raw cashews, raw pistachios, saffron and cardamom seeds and pulse until smooth.
2. Transfer the nut mixture into a saucepan over medium heat and bring to a boil, stirring occasionally.
3. Add in sugar, almond flour and salt and stir to combine well.
4. Adjust the heat to medium-low and cook for about 3-4 minutes, stirring frequently.
5. Remove from the heat and set aside to cool slightly.
6. Serve warm with the garnishing of chopped nuts.

Per Serving:
Calories: 242| Fat: 16.5g| Carbs: 22.2g| Fiber: 2g| Protein: 4.3g

## VERMICELLI PUDDING
**Prep Time: 15 mins.| Cook Time: 22 mins.|
Serves: 4**

- ✓ 2 tbsp. vegan butter
- ✓ ½ C. thin vermicelli
- ✓ 1 tbsp. cashews, chopped
- ✓ 1 tbsp. almonds, chopped
- ✓ 2½ C. unsweetened almond milk
- ✓ 3-4 tbsp. white sugar
- ✓ ½ tsp. ground cardamom
- ✓ ½ tbsp. raisins

1. In a heavy-bottomed skillet, melt 1 tbsp. of vegan butter over medium heat and cook the vermicelli for about 2-3 minutes, stirring continuously.
2. Transfer the vermicelli onto a plate and set aside.
3. In the same wok, melt remaining butter over medium heat and cook the cashews and almonds for about 2 minutes, stirring continuously.
4. With a slotted spoon, transfer the nuts onto a plate.
5. In the same wok, add the almond milk and bring to a boil.
6. Add in the roasted vermicelli and cook for about 5-7 minutes, stirring continuously.
7. Add in sugar, raisins and cardamom and cook for about 3-5 minutes, stirring continuously.
8. Remove from the heat and set aside to cool.
9. Transfer the vermicelli pudding into a large-sized serving bowl and refrigerate for 1-2 hours.
10. Serve with the garnishing of roasted almonds and cashews.

Per Serving:
Calories: 160| Fat: 9.6g| Carbs: 17.6g| Fiber: 1.1g| Protein: 2.2g

## CARROT PUDDING
**Prep Time: 15 mins.| Cook Time: 31 mins.|
Serves: 4**

- ✓ 2-2½ C. unsweetened almond milk
- ✓ ¼ C. raw cashews
- ✓ 1 tbsp. vegan butter
- ✓ 2 C. carrots, peeled and shredded
- ✓ 1-3 tbsp. coconut sugar
- ✓ ¼ tsp. ground cardamom
- ✓ Pinch of ground cinnamon
- ✓ Pinch of salt
- ✓ 3 tbsp. mixed nuts, chopped
- ✓ 3 tbsp. raisins

1. In a high-power blender, add almond milk and cashews and pulse until smooth and creamy.
2. Melt the vegan butter in a skillet over medium heat and cook the carrots for about 5-6 minutes, stirring occasionally.
3. Add in the almond milk and cook for about 10 minutes, stirring occasionally.
4. Reduce heat to medium-low and stir in the sugar, cardamom, cinnamon and salt
5. Add in the nuts and raisins and cook partially covered for about 10-15 minutes, stirring occasionally.
6. Serve warm.

Per Serving:
Calories: 184| Fat: 12.7g| Carbs: 19.5g| Fiber: 2.9g| Protein: 3.7g

## RICE PUDDING
**Prep Time: 10 mins.| Cook Time: 25 mins.|
Serves: 5**

- ✓ 1½ C. cooked white rice, lightly mashed
- ✓ 3 C. unsweetened almond milk
- ✓ 2 C. coconut milk
- ✓ 1/3 C. white sugar
- ✓ 2 tbsp. pistachios, crushed
- ✓ 2 tbsp. almonds, sliced
- ✓ 1 tbsp. raisins
- ✓ ¼ tsp. ground cardamom
- ✓ Pinch of saffron strands

7. In a heavy-bottomed saucepan, add all ingredients except for saffron over medium-high heat and bring to a boil.
8. Adjust the heat to medium-low and cook for about 20 minutes, stirring occasionally.
9. Remove from the heat and stir in saffron.
10. Serve warm or chilled.

Per Serving:

Calories: 377| Fat: 27g| Carbs: 34.1g| Fiber: 3.4g| Protein: 4.8g

# BRITISH RECIPES

### OATS & CHIA PUDDING
**Prep Time: 10 mins. | Serves: 1**

- ¼ C. rolled oats
- 1 tbsp. chia seeds
- 2/3 C. unsweetened coconut milk
- 1 tbsp. desiccated coconut
- 1 tsp. maple syrup
- ¼ tsp. ground cinnamon
- ½ banana, peeled and mashed

1. In a small-sized container, add all the ingredients except for banana and mix well.
2. Cover the container and refrigerate overnight.
3. In the morning, stir in the mashed banana and serve.

Per Serving:
Calories: 237 | Fat: 8.8g | Carbs: 39.4g | Fiber: 7.3g | Protein: 5g

### TOFU & ARUGULA SCRAMBLE
**Prep Time: 15 mins. | Cook Time: 8 mins. | Serves: 2**

- 1 tbsp. extra-virgin olive oil
- 1 garlic clove, minced
- ¼ lb. medium-firm tofu, drained, pressed and crumbled
- 1/3 C. vegetable broth
- 2½ C. fresh arugula
- ¼ C. tomato, finely chopped
- 2 tsp. low-sodium soy sauce
- 1 tsp. ground turmeric
- 1 tsp. fresh lemon juice

1. Heat olive oil in a frying pan over medium-high heat and sauté the garlic for about 1 minute.
2. Add the tofu and cook for about 2-3 minutes, slowly adding the broth.
3. Add the arugula, tomato, soy sauce and turmeric and stir fry for about 3-4 minutes or until all the liquid is absorbed.
4. Stir in the lemon juice and serve immediately.

Per Serving:
Calories: 125 | Fat: 10g | Carbs: 4.5g | Fiber: 1.5g | Protein: 6.8g

### CHOCOLATE PANCAKES
**Prep Time: 10 mins. | Cook Time: 48 mins. | Serves: 6**

- 1 C. all-purpose flour
- 1 tbsp. baking powder
- ¼ tsp. sea salt
- 1 C. warm almond milk
- 2 tbsp. white sugar
- 1 tbsp. coconut oil, melted
- 3 tbsp. vegan chocolate chips
- Non-stick cooking spray

1. In a bowl, blend the flour, baking powder and salt.
2. In another bowl, add the almond milk, sugar and coconut oil and beat until well blended.
3. Add the flour mixture and mix until just combined.
4. Gently fold in the chocolate chips.
5. Grease a non-stick skillet with cooking spray and heat over medium heat.
6. Add about ¼-1/3 C. of the mixture and cook for about 3-4 minutes per side.
7. Repeat with remaining mixture.
8. Serve warm.

Per Serving:
Calories: 215 | Fat: 12.5g | Carbs: 24.5g | Fiber: 1.6g | Protein: 3.2g

## POTATO PANCAKES
**Prep Time: 15 mins. | Cook Time: 22 mins. | Serves: 2**

- ✓ 2 large russet potatoes
- ✓ ¼ C. unsweetened almond milk
- ✓ 1-2 tbsp. nutritional yeast
- ✓ 1 tbsp. flaxseeds meal
- ✓ 3 tsp. olive oil, divided
- ✓ Salt and ground black pepper, as required
- ✓ ½ tsp. fresh lemon juice
- ✓ ¼-1/3 C. unbleached all-purpose flour
- ✓ ½ tsp. baking powder

1. Chop 1 potato and place in a pan of water.
2. Place the pan over medium heat and bring to a boil.
3. Cook for about 5-7 minutes or until done.
4. Drain the potato and set aside to cool slightly.
5. In a bowl, add boiled potato, almond milk, nutritional yeast, flaxseeds meal, 1 tsp. of oil, salt and black pepper and with a potato masher, mash well.
6. Grate the remaining potato and place in a second bowl.
7. In the bowl of grated potato, add lemon juice and mix well.
8. With a paper towel, squeeze the grated potato to remove excess moisture.
9. Add the grated potato in the bowl of mashed potatoes and mix well.
10. Add flour and baking powder and mix until well blended.
11. Make small-sized patties from the mixture.
12. In a skillet, heat oil over medium heat and cook for about 4-5 minutes per side.
13. Serve warm.

Per Serving:
Calories: 379 | Fat: 5.1g | Carbs: 74.6g | Fiber: 11.9g | Protein: 11.3g

## CHOCOLATE WAFFLES
**Prep Time: 15 mins. | Cook Time: 24 mins. | Serves: 4**

- ✓ ½ C. coconut flour
- ✓ 3 tbsp. granulated Erythritol
- ✓ 3 tbsp. unsweetened cocoa powder
- ✓ 2 tbsp. psyllium husk
- ✓ ½ tsp. baking powder
- ✓ Pinch of salt
- ✓ ¼ C. coconut oil, softened
- ✓ 1 C. unsweetened almond milk

1. Preheat the waffle iron and then grease it.
2. In a bowl, add the flour, Erythritol, cacao powder, psyllium husk, baking powder and salt and mix well.
3. Add the coconut oil and stir until a stiff dough forms.
4. Slowly add the almond milk, ¼ C. at a time, mixing well after each addition.
5. Set aside for about 3 minutes.
6. Place ¼ of the mixture into the preheated waffle iron and cook for about 5-6 minutes or until golden brown.
7. Repeat with the remaining mixture.
8. Serve warm

Per Serving:
Calories: 154 | Fat: 15.5g | Carbs: 6.2g | Fiber: 4.3g | Protein: 1.3g

## ENGLISH MUFFINS
**Prep Time: 20 mins. | Cook Time: 42 mins. | Serves: 12**

- ✓ 1 C. warm unsweetened almond milk
- ✓ 2 tsp. granulated white sugar
- ✓ 1 (¼-oz.) packet active dry yeast
- ✓ 3½ C. all-purpose flour plus more for dusting
- ✓ 1 tsp. salt
- ✓ 3 tbsp. vegan butter, melted and cooled
- ✓ Non-stick cooking spray
- ✓ Cornmeal, for coating the muffins

1. In a small-sized bowl, add the almond milk, sugar, and yeast and beat until well combined.
2. Set aside for about 5-10 minutes or until bubbly.
3. In a large-sized bowl, blend 3 C. of flour and salt.
4. Add the milk mixture and 3 tbsp of vegan butter and mix until a soft dough forms. (You can add the remaining ½ C. of flour if needed).
5. Place the dough onto a lightly floured surface and with your hands, knead until smooth and elastic.
6. Grease a bowl with cooking spray generously.
7. Place the dough into the greased bowl and cover it with a damp tea towel.

8. Set the bowl aside in a warm place for 1-2 hours or until doubled in size.
9. Place the dough onto a lightly floured surface and with a rolling pin, roll into ½ inch thickness.
10. Place the cornmeal onto a small-sized plate.
11. Line a baking sheet with parchment paper.
12. With a 3½-inch biscuit cutter, cut the dough into rounds.
13. Coat both sides of each dough round in the cornmeal lightly and then arrange onto the prepared baking sheet.
14. With a damp tea towel, cover the dough rounds and place in a warm place for about 30 minutes.
15. Lightly grease a large-sized non-stick skillet with cooking spray and heat over medium heat.
16. Place the dough rounds into the heated skillet in 3 batches and cook for about 5-7 minutes per side or until golden brown and puffy.
17. Transfer the cooked muffins onto a wire rack to cool before serving.
18. With a fork, split each muffin in half and serve.

Per Serving:
Calories: 164| Fat: 3.4g| Carbs: 28.7g| Fiber: 1.1g| Protein: 3.9g

## WHOLE-GRAIN BREAD
**Prep Time: 15 mins.| Cook Time: 45 mins.| Serves: 12**

- ½ C. warm water
- 4 tsp. active dry yeast
- 2 tsp. coconut sugar
- 2 C. white whole-wheat flour
- ½ C. whole spelt flour
- ¼ C. finely ground cornmeal
- 2 tsp. fine sea salt
- 1½ C. soy milk
- 1 tbsp. olive oil
- 1 tbsp. apple cider vinegar
- Non-stick cooking spray
- 1½ tsp. baking soda
- 2 tsp. coarse ground cornmeal

1. In a bowl, mix together the water, yeast, and coconut sugar. Set aside for about 5 minutes.
2. In a large-sized bowl, mix together the flours, fine cornmeal, and salt.
3. Add the flour mixture, soy milk, oil, vinegar, and oil to the yeast mixture and with a mixer, beat on medium speed for about 3 minutes.
4. With a clean kitchen towel, cover the bowl, and place in a warm place for 1½ hours or until doubled in size.
5. Preheat your oven to 375 °F. Grease an 8x4-inch loaf pan with cooking spray and then sprinkle the bottom with 1 tsp. of the coarse cornmeal evenly.
6. In the dough bowl, add the baking soda and beat on low for about 1 minute.
7. Place the dough into the prepared loaf pan evenly and sprinkle the top with the remaining coarse cornmeal.
8. Bake for approximately 20 minutes.
9. With a piece of foil, cover the loaf pan lightly and bake for approximately 20-25 minutes.
10. Remove the loaf pan from oven and place onto a wire rack for about 10-15 minutes.
11. Then invert the bread onto the wire rack to cool completely before serving.

Per Serving:
Calories: 114| Fat: 2.2g| Carbs: 20g| Fiber: 2.7g| Protein: 4.6g

## GRAPEFRUIT, BEET & CARROT SALAD
**Prep Time: 15 mins.| Serves: 6**

**For Dressing**
- ½ C. olive oil
- ½ tsp. maple syrup
- 1 tbsp. fresh lime juice
- 1 shallot, minced
- ½ tsp. fresh ginger, grated
- 1 tsp. ground cumin
- Pinch of red pepper flakes
- Salt and ground black pepper, as required

**For Salad**
- 4 carrots, peeled and sliced
- 3 beets, peeled and sliced
- 1 grapefruit, peeled, pith removed and sectioned
- 1/3 C. roasted almonds, chopped

1. For dressing: in a small-sized bowl, add all the ingredients and beat until well combined.
2. For salad: in a large-sized salad bowl, add all the ingredients and mix.
3. Place the dressing over salad and toss to coat well.
4. Serve immediately.

Per Serving:
Calories: 226| Fat: 19.7g| Carbs: 13.1g| Fiber: 3g| Protein: 2.6g

## VEGGIE SALAD
**Prep Time: 15 mins. | Serves: 4**

**For Dressing**
- 2 tbsp. red wine vinegar
- 2 tbsp. olive oil
- 1 tbsp. Dijon mustard
- ¼ tsp. garlic powder
- ¼ tsp onion powder
- Salt and ground black pepper, as required

**For Salad**
- 2 C. small cauliflower florets
- 2 C. small broccoli florets
- 1 large bell pepper, seeded and chopped
- ½ English cucumber, chopped
- ½ red onion, chopped
- 3 scallions

1. For dressing: in a small-sized bowl, add all the ingredients and beat until well combined.
2. For salad: in a large-sized salad bowl, add all the ingredients and mix.
3. Place the dressing over salad and toss to coat well.
4. Serve immediately.

Per Serving:
Calories: 118| Fat: 7.5g| Carbs: 11.9g| Fiber: 3.8g| Protein: 3.4g

## ROASTED VEGGIE SALAD
**Prep Time: 15 mins. | Cook Time: 1½ hrs. | Serves: 6**

**For Salad**
- ¼ C. kosher salt
- 1 lb. small beets
- 1 tbsp. extra-virgin olive oil
- 1 lb. baby carrots
- 2 tbsp. whisky
- 1½ tbsp. maple syrup
- 1 tsp. coconut oil, melted
- ¼ tsp. dried thyme
- 1/3 C. walnuts
- 6 C. mixed lettuce

**For Dressing**
- 2 tbsp. white wine vinegar
- 2 tbsp. sunflower oil
- 2 tbsp. maple syrup
- 1 tbsp. coarse mustard
- Salt and ground black pepper, as required

1. Preheat your oven to 350 °F.
2. Spread the kosher salt in the bottom of a baking dish.
3. Drizzle the beets with olive oil evenly and arrange over the kosher salt in baking dish.
4. Bake for approximately 1½ hours or until softened.
5. Meanwhile, in a large-sized bowl, add carrots, whiskey, coconut oil, maple syrup and thyme, and toss to coat well.
6. Arrange the carrots into another baking dish.
7. After 1 hour of baking, arrange the baking dish of carrots in the oven.
8. Remove the baking dishes of veggie from oven and set aside to cool for about 30 minutes.
9. Meanwhile, for dressing: in a small-sized bowl, add all the ingredients and beat until well combined.
10. Peel the beets and cut into slices.
11. Divide lettuce, beets and carrots onto serving plates and drizzle with dressing.
12. Top with walnuts and serve.

Per Serving:
Calories: 215| Fat: 12.3g| Carbs: 24.3g| Fiber: 4.6g| Protein: 3.8g

## GLAZED BRUSSELS SPROUT
**Prep Time: 15 mins. | Cook Time: 15 mins. | Serves: 6**

- 2 tbsp. white miso paste
- 1 tbsp. maple syrup
- 1 tbsp. olive oil
- 1 tbsp. wine vinegar
- 4½ C. Brussels sprout, trimmed and halved
- Salt and ground black pepper, as required
- 1¾ oz. walnuts, roughly chopped

1. Preheat your oven to 390 °F. Line a large-sized baking sheet with parchment paper.
2. For glaze: in a large-sized bowl, add the miso paste, maple syrup, oil, and vinegar and beat until well combined.
3. Add the sprouts and mix well.
4. Arrange the Brussels sprout onto the prepared baking sheet, flat side down, and sprinkle with salt and black pepper generously.
5. Bake for approximately 15 minutes.
6. After 10 minutes of baking, sprinkle the Brussels sprout with walnuts.
7. Serve hot.

Per Serving:
Calories: 111| Fat: 7.8g| Carbs: 13.7g| Fiber: 3.5g| Protein: 4.9g

## CABBAGE WITH LEEK
**Prep Time: 15 mins.| Cook Time: 20 mins.| Serves: 6**

- 3 tbsp. vegan butter
- 5 C. cabbage, sliced
- 1 leek, sliced
- Salt and ground black pepper, as required

1. In a large-sized skillet, melt the vegan butter over medium-high heat and cook the leek for about 5 minutes, stirring frequently.
2. Add in the cabbage and cook for about 15 minutes, stirring occasionally.
3. Stir in the salt and black pepper and serve hot.

Per Serving:
Calories: 74| Fat: 5.6g| Carbs: 5.5g| Fiber: 1.7g| Protein: 1g

## MUSHROOM WITH LEEKS
**Prep Time: 15 mins.| Cook Time: 20 mins.| Serves: 6**

- 2 tbsp. olive oil
- 2 lb. fresh mushrooms, sliced
- Salt, as required
- 2 leeks, sliced
- 1 tbsp. fresh tarragon, chopped

1. In a large-sized skillet, heat the oil over medium heat and cook the mushrooms with salt for about 10-15 minutes, stirring occasionally.
2. Add leeks and cook for about 3-4 minutes, stirring occasionally.
3. Stir in the tarragon and cook for about 1 minute.
4. Serve hot.

Per Serving:
Calories: 91| Fat: 5.2g| Carbs: 9.3g| Fiber: 2.1g| Protein: 5.3g

## VEGGIES WITH VEGAN SAUSAGE
**Prep Time: 15 mins.| Cook Time: 25 mins.| Serves: 8**

- 1 tsp. olive oil
- 2¼ C. potatoes, cut into small pieces
- 1 leek, sliced finely
- 1½ tsp. dried thyme
- 7 oz. vegan sausages
- 6 C. Brussels sprout, trimmed and halved
- 2¼ C. broccoli, cut into bite-sized florets
- 2½ tbsp. Dijon mustard

1. In a large-sized skillet, heat the oil over medium-high heat and cook the potatoes for about 10 minutes, stirring frequently.
2. Add the leeks and thyme and cook for about 2-3 minutes.
3. Add in the vegan sausages, Brussels sprout and broccoli and cook for about 10 minutes, stirring frequently.
4. Stir in the mustard, salt and black pepper and cook for about 12 minutes, stirring continuously.
5. Serve hot.

Per Serving:
Calories: 108| Fat: 1.2g| Carbs: 19.3g| Fiber: 5.9g| Protein: 7.1g

## MUSHROOM SOUP
**Prep Time: 20 mins.| Cook Time: 40 mins.| Serves: 6**

- 1 C boiling water
- ½ oz. dried porcini mushrooms
- 2 tsp. fresh rosemary, chopped
- 1 tbsp. olive oil
- 1 medium yellow onion, chopped
- 16 oz. fresh cremini mushrooms, sliced
- ½ C. raw cashews
- 2 whole garlic cloves, peeled
- 2 garlic cloves, minced
- Ground black pepper, as required
- 4 C. vegetable broth
- 2 tbsp. tamari
- 3 tbsp. arrowroot starch
- 1 C. water

1. In a bowl, add boiling water, porcinis and rosemary and set aside for about 20 minutes.

2. In a large-sized soup pan, heat oil over medium heat and sauté the onion for about 3-5 minutes.
3. Add the mushrooms, and cook for about 15-20 minutes, stirring occasionally.
4. Meanwhile, in a high-power blender, add porcini mushroom mixture, cashews and 2 whole garlic cloves and pulse until smooth. Set aside.
5. In the soup pan, add minced garlic, black pepper, and tamari, and cook for about 2-3 minutes, stirring frequently.
6. Add the broth and bring to a boil.
7. Meanwhile, in a bowl, dissolve the arrowroot in water.
8. In the soup pan, add the cashew mixture and stir to combine.
9. Now add the starch mixture and stir to combine.
10. Cook for about 3-5 minutes, stirring occasionally.
11. Serve hot.

Per Serving:
Calories: 169| Fat: 8.7g| Carbs: 15.1g| Fiber: 2.2g| Protein: 8.4g

## POTATO & LEEK SOUP
**Prep Time: 15 mins.| Cook Time: 45 mins.| Serves: 6**

- 3 large potatoes, peeled and cubed
- 3 tbsp. olive oil
- 3 tbsp. amaranth flour
- 1 leek, finely sliced
- 3 garlic cloves, finely minced
- 4 C. vegetable broth
- 1 C. light coconut milk
- 2-3 tsp. fresh thyme leaves
- Salt and ground black pepper, as required

1. In a large-sized pan of water, add the potatoes and bring to a boil.
2. Cook for about 8-10 minutes or until just tender.
3. Drain the potatoes and set aside.
4. In a large-sized soup pan, heat oil over medium heat and stir in the amaranth flour.
5. Cook for about 2 minutes, whisking continuously.
6. Add leeks and garlic and cook for about 2 minutes, stirring continuously.
7. Add the drained potatoes, broth, coconut milk and thyme and bring to a boil.
8. Adjust the heat to low and simmer for about 15-20 minutes.
9. Stir in salt and black pepper and serve hot.

Per Serving:
Calories: 340| Fat: 18.1g| Carbs: 38.7g| Fiber: 6.3g| Protein: 8.5g

## VINEGAR BLACK-EYED PEAS
**Prep Time: 10 mins.| Cook Time: 3 hours 5 mins.| Serves: 6**

- 2½ C. black-eyed peas, rinsed
- Pinch of baking soda
- 1 carrot, peeled and thickly sliced
- 1 celery stalk, roughly chopped
- 1 onion, roughly chopped
- 2 tbsp. malt vinegar
- Salt, as required

1. In a large-sized saucepan of water, soak the black-eyed peas with baking soda overnight.
2. Drain the peas in a colander and rinse well.
3. In the same pan, add the peas and cover with fresh water.
4. Add the carrot, celery, and onion and stir to combine.
5. Place the pan over high heat and bring to a boil.
6. Adjust the heat to medium and simmer for about 2-3 hours or until the peas are soft, stirring occasionally.
7. Stir in vinegar and salt and serve hot.

Per Serving:
Calories: 88| Fat: 0.8g| Carbs: 16.2g| Fiber: 4g| Protein: 5.3g

## LENTIL SOUP
**Prep Time: 15 mins.| Cook Time: 35 mins.| Serves: 4**

- 6 C. vegetable broth
- 7 oz. red lentils, rinsed
- 1 (14-oz.) can diced tomatoes
- 1 tbsp. fresh tarragon leaves
- Salt and ground black pepper, as required

1. In a large-sized soup pan, add broth and lentils over medium-high heat and bring to a boil.
2. Cook uncovered for about 10 minutes.
3. Adjust the heat to low and simmer, covered for about 15 minutes.

4. Remove from the heat and stir in the tomatoes, tarragon, salt and black pepper.
5. With an immersion blender, blend the soup until smooth.
6. Return the soup over medium heat and cook for about 3-5 minutes.
7. Serve hot.

Per Serving:
Calories: 252| Fat: 2.8g| Carbs: 35.3g| Fiber: 16.4g| Protein: 21g

## IRISH STEW
**Prep Time: 20 mins.| Cook Time: 1¼ hrs.| Serves: 8**

- 2 tbsp. olive oil
- 3 large carrots, peeled and cut into ½-inch chunks
- 2 celery stalks, chopped
- 1 large onion, chopped
- 9 oz. portobello mushrooms, sliced
- 5 garlic cloves, minced
- 4 tbsp. all-purpose flour
- 11 oz. Guinness
- 4 large potatoes, cut into large chunks
- 1 medium rutabaga, cut into chunky pieces
- ¼ head green cabbage, shredded
- 4 C. vegetable broth
- ¼ C. soy sauce
- 1 tbsp. white sugar
- 1½ tsp. dried rosemary
- 1 tsp. dried thyme
- 2 bay leaves
- Salt and ground black pepper, as required

1. In a large-sized Dutch oven, heat the oil over medium heat and sauté the carrots, celery and onion for about 4-5 minutes.
2. Add the mushrooms and cook for about 4-5 minutes, stirring occasionally.
3. Add the garlic and sauté for about 1 minute.
4. Stir in the flour and cook for about 1-2 minutes, stirring continuously.
5. Stir in the Guinness and cook for about 1 minute, stirring continuously.
6. Add the potatoes, rutabaga, cabbage, broth, soy sauce, sugar, dried herbs, bay leaves, salt and black pepper and bring to a boil, stirring frequently.
7. Adjust the heat to medium-low and simmer, covered for about 50-60 minutes, stirring occasionally.
8. Serve hot.

Per Serving:
Calories: 286| Fat: 4.7g| Carbs: 47.2g| Fiber: 8g| Protein: 8.9g

## RICE & VEGGIE STEW
**Prep Time: 15 mins.| Cook Time: 35 mins.| Serves: 4**

- 2¾ C. vegetable broth
- ¼ C. uncooked white rice
- 2 carrots, peeled and chopped
- 2 potatoes, scrubbed and chopped
- 1 parsnip, peeled and chopped
- 1 turnip, peeled and chopped
- 1 onion, chopped
- ½ tsp. cayenne powder
- Salt and ground black pepper, as required
- tbsp. fresh parsley, chopped

1. In a large-sized soup pan, add the broth over medium-high heat and bring to a boil.
2. Add the remaining ingredients except the parsley and again, bring to a boil.
3. Adjust the heat to medium and cook, covered for about 30 minutes or until desired doneness.
4. Serve hot with the garnishing of parsley.

Per Serving:
Calories: 203| Fat: 1.3g| Carbs: 41.5g| Fiber: 6.7g| Protein: 7g

## YORKSHIRE STEW
**Prep Time: 15 mins.| Cook Time: 40 mins.| Serves: 6**

- 4¼ C. vegetable broth
- 2 potatoes, chopped
- 2 carrots, peeled and chopped
- 1 swede, chopped
- 1 leek, chopped
- 1 onion, chopped
- 1 (14-oz.) can diced tomatoes
- 2 garlic cloves, chopped
- 1 tbsp. tomato paste
- 1 tsp. olive oil

- 2-3 fresh thyme sprigs
- 2 bay leaves
- 1 tsp. cayenne powder
- Salt and ground black pepper, as required
- 1 C. cooked barley

1. In a large-sized soup pan, add broth, potatoes, carrots, swede, leek, and onion over high heat and bring to a boil.
2. Add the tomatoes, garlic, tomato paste, oi, thyme, bay leaves and cayenne powder and stir to combine.
3. Adjust the heat to low and simmer, covered for about 30 minutes, stirring occasionally.
4. Stir in the barley, salt and black pepper and cook for about 5 minutes.
5. Serve hot.

Per Serving:
Calories: 255| Fat: 2.9g| Carbs: 48.8g| Fiber: 10.7g| Protein: 10.6g

### VEGGIE CASSEROLE
**Prep Time: 20 mins.| Cook Time: 30 mins.| Serves: 8**

#### For Veggies
- 2 lb. potatoes, peeled
- 1 eggplant, sliced
- 1 zucchini, sliced
- 1 bell pepper, seeded and sliced
- 1 C. fresh corn

#### For Sauce
- 2 tsp. tahini
- 7 oz. coconut milk
- 1 C. vegetable broth
- 2-3 tbsp. water
- 1 tsp. potato starch
- 1 garlic clove

#### For Topping
- 1 C. vegan breadcrumbs
- ¾ C. macadamia nuts

1. Preheat your oven to 390 °F. Line a large-sized baking sheet with parchment paper.
2. In a pan of water, add the potatoes and cook for about 10-15 minutes.
3. Drain the potatoes and set aside to cool.
4. Then cut the potatoes into slices.
5. Arrange the vegetables and corn onto the prepared baking sheet and sprinkle with salt and black pepper.
6. Roast for about 10 minutes.
7. Meanwhile, for sauce: in a saucepan, add coconut milk, broth and tahini over medium heat and bring to a boil.
8. In a small-sized bowl, dissolve the potato starch in water.
9. In the pan of broth mixture, add the starch mixture, stirring continuously.
10. Stir in garlic, salt and black pepper and remove from the heat.
11. For topping: place breadcrumbs and macadamias in a food processor and pulse until a crumbly mixture forms.
12. Remove the vegetables from oven.
13. In a casserole dish, place half of the vegetables and top with half of sauce.
14. Repeat the layers and top with the crumbly mixture.
15. Again, set your oven to 390 °F and bake for approximately 15-20 minutes or until the top becomes golden brown.
16. Serve hot.

Per Serving:
Calories: 333| Fat: 17.5g| Carbs: 40.5g| Fiber: 8.1g| Protein: 7.8g

### SAUSAGE VEGGIES & BEANS
**Prep Time: 15 mins.| Cook Time: 45 mins.| Serves: 4**

- 1 tsp. olive oil
- 8 vegan sausages
- 2 red onions, chopped
- 4 garlic cloves, crushed
- 1 tsp. smoked paprika
- 2 bay leaves
- 1 tbsp. tomato puree
- 4½ C. carrots, peeled and chopped
- 1¾ C. canned tomatoes
- 2 tsp. fresh thyme, chopped
- 1½ C. red wine
- 1 C. vegetable broth
- 1 C. canned butterbeans

1. In a large-sized ovenproof wok, heat oil over medium heat and cook the sausages for about 5 minutes or until browned from all sides. Transfer the sausages onto a plate.
2. In the same wok, add onions, garlic, paprika and bay leaves and sauté for about 3-5 minutes.
3. Stir in the tomato puree and mix well.
4. Stir in the carrots, tomatoes, thyme wine, and broth and bring to a boil.
5. Add the cooked sausage and stir to combine.
6. Adjust the heat to low and simmer uncovered for about 20 minutes.

7. Stir the butterbeans and simmer for about 10 minutes.
8. Stir in the salt and black pepper and serve hot.

Per Serving:
Calories: 353| Fat: 2.2g| Carbs: 46.8g| Fiber: 13.6g| Protein: 20.6g

## MINI SHEPHERD PIES
**Prep Time: 25 mins.| Cook Time: 53 mins.| Serves: 6**

### For Topping
- 3 medium Yukon Gold potatoes, peeled and cubed
- 3 C. fresh kale, trimmed and chopped
- 1 scallion, chopped
- 1½ tbsp. coconut oil, softened
- ¾ C. coconut milk
- 1/8 tsp. freshly ground nutmeg
- Salt, as required

### For Filling
- 1½ tbsp. olive oil, divided
- 14 oz. vegan sausages, crumbled
- 2 medium carrots, peeled and finely chopped
- 1 medium onion, chopped
- 3 celery stalks, chopped
- 1 C. cabbage, chopped
- 2 garlic cloves, minced
- Salt and ground black pepper, as required
- 2 tbsp. all-purpose flour
- ½ C. vegetable broth
- ½ C. Guinness stout
- 2 tsp. Worcestershire sauce
- 1 C. frozen green peas, thawed
- ¼ C. fresh parsley, chopped

1. Preheat your oven to 400 °F.
2. For topping: in a pan of water, add the potatoes over high heat and bring to a boil.
3. Adjust the heat to low and simmer for about 25 minutes.
4. Drain the potatoes and return in the same pan.
5. With a potato masher, mash the potatoes and cover the pan.
6. Meanwhile, in another pan, add the remaining topping ingredients and bring to a gentle simmer.
7. Simmer, covered for about 10-12 minutes, stirring occasionally.
8. Transfer the kale mixture in the pan of potatoes and stir to combine.
9. Meanwhile, for filling: in skillet, heat 1 tbsp. of the oil over medium-high heat and cook the vegetarian sausage for about 4-5 minutes or until browned completely.
10. Transfer the cooked sausage onto a plate.
11. In the same skillet, heat the remaining oil and cook onion, carrot, celery, cabbage, garlic, salt and black pepper for about 10-12 minutes.
12. Add the flour and stir until well coated with vegetables.
13. Add the broth, Guinness and Worcestershire sauce and cook until mixture becomes thick, stirring continuously.
14. Add the sausage, peas and parsley and cook for about 2-3 minutes
15. In 6 mason jars, divide filling mixture and top with the topping mixture evenly.
16. Arrange the jars onto a rimmed baking sheet and bake for approximately 20 minutes.
17. Now, switch the oven settings to broiler.
18. Broil for about 1-3 minutes or until top becomes golden brown
19. Remove from the oven and serve warm.

Per Serving:
Calories: 392| Fat: 18.9g| Carbs: 36.5g| Fiber: 8.3g| Protein: 19.5g

## BARLEY & LENTIL SHEPHERD PIE
**Prep Time: 20 mins.| Cook Time: 1 hr. 20 mins.| Serves: 8**

- ¼ C. pearl barley
- ½ C. lentils
- 1 tsp. nutritional yeast
- 2 C. vegetable broth, divided
- 3 potatoes, scrubbed and chopped
- ½ C. walnuts, chopped
- ½ of onion, chopped
- 1 large carrot, peeled and chopped
- ½ tsp. water
- 1 tsp. all-purpose flour
- Salt and ground black pepper, as required

1. Preheat your oven to 350 °F.
2. In a large-sized pan, add barley, lentils, nutritional yeast and 1¼ C. of broth over medium-low heat

and cook, covered for about 30 minutes or until all the liquid is absorbed.
3. Transfer the barley mixture into a large-sized bowl.
4. In a pan of salted boiling water, add the potatoes and boil for about 15 minutes.
5. Drain the potatoes well and set aside to cool slightly.
6. Then with a potato masher, mash the potatoes completely.
7. Meanwhile, in another pan, add walnuts, onion, carrot and remaining broth over medium heat and cook for about 15 minutes.
8. Meanwhile, in a bowl, mix together water and flour.
9. Add flour mixture in carrot mixture, stirring continuously.
10. Cook for about 2-3 minutes or until thickened.
11. Transfer the carrot mixture into bowl with barley mixture.
12. Add salt and black pepper and stir to combine.
13. Transfer the mixture into a casserole dish evenly.
14. Spread mashed potatoes on top evenly.
15. Bake for approximately 30 minutes or until top becomes golden brown.
16. Serve hot.

Per Serving:
Calories: 186| Fat: 5.3g| Carbs: 27.6g| Fiber: 7.6g| Protein: 8.5g

## YORKSHIRE PUDDING
**Prep Time: 20 mins.| Cook Time: 40 mins.| Serves: 8**

- ½ C. all-purpose flour
- 2/3 C. chickpea flour
- 2¼ tsp. baking powder
- ¼ tsp. ground turmeric
- ¼ tsp. fine salt
- 6 tbsp. aquafaba (the liquid from a can of chickpeas)
- ¾ tsp. apple cider vinegar
- ½ tsp. Dijon mustard
- 1½ C. water
- 12 tsp. olive oil

1. Preheat your oven to 425 °F.
2. Arrange a large-sized baking sheet in the oven while preheating.
3. In a medium-sized bowl, add the flours, baking powder, turmeric and salt and mix well.
4. In another bowl, the aquafaba, vinegar, mustard and water and whisk until well combined.
5. In the bowl of flour mixture, add the water mixture and whisk until smooth and bubbly.
6. Set aside for about 10 minutes.
7. In each of 8 metal muffin pans, add 1¼ tsp. of oil and tilt to spread evenly.
8. Arrange the muffin cups onto the preheated baking sheet.
9. Again, place the baking sheet in oven for about 10 minutes.
10. Remove the baking sheet of muffin pans from oven.
11. Immediately pour the mixture into the pans evenly.
12. Bake for approximately 35-40 minutes.
13. Serve immediately.

Per Serving:
Calories: 122| Fat: 7.6g| Carbs: 12g| Fiber: 1.1g| Protein: 2.6g

## STRAWBERRIES WITH CREAM
**Prep Time: 15 mins.| Serves: 3**

- 2 (12-oz.) cans full-fat coconut milk, chilled overnight
- ½ C. icing sugar
- 2½ C. fresh strawberries, hulled and halved

1. Carefully scoop the thickened cream from each can of coconut milk and transfer into a bowl.
2. In the bowl of coconut cream, add the icing sugar and with a handheld electric mixer, beat until fluffy.
3. In each serving glass, place a layer of coconut cream and top with some strawberries.
4. Repeat the layers.
5. Serve chilled

Per Serving:
Calories: 326| Fat: 21.3g| Carbs: 32.6g| Fiber: 2.4g| Protein: 2.6g

## BANOFFEE PIE
**Prep Time: 20 mins.| Cook Time: 6 mins.| Serves: 10**

**For Base**
- ✓ 2 C. Digestive biscuit crumbs, crushed finely
- ✓ ¼ C. plus 2 tbsp. vegan margarine, melted

**For Filling**
- ✓ 1 C. soy milk
- ✓ 2 tbsp. cornflour
- ✓ 1/3 C. plus 1 tbsp. brown sugar
- ✓ 3 tsp. vanilla extract
- ✓ 2 tbsp. vegan margarine
- ✓ 3 medium-sized ripe bananas, peeled and sliced

**For Topping**
- ✓ ½ C. vegan whipped cream
- ✓ ¼ C. vegan chocolate shavings

1. For base: in a large-sized bowl, add the biscuit crumb and melted margarine and mix until well combined.
2. Place the crumb mixture into a 9-inch tart pan and press in the bottom and sides.
3. Refrigerate the tart pan before using.
4. For caramel filling: in a bowl, add 2 tbsp. of the soy milk and cornflour and mix until smooth.
5. Add the remaining soy milk and whisk until well combined.
6. In a small-sized saucepan, add the cornstarch mixture with brown sugar and vanilla and mix well.
7. Add in the vegan margarine and place the pan over low heat.
8. Cook for about 2-3 minutes, stirring continuously.
9. Adjust the heat to high and cook for about 2-3 minutes, stirring continuously.
10. Place the caramel over the base evenly and refrigerate for 1 hour before serving.
11. Just before serving, arrange the banana slices over the pie evenly.
12. Top with whipped cream and chocolate shaving and serve.

Per Serving:
Calories: 248| Fat: 12.4g| Carbs: 31.8g| Fiber: 1.6g| Protein: 2.9g

## BLUEBERRY SCONES
**Prep Time: 15 mins.| Cook Time: 22 mins.| Serves: 8**

- ✓ 1 tbsp. ground flaxseeds
- ✓ 3 tbsp. water
- ✓ 1 C. blanched almond flour
- ✓ ¼ C. coconut flour
- ✓ 3 tbsp. granulated Erythritol
- ✓ ½ tsp. baking powder
- ✓ Salt, as required
- ✓ ¼ C. unsweetened almond milk
- ✓ 2 tbsp. coconut oil, melted
- ✓ 1 tsp. vanilla extract
- ✓ ½ C. fresh blackberries

1. Preheat your oven to 350 °F. Line a baking sheet with parchment paper.
2. For scones: in a large-sized bowl, add the ground flaxseeds and water and mix until seeds are absorbed completely.
3. Set aside for about 5 minutes.
4. Add the flours, Erythritol, baking powder and salt in a bowl and mix until well combined.
5. In the bowl of the flaxseeds mixture, add the almond milk, coconut oil and vanilla extract and beat until well combined.
6. Add the flour mixture and mix until a pliable dough forms.
7. Gently fold in the blackberries.
8. Arrange the dough onto the prepared baking sheet and with your hands, pat into about 1-inch thick circle.
9. Carefully cut the circle into 8 equal-sized wedges.
10. Now, arrange the scones in a single layer about 1-inch apart
11. Bake for approximately 18-22 minutes or until the top becomes golden brown
12. Remove from the oven and place the baking sheet onto a wire rack to cool completely before serving.

Per Serving:
Calories: 128| Fat: 11.1g| Carbs: 3.9g| Fiber: 2.2g| Protein: 0.2g

## CHOCOLATE CUPCAKES
**Prep Time: 15 mins.| Cook Time: 20 mins.| Serves: 12**

**For Cupcakes**
- ✓ 1 C. rice milk
- ✓ 1 tsp. white vinegar
- ✓ 1/3 C. vegetable oil
- ✓ ¾ C. white sugar

- ✓ 1½ tsp. vanilla extract
- ✓ 1 C. all-purpose flour
- ✓ 1/3 C. cocoa powder
- ✓ ¾ tsp. baking soda
- ✓ ½ tsp. baking powder
- ✓ ¼ tsp. salt

**For Frosting**
- ✓ 1 C. confectioners' sugar
- ✓ ¼ C. cocoa powder, sifted
- ✓ 3 tbsp. rice milk

1. Preheat your oven to 350 °F. Line a 12 cups muffin tin with paper liners.
2. For cupcakes: in a large-sized bowl, add the rice milk, vinegar, oil, sugar, and vanilla extract and beat until well combined.
3. In another bowl, sift together the flour, cocoa powder, baking soda, baking powder and salt.
4. In the bowl of rice milk mixture, add the flour mixture and mix until just combined.
5. Transfer the mixture into paper muffin cups about ¾ of full.
6. Bake for 20 minutes or until a toothpick inserted in the center comes out clean.
7. Remove the muffin tin from oven and place onto a wire rack to cool for about 10 minutes.
8. Carefully invert the cupcakes onto a wire rack to cool completely before frosting.
9. For frosting: in a bowl, add all ingredients and beat until smooth.
10. Spread frosting over each cupcake evenly and serve.

Per Serving:
Calories: 200| Fat: 6.9g| Carbs: 35g| Fiber: 1.6g| Protein: 1.9g

## CHERRY CRUMBLE
**Prep Time: 10 mins.| Cook Time: 50 mins.| Serves: 12**

- ✓ 3¾ C. cherry pie filling
- ✓ 1 package yellow cake mix
- ✓ ½ C. brown sugar
- ✓ ½ C. cold vegan butter, cut in small pieces

1. Preheat your oven to 375 °F.
2. Line the inside of a Dutch oven with a piece of foil.
3. In the bottom of the prepared Dutch oven, spread the cherry pie filling in an even layer.
4. Sprinkle the top of cherry pie filling with cake mix, followed by brown sugar.
5. Place the butter pieces on top in the shape of dots.
6. Cover the Dutch oven with a lid and bake for approximately 45-50 minutes or until the top is golden brown.
7. Remove from oven and let it cool slightly before serving.

Per Serving:
Calories: 224| Fat: 8.7g| Carbs: 35.6g| Fiber: 1g| Protein: 0.5g

## PEACH COBBLER
**Prep Time: 15 mins.| Cook Time: 1 hr. 2 mins.| Serves: 10**

**For Filling**
- ✓ 6 tbsp. coconut oil, melted
- ✓ 3 lb. ripe peaches
- ✓ 1/3 C. maple syrup
- ✓ 2 tbsp. cornstarch
- ✓ 1 tsp. vanilla extract
- ✓ ½ tsp. ground cinnamon
- ✓ ½ tsp. ground ginger

**For Topping**
- ✓ ¾ C. granulated white sugar
- ✓ 1/3 C. all-purpose flour
- ✓ 1/3 C. white whole-wheat flour
- ✓ 2 tsp. baking powder
- ✓ ½ tsp. salt
- ✓ ½ C. unsweetened almond milk

1. Preheat your oven to 350 °F.
2. In a 10-inch Dutch oven, add the coconut oil and place in the oven until butter is melted.
3. In another large-sized Dutch oven of boiling water, add the peaches in 2 batches and cook for about 1 minute.
4. With a slotted spoon, remove the peaches from the pan and plunge into a bowl of ice bath to stop the cooking.
5. Remove the peaches from ice bath and with your fingers, slip off the skin of each peach.

6. Then, cut the peaches into 1/3-inch wide slices
7. In a large-sized bowl, add the peach slices, maple syrup, cornstarch, vanilla extract, cinnamon, and ginger and gently stir to combine.
8. For topping: in another bowl, add the sugar, flours, baking powder and salt and mix well.
9. Add the almond milk and beat until well combined.
10. After melting of butter, remove the Dutch oven from the oven.
11. In the Dutch oven, place the flour mixture over melted coconut oil evenly and top with the peach mixture.
12. Bake for approximately 50-60 minutes or until a toothpick inserted in the center comes out clean.
13. Remove from oven and let it cool slightly before serving.
14. Serve warm.

Per Serving:
Calories: 213| Fat: 7.4g| Carbs: 37.2g| Fiber: 1.3g| Protein: 1.9g

## BLACKBERRY & BANANA CRUMBLE
**Prep Time: 10 mins.| Cook Time: 40 mins.| Serves: 4**

- Non-stick cooking spray
- ¼ C. coconut flour
- ¼ C. arrowroot flour
- ¾ tsp. baking soda
- ¼ C. ripe banana, peeled and mashed
- 2 tbsp. coconut oil, melted
- 3 tbsp. water
- ½ tbsp. fresh lemon juice
- 1½ C. fresh blackberries

1. Preheat your oven to 300 °F. Lightly grease an 8x8-inch baking dish with cooking spray.
2. In a large-sized bowl, add all the ingredients except the blueberries and mix until well combined.
3. In the bottom of the prepared baking dish, place the blueberries and top them with the flour mixture evenly.
4. Bake for approximately 40 minutes or until the top becomes golden brown.
5. Serve warm.

Per Serving:
Calories: 107| Fat: 7.2g| Carbs: 11.6g| Fiber: 2g| Protein: 1g

## APPLE CRISP
**Prep Time: 15 mins.| Cook Time: 20 mins.| Serves: 8**

**For Filling**
- Non-stick cooking spray
- 2 large apples, peeled, cored, and chopped
- 2 tbsp. water
- 2 tbsp. fresh apple juice
- ¼ tsp. ground cinnamon

**For Topping**
- ½ C. quick rolled oats
- ¼ C. unsweetened coconut flakes
- 2 tbsp. pecans, chopped
- ½ tsp. ground cinnamon
- ¼ C. water

1. Preheat your oven to 300 F. Lightly grease a baking dish with cooking spray.
2. To make the filling add all of the ingredients in a large-sized bowl and gently mix. Set aside.
3. Make the topping by adding all of the ingredients to another bowl and mix well.
4. Place the filling mixture into the prepared baking dish then spread the topping over the filling mixture evenly.
5. Bake for approximately 20 minutes or until the top becomes golden brown.
6. Serve warm.

Per Serving:
Calories: 100| Fat: 2.7g| Carbs: 19.1g| Fiber: 2.6g| Protein: 1.2g

## BLUEBERRY CRUMBLE
**Prep Time: 10 mins.| Cook Time: 17 mins.| Serves: 1**

- 1 tsp. stevia powder
- ¼ C. oats
- 1 scoop vegan vanilla protein powder
- 2 tbsp. fresh lemon juice
- 10 almonds, finely chopped
- 1 C. fresh blueberries

1. Preheat your oven to 350 °F.

2. In a bowl, add the oats, protein powder and lemon juice and mix until a crumbly mixture forms.
3. Add the almonds and mix well.
4. In the bottom of a small-sized Pyrex dish, place the blueberries and sprinkle with a little stevia.
5. Spread the crumble on top of the blueberries evenly.
6. Bake for approximately 15 minutes.
7. Now, set the oven to broiler and broil for about 1-2 minutes.
8. Remove from the oven and set aside to cool slightly before serving.

Per Serving:
Calories: 346| Fat: 9.9g| Carbs: 39g| Fiber: 7.2g| Protein: 28.4g

# FRENCH RECIPES

## CREPES
**Prep Time: 10 mins.| Cook Time: 18 mins.| Serves: 6**

- 1½ C. all-purpose flour
- 1 tbsp. cornstarch
- 1 tbsp. granulated white sugar
- ¼ tsp. salt
- 1 C. water
- 1 C. unsweetened soy milk
- 2 tbsp. avocado oil
- 2-4 tbsp. vegan butter
- 2-4 tbsp. powdered sugar

1. In a large-sized bowl, blend the flour, cornstarch, sugar and salt.
2. Add the water, soy milk and oil and beat until smooth.
3. In a medium-sized-sized, non-stick wok, melt 1 tbsp. of vegan butter over medium heat.
4. Add about 1/3 C. of the mixture and immediately tilt the pan to spread in a thin circle.
5. Cook for about 2 minutes or until golden brown.
6. Carefully flip the crepe and cook for 30-60 seconds.
7. Repeat with remaining mixture.
8. Dust with powdered sugar and serve with fresh berries of your choice.

Per Serving:
Calories: 198| Fat: 5.3g| Carbs: 32.5g| Fiber: 1.3g| Protein: 4.6g

## FRENCH TOAST
**Prep Time: 15 mins.| Cook Time: 36 mins.| Serves: 3**

- 1 C. unsweetened soy milk
- 2 tsp. pure maple syrup
- 1 tsp. vanilla extract
- ¼ C. cornstarch
- 1 tsp. ground flaxseeds
- ½ tsp. baking powder
- 1 tsp. ground cinnamon
- 2-3 tbsp. coconut oil
- 6 French bread slices

1. In a shallow bowl, whisk together the soy milk, maple syrup, vanilla extract, cornstarch, ground flaxseeds, baking powder and cinnamon until well blended.
2. In a non-stick skillet, melt a little coconut oil over medium-high heat.

3. Dip both sides of 1 bread slice in soy milk mixture and cook in the skillet for about 3 minutes per side.
4. Repeat with remaining slices.
5. Serve warm.

Per Serving:
Calories: 260| Fat: 11.5g| Carbs: 34.3g| Fiber: 1.7g| Protein: 4.9g

## FRENCH BREAD
**Prep Time: 15 mins.| Cook Time: 16 mins.| Serves: 8**

- 1 C. warm water
- 1 tsp. white sugar
- 1 (¼-oz.) envelope active dry yeast
- 2-3 C. bread flour
- 1 tsp. salt
- 2 tbsp. olive oil

1. Place water, sugar and yeast in a bowl and mix until dissolved.
2. Let it rest for 5 minutes or until it begins to foam.
3. In the bowl of an electric mixer, fitted with a dough hook, place yeast mixture, 2 C. of flour, salt and oil and mix on low speed for about 1 minute.
4. Slowly add enough flour and mix until a soft and smooth dough forms.
5. Now, mix on medium speed for 5 minutes.
6. With a plastic wrap, cover the dough bowl and set aside in warm for 30 minutes or until doubled in size.
7. Preheat your oven to 400°F.
8. Lightly grease a baking sheet.
9. Uncover the bowl and with your hands, punch the dough down.
10. Set aside for 10 minutes.
11. Place the dough onto a lightly floured surface and shape into a 12-inch long loaf.
12. Now, arrange the loaf onto the prepared baking sheet.
13. Cut 3 (¼-inch deep) slits across top of the loaf with a sharp paring knife.
14. Bake for approximately 16 minutes or until golden brown and sounds hollow when tapped.
15. Remove the baking sheet from oven and place onto a wire rack to cool for about 10 minutes.
16. Now, invert the bread onto the wire rack to cool completely before slicing.
17. Cut the bread loaf into desired-sized pieces and serve.

Per Serving:
Calories: 148| Fat: 3.9g| Carbs: 24.7g| Fiber: 1g| Protein: 3.6g

## CROISSANTS
**Prep Time: 20 mins.| Cook Time: 18 mins.| Serves: 20**

- 17½ oz. vegan puff pastry
- 20 tsp. vegan chocolate spread
- ½ C. unsweetened soy milk
- 10-12 tsp. icing sugar

1. Preheat your oven to 375 °F. Line 2 large baking sheets with baking paper.
2. Separate the puff pastry from the packaged baking paper and place onto a smooth surface.
3. Lightly dust both sides of the pastry with flour.
4. Cut the puff pastry into 20 narrow triangles.
5. Spread chocolate spread on the broader side of each pastry triangle.
6. Brush the spike of each triangle with a little soy milk.
7. Roll each pastry triangle from the broad side to the spike and then pinch the sides together.
8. Brush the top of each croissant with a little soy milk.
9. Arrange the croissants onto the prepared baking sheet in a single layer.
10. Bake for approximately 15-18 minutes or until the croissants become golden brown.
11. Remove the baking sheet from the oven and place onto a cooling rack to cool.

12. Dust with icing sugar and serve.

Per Serving:
Calories: 177| Fat: 11.6g| Carbs: 16.2g| Fiber: 0.6g| Protein: 2.4g

## MUSHROOM & BROCCOLI QUICHE
**Prep Time: 20 mins.| Cook Time: 1 hr.| Serves: 4**

- Non-stick cooking spray
- 1 C. water
- Pinch of salt
- 1/3 C. bulgur wheat
- ¾ tbsp. light sesame oil
- 1½ C. fresh cremini mushrooms, sliced
- 2 C. fresh broccoli, chopped
- 1 yellow onion, chopped
- 16 oz. firm tofu, pressed and cubed
- ¾ tbsp. white miso
- 1¼ tbsp. tahini
- 1 tbsp. low-sodium soy sauce

1. Preheat your oven to 350 °F. Lightly grease a pie dish with cooking spray.
2. In a pan, add the water over medium heat and salt bring to a boil.
3. Stir in the bulgur and again bring to a rolling boil.
4. Adjust the heat to low and simmer, covered for about 12-15 minutes or until all the liquid is absorbed.
5. Remove from heat and set the pan aside to cool slightly.
6. Now, place the cooked bulgur into the pie dish evenly and with your fingers, press into the bottom.
7. Bake for approximately 12 minutes.
8. Remove from the oven and set aside to cool slightly.
9. Meanwhile, in a skillet, heat oil over medium heat.
10. Add the mushrooms, broccoli and onion and cook for about 10 minutes, stirring occasionally.
11. Remove from the heat and transfer into a large-sized bowl to cool slightly.
12. Meanwhile, in a food processor, add the remaining ingredients and pulse until smooth.
13. Transfer the tofu mixture into the bowl with veggie mixture and mix until well combined.
14. Place the veggie mixture over the baked crust evenly.
15. Bake for approximately 30 minutes or until top becomes golden brown.
16. Remove from the oven and set the pie dish aside for at least 10 minutes.
17. Cut into 4 equal-sized slices and serve.

Per Serving:
Calories: 211| Fat: 10.4g| Carbs: 19.6g| Fiber: 5.7g| Protein: 14.4g

## SPINACH & MUSHROOM QUICHE
**Prep Time: 15 mins.| Cook Time: 56 mins.| Serves: 6**

- Non-stick cooking spray
- 2 tbsp. olive oil
- 1 small onion, chopped
- 8 oz. cremini mushroom, sliced
- 3 garlic cloves, minced
- 3 C. fresh spinach
- Salt and ground black pepper, as required
- 1 (14-oz.) block extra-firm tofu, pressed and drained
- 1 (9-inch) vegan frozen pie shell
- 2 tbsp. all-purpose flour
- ½ tsp. ground turmeric
- ¾ tsp. granulated garlic
- ½ tsp. granulated onion
- 1-2 tbsp. unsweetened almond milk
- 1/3 C. cherry tomatoes, cut in half

1. Preheat your oven to 375 °F. Lightly grease a pie dish with cooking spray.
2. Heat oil in a large-sized skillet over medium heat and sauté the onion for about 3-5 minutes.
3. Add garlic and sauté for about 30-60 seconds.
4. Add in mushrooms and sauté for about 5-7 minutes.
5. Add spinach and cook for about 2-3 minutes.
6. Stir in salt and black pepper and remove from heat.
7. Set aside to cool slightly.
8. In a food processor, add the tofu, almond milk, flour, spices, salt and black pepper and pulse until smooth.
9. Transfer the tofu mixtue into a bowl and fold in the mushrooms mixture.
10. Arrange the pie crust into the prepared pie dish.
11. Place the tofu mixture in the pie crust evenly.

12. Arrange the cherry tomatoes on top and gently press down.
13. Bake for approximately 30-40 minutes or until the quiche is golden.
14. Remove from oven and set aside to cool for 10 minutes before serving.

Per Serving:
Calories: 220| Fat: 13.3g| Carbs: 18.3g| Fiber: 1.5g| Protein: 9.9g

## POTATO SALAD

**Prep Time: 15 mins.| Cook Time: 15 mins.| Serves: 6**

**For Salad**
- 2 lb. fresh potatoes, cut into ¼-inch thick slices
- 2 tbsp. salt
- 2 large garlic cloves
- ¼ C. fresh flat-leaf parsley, roughly chopped
- 2 tbsp. fresh tarragon, roughly chopped
- 2 tbsp. fresh chives, minced

**For Vinaigrette**
- 1 tbsp. Dijon mustard
- ¼ C. champagne vinegar
- 1/3 C. olive oil
- ¼ tsp. ground black pepper

1. Place the potato slices and salt in a large-sized saucepan of water and bring to a boil.
2. Add garlic, reduce heat and cook for about 5-10 minutes.
3. Drain the potatoes and set aside to cool slightly.
4. For vinaigrette: in a bowl, add all ingredients and whisk until well blended
5. Drizzle the vinaigrette over the warm potatoes and set aside at room temperature for about 10-15 minutes.
6. Top with fresh herbs and serve.

Per Serving:
Calories: 209| Fat: 11.5g| Carbs: 24.9g| Fiber: 3.9g| Protein: 3g

## NICOISE SALAD

**Prep Time: 20 mins.| Cook Time: 10 mins.| Serves: 6**

**For Dressing**
- 2 tsp. wholegrain mustard
- 2 tbsp. fresh lemon juice
- 2 tbsp. extra-virgin olive oil
- 1 tsp. white sugar
- 1 small garlic clove, finely grated
- Salt and ground black pepper, as required

**For Salad**
- 2 tbsp. olive oil, divided
- 4 cooked medium potatoes, cut into thick slices
- 7 oz. green beans, trimmed and sliced
- 1 garlic clove, sliced thinly
- 2 ripe tomatoes, chopped
- 20 cherry tomatoes, sliced
- 1 large cucumber, sliced
- 1 small red onion, finely chopped
- 20 small Romaine lettuce leaves
- 2 C. fresh arugula

1. For dressing: in a bowl, add all ingredients and whisk until well blended. Set aside.
2. For salad: in a non-stick skillet, heat 1 tbsp. of oil over medium heat and cook the potato slices for about 3-5 minutes or until browned completely.
3. Transfer the potato slices into a serving bowl.
4. In the same skillet, heat remaining oil over medium-high heat and cook the green beans and garlic for about 5 minutes, stirring frequently.
5. Transfer the green beans into the bowl with potatoes.
6. Add remaining salt ingredients and mix well.
7. Drizzle with dressing and serve.

Per Serving:
Calories: 230| Fat: 9.8g| Carbs: 31.7g| Fiber: 6g| Protein: 4.3g

## LENTIL SALAD

**Prep Time: 15 mins.| Cook Time: 7 mins.| Serves: 2**

- ½ tbsp. plus 1 tsp. olive oil
- 3 tbsp. red wine vinegar
- 1 tbsp. Dijon mustard
- 1 ½ tsp. Herbs de Provence
- Salt and ground black pepper, as required
- 1 large carrot, chopped
- ½ medium onion, chopped
- 1 clove garlic, minced
- 1 C. cooked lentils
- 1 tbsp. fresh parsley, chopped

1. In a small-sized bowl, whisk together ½ tbsp. olive oil, vinegar, mustard, Herbs de Provence, salt and black pepper and whisk until well combined. Set aside.
2. In a large-sized skillet, heat 1 tsp. oil over medium heat and cook the carrots, onion, and garlic for about 5 minutes, stirring occasionally.
3. Add in the cooked lentils and cook for about 2 minutes.

4. Remove from the heat and stir in the dressing.
5. Set aside to cool slightly before serving.
6. Serve with the garnishing of parsley.

Per Serving:
Calories: 181| Fat: 4.3g| Carbs: 26.7g| Fiber: 9.7g| Protein: 10g

## FRENCH ONION SOUP
**Prep Time: 20 mins.| Cook Time: 1 hr. 25 mins.| Serves: 6**

**For Soup**
- ¼ C. olive oil
- 4 medium yellow onions, sliced
- ¾ tsp. granulated white sugar
- 4 garlic cloves, minced
- 1½ tsp. dried thyme
- ¾ C. red wine
- 3 tbsp. all-purpose flour
- 8 C. low-sodium vegetable broth
- 2 bay leaves
- Salt and ground black pepper, as required
- 6 baguette slices, toasted

**For Cashew Cheese**
- ¼ C. raw cashews, soaked in water for 2 hours and drained
- 1¼ C. hot unsweetened almond milk
- 2 tbsp. tapioca flour
- 1 tbsp. nutritional yeast
- 2 tsp. fresh lemon juice
- ½ tsp. garlic powder
- ¾ tsp. salt

1. For soup: in a large-sized saucepan, heat the oil over medium-low heat and cook the onions and sugar for about 40-50 minutes or until the onions are caramelized, stirring occasionally.
2. Add in the garlic and thyme and sauté for about 30-60 seconds.
3. Add the red wine and stir to combine.
4. Adjust the heat to medium-high and bring to a boil.
5. Adjust the heat to medium-low and simmer for about 10-15 minutes, stirring occasionally.
6. Adjust the heat to low and stir in the flour.
7. Cook for about 1 minute, stirring continuously.
8. Add the broth, bay leaves, salt, and black pepper and stir t combine.
9. Adjust the heat to medium and simmer for about 10-15 minutes.
10. Meanwhile, preheat the broiler of your oven.
11. Meanwhile, for cashew cheese: place all ingredients in a high-power blender and pulse on high until smooth.
12. Transfer the mixture into a small-sized saucepan over medium heat and cook for about 3-5 minutes, stirring occasionally.
13. Remove the pan of cheese from the heat.
14. Remove the soup pan from heat and discard the bay leaves.
15. Carefully divide the soup into ovenproof bowls, filling halfway.
16. Arrange 1 bread slice into each bowl and top with more soup.
17. Top each bowl with cashew cheese and broil for about 2-3 minutes.
18. Serve hot.

Per Serving:
Calories: 285| Fat: 15g| Carbs: 25.3g| Fiber: 2.8g| Protein: 7.7g

## POTATO SOUP
**Prep Time: 15 mins.| Cook Time: 25 mins.| Serves: 6**

- 4 tbsp. olive oil, divided
- 2 lb. carrots, peeled and sliced thinly
- ½ large sweet onion, sliced thinly
- 1 fresh thyme sprig
- ¼ tsp. white sugar
- Salt, as required
- 10 oz. potatoes, peeled and cut into small cubes
- 4 C. water
- 2 tbsp. coconut cream
- ½ bread roll, cut into small cubes
- 2 tbsp. fresh chervil

1. In a soup pan heat 2 tbsp. of oil over medium heat and sauté the carrots, onion, thyme, sugar and salt for about 5 minutes.
2. Add the potatoes and water and cook for about 15 minutes.
3. Meanwhile, in a non-stick skillet, heat remaining oil over medium-high heat and cook the bread

cubes for about 2-4 minutes or until golden and crisp.
4. Place the bread cubes onto a paper towel-lined plate to drain.
5. Remove the soup pan from heat and discard the thyme sprig.
6. With a stick blender, blend the soup until smooth.
7. Return the pan over medium heat and stir in the coconut cream.
8. Cook for about 3-5 minutes.
9. Serve hot with the topping of bread cubes and chervil.

Per Serving:
Calories: 256| Fat: 10.3g| Carbs: 38.1g| Fiber: 5.9g| Protein: 4.6g

## PASTA E FAGIOLI
**Prep Time: 15 mins.| Cook Time: 45 mins.| Serves: 6**

- 2 tbsp. extra-virgin olive oil
- 1 onion, chopped
- 2 celery stalks, chopped
- Salt and ground black pepper, as required
- 3 C. butternut squash, peeled and cubed
- 4 garlic cloves, minced
- 1 tsp. dried oregano
- 30 oz. cannellini beans, rinsed
- 56 oz. crushed tomatoes
- 3½-4 C. vegetable broth
- 3 C. Swiss chard, chopped
- ½ lb. cooked elbow pasta
- ¼ C. fresh parsley, minced

1. In a Dutch oven, heat the olive oil over medium-high heat and sauté the onions, celery, salt and black pepper for about 5-7 minutes.
2. Stir in the butternut squash, garlic, and oregano and cook for about 6-8 minutes, stirring occasionally.
3. Add in the beans, tomatoes and broth and bring to a boil.
4. Add the Swiss chard and mix well.
5. Adjust the heat to low and simmer for about 15-20 minutes.
6. Add in the cooked pasta and cook for about 3-5 minutes.
7. Stir in the parsley, salt and black pepper and remove from the heat.
8. Serve hot with the garnishing of parsley.

Per Serving:
Calories: 385| Fat: 6.6g| Carbs: 64.9g| Fiber: 18.5g| Protein: 20.1g

## BAKED VEGGIE STEW
**Prep Time: 20 mins.| Cook Time: 1 hr. 5 mins.| Serves: 5**

- 2 tbsp. olive oil
- 1 medium yellow onion, rough chopped
- 2 tbsp. garlic, minced
- 1 tbsp. all-purpose flour
- 2 tbsp. tomato paste
- ¼ C. white wine
- 1 (14½-oz.) can petite diced tomatoes
- ½ C. vegetable broth
- ½ C. water
- ¼ tsp. baking soda
- 1½ tsp. dried thyme, crushed
- ½ tsp. dried oregano
- 1 tsp. garlic powder
- 1 tsp. onion powder
- 2 tbsp. dried onions, minced
- ½ tsp. mustard powder
- 2 bay leaves
- Pinch of saffron threads
- Salt and ground black pepper, as required
- 2 lb. Russet potatoes, scrubbed and cut into wedges
- 10 oz. fresh mushrooms, sliced
- 3 carrots, peeled and cut into chunks
- 2 celery ribs, cut into chunks
- 1 (15½-oz.) can cannellini beans, drained and rinsed
- 3 tbsp. fresh parsley, chopped

1. Preheat your oven to 400 °F.
2. In a large-sized Dutch oven, heat the oil over medium-high heat and sauté the onion for about 4 minutes.
3. Add the garlic, tomato paste and flour and sauté for about 1 minute.
4. Add in the white wine and cook for about 2-3 minutes, stirring continuously.

5. Add the tomatoes, broth, baking soda, dried herbs, spices, bay leaves and saffron and simmer for about 2 minutes, stirring continuously.
6. Remove from the heat and stir in the potatoes, mushrooms, carrots and celery.
7. With a tight-fitting lid, cover the pan and immediately transfer into the oven.
8. Bake for approximately 40 minutes.
9. Remove the pan from oven and gently stir in the cannellini beans.
10. Again, cover the pan and bake for approximately 5 minutes.
11. Remove the pan from oven and place over medium heat.
12. Remove the lid and cook for about 10 minutes.
13. Discard the bay leaves and serve hot with the garnishing of parsley.
14. Serve hot.

Per Serving:
Calories: 331| Fat: 6.3g| Carbs: 59.7g| Fiber: 14.2g| Protein: 12.6g

## TEMPEH & BEANS STEW
**Prep Time: 15 mins.| Cook Time: 30 mins.| Serves: 8**

- 1 tbsp. extra-virgin olive oil
- 8 oz. package tempeh, cubed into ½-inch pieces
- 2 medium carrots, peeled and sliced
- 2 celery stalks, chopped
- 1 medium onion, chopped
- 5 garlic cloves, finely minced
- Salt and ground black pepper, as required
- 15 fresh mushrooms, sliced
- ½ C. red wine
- 3 C. canned navy beans, drained
- 2 tomatoes, chopped
- 1-1½ C. water
- 2 tbsp. fresh parsley, chopped
- 1 tbsp. fresh sage, chopped
- 1 tbsp. fresh thyme, chopped
- 2 bay leaves

1. In a large-sized saucepan, heat oil over medium heat and sauté the tempeh cubes for about 4-5 minutes, stirring frequently.
2. Add the carrots, celery, onion, garlic, salt and black pepper and sauté for about 5 minutes.
3. Add the mushrooms and wine and cook for about 4-5 minutes.
4. Add the beans, tomatoes, water, fresh herbs and bay leaves and bring to a boil.
5. Adjust the heat to low and simmer, covered for about 5-10 minutes.
6. Serve hot.

Per Serving:
Calories: 208| Fat: 5.5g| Carbs: 27.1g| Fiber: 8.9g| Protein: 12.7g

## GLAZED CARROTS
**Prep Time: 15 mins.| Cook Time: 20 mins.| Serves: 3**

- 1 lb. carrots, peeled and cut into ¼-inch slices cross-wise
- 1 C. water
- 2 tbsp. coconut oil
- 2 tsp. white sugar
- Salt, as required

1. In a skillet, melt coconut oil over medium heat and stir in carrots and sugar.
2. Add in water and bring to a boil.
3. Cover the skillet and simmer for about 10 minutes.
4. Uncover and cook for about 5 minutes.
5. Stir in salt and serve hot.

Per Serving:
Calories: 160| Fat: 9.1g| Carbs: 17.5g| Fiber: 3.7g| Protein: 1.2g

## GARLIKY POTATOES
**Prep Time: 10 mins.| Cook Time: 1 hr.| Serves: 6**

- 4 large Russet potatoes, peeled and cut into ¼-inch thick slices
- 6 tbsp. olive oil, divided
- 2 yellow onions, cut into ¼-inch slices
- 4 garlic cloves, minced
- Salt and ground black pepper, as required
- 2 tbsp. fresh parsley, minced

1. Preheat your oven to 425 °F.
2. In a large-sized saucepan of water, add the potatoes over high heat and bring to a boil.
3. Cook for about 5-6 minutes.

4. Drain the potatoes well and set aside.
5. In a large-sized, ovenproof skillet, heat 4 tbsp. of oil over medium heat and cook the onions for about 10-12 minutes, stirring occasionally.
6. Add the garlic and sauté for about 1 minute.
7. Remove from the heat and transfer the onions and garlic into a bowl. Set aside.
8. In the same skillet, arrange half of the potatoes and sprinkle with salt and black pepper.
9. Spread the onions and garlic across the potatoes.
10. Top with remaining potatoes and sprinkle with salt and black pepper.
11. Drizzle with remaining olive oil evenly.
12. Bake for approximately 40 minutes.
13. Garnish with parsley and serve.

Per Serving:
Calories: 308 | Fat: 14.3g | Carbs: 42.8g | Fiber: 6.8g | Protein: 4.7g

## SCALLOPED POTATOES
**Prep Time: 15 mins. | Cook Time: 1 hr. 5 mins. | Serves: 4**

- Non-stick cooking spray
- 2½ tbsp. olive oil
- 4 garlic cloves, minced
- Salt and ground black pepper, as required
- 2½ tbsp. cornstarch
- 1½ C. unsweetened almond milk
- ½ C. vegetable broth
- 4-5 tbsp. nutritional yeast
- 1/8 tsp. ground nutmeg
- 2-3 medium Yukon gold potatoes, very thinly sliced
- 1/3 C. vegan cheese, divided

1. Preheat your oven to 350 °F. Arrange a rack in the center of oven.
2. Generously grease a casserole dish with cooking spray.
3. In a large-sized rimmed, 10-inch cast-iron skillet, heat oil over medium heat and sauté the garlic, salt, and black pepper for about 1 minute.
4. Stir in cornstarch and cook for about 1 minute, stirring continuously.
5. Add in the almond milk and stir to combine well.
6. Add the broth and stir to combine well.
7. Reduce heat to low and simmer for about 4-5 minutes, stirring frequently.
8. Remove from the heat and set aside to cool slightly.
9. In a high-power blender, add mushroom sauce, nutritional yeast and nutmeg and pulse on high until creamy and smooth.
10. In the bottom of the prepared casserole dish, arrange half of the potato slices and sprinkle with salt, black pepper and 2 tbsp. of vegan cheese.
11. Repeat the layers.
12. Place the mushroom sauce over the potatoes evenly and sprinkle with remaining vegan cheese.
13. With a piece of foil, cover the casserole dish and bake for approximately 20 minutes.
14. Remove the foil and bake for approximately 40-45 minutes.
15. Remove from oven and set aside to cool for about 10 minutes before serving.

Per Serving:
Calories: 251 | Fat: 12.6g | Carbs: 29.1g | Fiber: 6.3g | Protein: 8.3g

## GREEN BEANS WITH SHALLOT
**Prep Time: 15 mins. | Cook Time: 28 mins. | Serves: 4**

- 2 tbsp. olive oil
- 2 large shallots, thinly sliced
- ½ C. water
- ¾ lb. French string beans, trimmed
- ½ tsp. salt
- ¼ tsp. ground black pepper
- Pinch of white sugar

1. Heat the oil in a large-sized skillet over medium-low heat and cook the shallots for about 8 minutes, stirring frequently.
2. Add the beans, salt, black pepper and water and bring to a boil.
3. Adjust the heat to low, and cook, covered for about 8 minutes.
4. Remove the lid of skillet and Adjust the heat to high.
5. Cook for about 6 minutes, stirring frequently.
6. Stir in the sugar and remove from heat.
7. Serve hot.

Per Serving:
Calories: 83| Fat: 7g| Carbs: 4.9g| Fiber: 1.9g| Protein: 1g

### MUSHROOM BOURGUIGNON
**Prep Time: 15 mins.| Cook Time: 45 mins.| Serves: 4**

- 1 tbsp. olive oil
- 10 oz. fresh mushrooms, sliced
- 1 small onion, chopped
- 4 garlic cloves, minced
- ¼ C. red wine
- 1 tbsp. tomato paste
- 1 tsp. fresh thyme, chopped
- 1 tsp. onion powder
- ¼ tsp. red pepper flakes
- Salt, as required
- 2 C. vegetable broth
- 1 C. carrots, chopped
- 1 C. celery, chopped
- 1 tbsp. vegan butter
- 1 tbsp. all-purpose flour
- 2 tbsp. water
- ¼ C. parsley, chopped

1. In a deep non-stick skillet, heat the oil over medium heat and sauté the mushrooms, onion, and garlic for about 4-5 minutes.
2. Add the red wine and cook for about 1-2 minutes, stirring frequently.
3. Add in the tomato paste, thyme, onion powder, red pepper flakes and salt and cook for about 1 minute, stirring frequently.
4. Add in the broth, carrots and celery and bring to a boil.
5. Adjust the heat to medium-low and cook, covered for about 30 minutes.
6. Meanwhile, for flour slurry: in a small-sized bowl, dissolve the flour into water.
7. In the pan, add the flour slurry, stirring continuously.
8. Cook for about 1-2 minutes, stirring continuously.
9. Stir in the parsley and serve hot.

Per Serving:
Calories: 143| Fat: 7.3g| Carbs: 12.5g| Fiber: 2.7g| Protein: 6g

### VEGGIE COQ AU VIN
**Prep Time: 15 mins.| Cook Time: 20 mins.| Serves: 4**

- 1 tbsp. olive oil
- 2 medium onions, chopped
- 3 garlic cloves, sliced
- 3 large potatoes, cut into chunky wedges
- 2 medium carrots, peeled and sliced
- 1 C. fresh mushrooms, sliced
- 2 tbsp. all-purpose flour
- 1 tbsp. tomato paste
- 9 fluid oz. red wine
- ¾ C. vegetable broth
- 2-3 tbsp. fresh thyme, chopped

1. In a deep saucepan, heat the olive oil over medium heat and sauté the onions for about 5 minutes/
2. Add the garlic and sauté for about 1 minute.
3. Add in the potatoes, carrots and mushrooms and stir fry for about 3-4 minutes.
4. Add the flour and tomato paste and stir fry for about 1-2 minutes.
5. Add in the red wine and simmer for about 3 minutes, stirring frequently.
6. Add the broth and the thyme and simmer for about 5 minutes, stirring occasionally.
7. Serve hot with the garnishing of thyme.

Per Serving:
Calories: 340| Fat: 4.2g| Carbs: 58.6g| Fiber: 9.1g| Protein: 7.7g

### RATATOUILLE
**Prep Time: 20 mins.| Cook Time: 45 mins.| Serves: 4**

- 6 oz. tomato paste
- 3 tbsp. olive oil, divided
- ½ onion, chopped
- 3 tbsp. garlic, minced
- Salt and ground black pepper, as required
- ¾ C. water
- 1 zucchini, sliced into thin circles
- 1 yellow squash, sliced into circles thinly
- 1 eggplant, sliced into circles thinly
- 1 red bell pepper, seeded and sliced into circles thinly
- 1 yellow bell pepper, seeded and sliced into circles thinly

130

- ✓ 1 tbsp. fresh thyme leaves, minced
- ✓ 1 tbsp. fresh lemon juice

4. Preheat your oven to 375 °F.
5. In a bowl, add the tomato paste, 1 tbsp. of oil, onion, garlic, salt and black pepper and blend nicely.
6. In the bottom of a 10x10-inch baking dish, spread the tomato paste mixture evenly.
7. Arrange alternating vegetable slices, starting at the outer edge of the baking dish and working concentrically towards the center.
8. Drizzle the vegetables with the remaining oil and sprinkle with salt and black pepper, followed by the thyme.
9. Arrange a piece of parchment paper over the vegetables.
10. Bake for approximately 45 minutes.
11. Serve hot.

Per Serving:
Calories: 206| Fat: 11.4g| Carbs: 54g| Fiber: 26.4g| Protein: 5.4g

## CHICKPEA RATATOUILLE

**Prep Time: 15 mins.| Cook Time: 1 hr. 25 mins.| Serves: 6**

- ✓ 2 tbsp. olive oil, divided
- ✓ 2 large bell peppers, seeded and chopped
- ✓ 1 medium onion, chopped
- ✓ 4 garlic cloves, minced
- ✓ 1¼ lb. grape tomatoes, cut in half
- ✓ 2 medium zucchinis, chopped
- ✓ 1 eggplant, chopped
- ✓ 2 tbsp. fresh basil leaves, chopped
- ✓ 2 tsp. Herbs de Provence
- ✓ Pinch of red pepper flakes
- ✓ Salt and ground black pepper, as required
- ✓ 3 C. cooked chickpeas

1. In a heavy-bottomed saucepan, heat the olive oil over medium heat and sauté the bell peppers, onions and garlic for 3-4 minutes.
2. Add tomatoes and cook for about 5 minutes, stirring frequently.
3. Add in the zucchinis, eggplant, basil, Herbs de Provence, red pepper flakes, salt and black pepper and stir to combine.
4. Adjust the heat to a low and simmer uncovered for about 15 minutes.
5. Add in the chickpeas and simmer, covered for about 45-60 minutes.
6. Serve hot.

Per Serving:
Calories: 253| Fat: 6.6g| Carbs: 42.9g| Fiber: 10.8g| Protein: 9.1g

## ONION GALETTE

**Prep Time: 20 mins.| Cook Time: 1 hr. 10 mins.| Serves: 4**

**For Dough**
- ✓ ½ C. all-purpose flour plus more for dusting
- ✓ ½ C. whole-wheat flour
- ✓ ¼ tsp. salt
- ✓ 6 tbsp. chilled vegan butter, cut into pieces
- ✓ 5 tbsp. ice cold water

**For Filling**
- ✓ 2 tbsp. vegan butter
- ✓ 3 medium onions, thinly sliced
- ✓ 1 tsp. ground thyme
- ✓ Salt and ground black pepper, as required
- ✓ Unsweetened almond milk, for brushing

1. For dough: in a bowl, blend the flour and salt.
2. Cut the vegan butter into the flour mixture with a pastry cutter until a coarse meal is formed.
3. Slowly add the water and stir until just blended.
4. With your hands, gently knead until dough comes together.
5. With your hands, flatten the dough into a disk.
6. With plastic wrap, cover the dough disk and refrigerate for about 1 hour.
7. For filling: in a skillet, melt the vegan butter over medium-high heat and cook the onions and thyme for about 10 minutes, stirring occasionally.
8. Adjust the heat to low and cook for about 10-15 minutes, stirring occasionally.
9. Stir in the salt and black pepper and remove from the heat. Set aside to cool.
10. Preheat your oven to 375 °F.
11. Arrange a pizza stone on the bottom rack of the oven.
12. Line a baking sheet with parchment paper.
13. Unwrap the dough and place onto a lightly floured surface.

14. With a rolling pin, roll the dough into a 12-inch circle.
15. Arrange the dough circle onto the prepared baking sheet.
16. Place the onions on the dough circle, leaving about a 1½-inch border.
17. Fold the edge of dough over the filling and then brush the edges with almond milk.
18. Arrange the baking sheet over pizza stone and bake for approximately 40 minutes.
19. Now arrange the baking sheet onto the top rack of oven and bake for approximately 5 minutes.
20. Remove the galette from oven and place onto a rack to cool slightly.
21. Serve warm.

Per Serving:
Calories: 356| Fat: 22.8g| Carbs: 4.3g| Fiber: 3.5g| Protein: 15g

## MUSHROOM GALETTE
**Prep Time: 20 mins.| Cook Time: 50 mins.| Serves: 6**

### For Crust
- 2 C. all-purpose flour plus more for dusting
- ½ tsp. baking powder
- ½ tsp. salt
- 8 tbsp. chilled vegan butter, cut into pieces
- ½ C. water, plus more if needed

### For Filling
- 2 tbsp. vegan butter
- 1½ lb. mixed fresh mushrooms, sliced
- ½ of onion, sliced
- 4 large garlic cloves, minced
- 2 tsp. fresh thyme, chopped
- 1 tsp. Italian seasoning
- Salt and ground black pepper, as required
- ¼ C. vegetable broth
- ¼ C. vegan cheese
- Unsweetened almond milk, for brushing

1. For crust: sift together the flour, baking powder, and salt in a large-sized bowl.
2. Cut the vegan butter into the flour with a pastry cutter until a coarse meal is formed.
3. Slowly add the water and stir until just blended.
4. With your hands, gently knead until dough comes together.
5. With your hands, flatten the dough into a disk.
6. With plastic wrap, cover the dough disk and refrigerate for at least 30 minutes.
7. Meanwhile, for filling: in a skillet, melt 1 tbsp. of vegan butter over medium heat and sauté the mushrooms for about 5 minutes.
8. Add in the remaining butter, onion, garlic, thyme, Italian seasoning, salt and black pepper and sauté for about 4-6 minutes.
9. Add in the broth and the cheese and cook for about 2-3 minutes, stirring frequently.
10. Remove from the heat and set aside.
11. Preheat your oven to 400 °F. Line a baking sheet with parchment paper.
12. Unwrap the dough and place onto a lightly floured surface.
13. With a rolling pin, roll the dough into a ¼-in thick circle.
14. Arrange the dough circle onto the prepared baking sheet.
15. Place the mushroom mixture on the dough circle, leaving about a 1-inch border.
16. Fold the edge of dough over the filling and then brush the edges with almond milk.
17. Bake for approximately 25 minutes or until golden brown.
18. Remove the galette from oven and place onto a rack to cool slightly.
19. Serve warm.

Per Serving:
Calories: 366| Fat: 20.2g| Carbs: 38.3g| Fiber: 3g| Protein: 8.7g

## SPINACH GRATIN
**Prep Time: 20 mins.| Cook Time: 53 mins.| Serves: 8**

### For Sauce
- 4-5 C. small cauliflower florets
- ½ C. cashews, soaked in hot water for 15-30 minutes and drained
- 2 tsp. olive oil
- 1 onion, chopped
- 2 garlic cloves, chopped
- 1 C. vegetable broth
- 1 tbsp. nutritional yeast

- ✓ Pinch of ground nutmeg
- ✓ Salt and ground black pepper, as required

**For Topping**
- ✓ ¼ C. sunflower seeds
- ✓ ¼ C. cashews
- ✓ 2 tbsp. sesame seeds
- ✓ 1 tbsp. nutritional yeast
- ✓ Salt and ground black pepper, as required
- ✓ ¼ C. vegan breadcrumbs

**For Spinach**
- ✓ 1 tbsp. olive oil
- ✓ 1 onion, finely chopped
- ✓ 1 garlic clove, finely chopped
- ✓ 1 lb. baby spinach, roughly chopped
- ✓ Pinch of ground nutmeg
- ✓ ¼ tsp. salt

1. Preheat your oven to 430 °F.
2. For sauce: in a pot of salted boiling water, cook the cauliflower for about 10 minutes.
3. Meanwhile, heat olive oil in a frying pan over medium-low hear and sauté onion and garlic for about 4-5 minutes.
4. Drain the cauliflower and add transfer into a high-power blender.
5. Add the cooked onion mixture and remaining ingredients and pulse until smooth.
6. Transfer the sauce into a bowl and set aside.
7. For topping: in a food processor, add all ingredients except for breadcrumbs and pulse until a crumbly mixture is formed.
8. Add the breadcrumbs and pulse until just combined.
9. For spinach: heat olive oil in a large-sized, deep skillet over medium heat and cook the onion and garlic for about 5-10 minutes, stirring frequently.
10. Add the spinach and cook for about 2-3 minutes, stirring frequently.
11. Drain the liquid from the skillet completely and transfer the spinach into a bowl with nutmeg and salt.
12. Place the spinach mixture into a casserole dish and with the back of a spoon, smooth the top surface.
13. Spread the crumb mixture on top evenly.
14. Bake for approximately 25-30 minutes until the topping is golden brown.
15. Serve hot.

Per Serving:
Calories: 186| Fat: 11.5g| Carbs: 16.4g| Fiber: 4.7g| Protein: 8g

## POTATO GRATIN
**Prep Time: 15 mins.| Cook Time: 55 mins.| Serves: 6**

- ✓ 2 tbsp. olive oil
- ✓ 1 medium red onion, thinly sliced
- ✓ 4 garlic cloves, finely chopped
- ✓ 1½ C. unsweetened soy milk
- ✓ 1 C. coconut cream
- ✓ 1 tsp. apple cider vinegar
- ✓ 4 tbsp. nutritional yeast
- ✓ 1 fresh rosemary sprig, finely chopped
- ✓ ¼ tsp. ground nutmeg
- ✓ Salt and ground black pepper, as required
- ✓ 2¼ lb. yellow flesh potatoes, peeled and cut into ¼-inch thick slices

1. Preheat your oven to 390 °F.
2. In a large-sized saucepan, heat the oil over medium-high heat and sauté the onion for about 3-5 minutes.
3. Add in the garlic and sauté for about 2 minutes.
4. Add in the remaining ingredients except for potatoes and bring to a gentle simmer.
5. Cook for about 3 minutes, stirring occasionally.
6. Remove from the heat and set aside.
7. Add the potato slices into the saucepan and gently blend with sauce.
8. Transfer the potato slices into a 9½ x9½-inch baking dish and spread in an even layer.
9. Cover the baking dish with a piece of baking paper and gently press down onto the potatoes.
10. Bake for approximately 20 minutes.
11. Remove the baking paper and bake for approximately 20 minutes.
12. Serve hot.

Per Serving:
Calories: 317| Fat: 15.9g| Carbs: 38.3g| Fiber: 7.5g| Protein: 9.2g

## BEANS & VEGGIE CASSEROLE
**Prep Time: 20 mins.| Cook Time: 50 mins.| Serves: 6**

**For Casserole**
- ✓ 8 oz. cremini mushrooms, halved
- ✓ 2 medium carrots, peeled and cut into 1-inch chunks
- ✓ 1 small fennel bulb, cored and sliced
- ✓ 3 tbsp. olive oil, divided
- ✓ Salt and ground black pepper, as required
- ✓ 1 medium yellow onion, diced
- ✓ 5 medium garlic cloves, minced
- ✓ 1 tsp. Herbs de Provence
- ✓ 1 tsp. smoked paprika

- ✓ 4 C. cooked white beans
- ✓ 1 (15-oz.) can tomato sauce
- ✓ ¾ C. vegetable broth

**For Topping**
- ✓ ¾ C. vegan panko breadcrumbs
- ✓ 1 tbsp. nutritional yeast
- ✓ 2 tbsp. fresh parsley, minced
- ✓ 2 tbsp. olive oil
- ✓ Pinch of salt

1. Preheat your oven to 425 °F.
2. For casserole: arrange the mushrooms, carrots, and fennel onto a rimmed baking sheet and drizzle with 2 tbsp. of oil.
3. Sprinkle with salt and black pepper and toss to coat.
4. Roast for about 25 minutes, stirring once halfway through.
5. Meanwhile, in a large-sized high-sided skillet, heat remaining oil over medium-low heat and cook the onion, garlic, Herbs de Provence, paprika, and salt for about 5-7 minutes, stirring frequently.
6. Add the beans, tomato sauce, and broth and simmer for about 5 minutes.
7. Remove from the heat and set aside.
8. Remove the baking sheet of vegetables from oven and set aside.
9. Again, set the temperature of oven to 400 °F.
10. For topping: in a bowl, add the breadcrumbs, nutritional yeast and parsley, and mix well.
11. Add the oil and salt and with your fingers, rub the mixture to combine well.
12. In a large-sized bowl, add roasted vegetables and beans mixture and mix well.
13. Place the mixture into a casserole dish and spread in an even layer and sprinkle with breadcrumb mixture.
14. Bake for approximately 20-25 minutes.
15. Serve hot.

Per Serving:
Calories: 372| Fat: 13.3g| Carbs: 52.2g| Fiber: 71.7g| Protein: 15.2g

## BERRIES COMPOTE
**Prep Time: 10 mins.| Cook Time: 8 mins.| Serves: 3**

- ✓ 1½ C. fresh mixed berries (strawberries, raspberries, blueberries and blackberries)
- ✓ 1 tbsp. fresh lemon juice
- ✓ 1 tbsp. maple syrup

1. In a medium-sized-sized saucepan, add the berries and lemon juice and heat over medium-high heat and ring to a boil, stirring frequently.
2. Adjust the heat to low and cook for about 2-3 minutes, pressing the berries occasionally.
3. Add in the maple syrup and stir to combine.
4. Remove from the heat and serve warm.

Per Serving:
Calories: 59| Fat: 0.3g| Carbs: 13.1g| Fiber: 2.5g| Protein: 0.5g

## RASPBERRY MOUSSE
**Prep Time: 10 mins.| Serves: 6**

- ✓ 1½ C. fresh strawberries, hulled
- ✓ 1 2/3 C. chilled unsweetened coconut milk
- ✓ 2 tsp. powdered sugar
- ✓ 1 tsp. vanilla extract

1. In a food processor, add all the ingredients and pulse until smooth.
2. Transfer into serving bowls and serve.

Per Serving:
Calories: 170| Fat: 16g| Carbs: 7.4g| Fiber: 2.2g| Protein: 1.8g

## BANANA MOUSSE
**Prep Time: 15 mins.| Serves: 4**

- ✓ 2 bananas, peeled and sliced
- ✓ 1/3 C. coconut cream
- ✓ 1 tsp. unsweetened coconut, shredded
- ✓ ½ tsp. ground cinnamon

1. In a food processor, add all the ingredients except for cinnamon and pulse until smooth.
2. Transfer the mixture into serving bowls.
3. Refrigerate to chill before serving.
4. Sprinkle with cinnamon and serve.

Per Serving:

Calories: 157| Fat: 5.2g| Carbs: 29.9:g| Fiber: 2.7g| Protein: 1.6g

## CRÈME BRULEE
**Prep Time: 20 mins.| Cook Time: 6 mins.| Serves: 4**

- ✓ 1 (13½-oz.) can full-fat coconut milk
- ✓ ¼ C. raw cashews
- ✓ ½ C. granulated white sugar, divided
- ✓ 1 tbsp. arrowroot powder
- ✓ 1 tsp. nutritional yeast flakes
- ✓ 1 tsp. vanilla extract

1. In a saucepan, add the coconut milk, cashews, ¼ C. of sugar and arrowroot powder and stir to combine well.
2. Place the saucepan over medium heat and cook for about 6 minutes, stirring continuously.
3. Remove from heat and set aside to cool slightly.
4. In a high-power blender, add the milk mixture, nutritional yeast flakes, vanilla extract and turmeric and pulse until smooth and creamy.
5. Divide the mixture into 4 ramekins and refrigerate overnight.
6. Just before serving, sprinkle 1 tbsp. of sugar on top of each ramekin.
7. Holding a kitchen torch about 4-5-inch from the top, caramelize the sugar for about 2 minutes.
8. Set aside for 5 minutes before serving.

Per Serving:
Calories: 330| Fat: 21.7g| Carbs: 32.1g| Fiber: 0.4g| Protein: 3.2g

## CHOCOLATE POT DE CREME
**Prep Time: 15 mins.| Cook Time: 2 mins.| Serves: 8**

- ✓ 10 oz. vegan dark chocolate
- ✓ 15 oz. coconut cream
- ✓ ¼ C. maple syrup
- ✓ 1 tsp. vanilla extract
- ✓ ½ tsp. peppermint extract
- ✓ Pinch of salt

1. In a microwave-safe bowl, add chocolate and microwave on high for about 1½-2 minutes, stirring after every 20 seconds.
2. Remove from microwave and stir until smooth.
3. In a high-power blender, add the remaining ingredients and pulse until smooth.
4. While the motor is running, slowly add the melted chocolate and pulse until well blended.
5. Divide the chocolate mixture into 8 ramekins evenly and refrigerate for about 4 hours before serving.

Per Serving:
Calories: 339| Fat: 23.2g| Carbs: 30.7g| Fiber: 2.4g| Protein: 3.9g

## ALMOND FINANCIERS
**Prep Time: 15 mins.| Cook Time: 35 mins.| Serves: 6**

- ✓ 1½ C. almond meal
- ✓ 1/3 C. self-rising flour
- ✓ 3 tbsp. maple syrup
- ✓ ¾ C. unsweetened almond milk
- ✓ ¼ C. blackcurrant jam
- ✓ 1 tsp. vanilla extract
- ✓ 1 tsp. almond extract
- ✓ 2-3 tbsp. almond flakes

1. Preheat your oven to 350 °F. Line a muffin pan with paper liners.
2. In a bowl, add all ingredients except for almond flakes and mi until well combined.
3. Place about ½-inch thick layer mixture into each prepared muffin cup.
4. Top each cup with almond flakes.
5. Bake for approximately 30-35 minutes.
6. Remove the muffin tin from oven and place onto a wire rack to cool completely before serving.

Per Serving:
Calories: 232| Fat: 13.4g| Carbs: 24.1g| Fiber: 3.6g| Protein: 6.3g

## BLUEBERRY FINANCIERS
**Prep Time: 15 mins.| Cook Time: 30 mins.| Serves: 9**

- ✓ Non-stick cooking spray
- ✓ 3 tbsp. vegan egg replacer
- ✓ 6 tbsp. warm water
- ✓ ¼ C. vegan margarine

- ✓ ¼ C. brown sugar
- ✓ ½ C. almond flour
- ✓ ¼ C. whole-wheat pastry flour
- ✓ ¼ C. fresh blueberries

1. Preheat your oven to 320 °F. Grease a mini muffin tin with cooking spray.
2. In a bowl, blend the egg replacer and water until smooth.
3. Set aside for 5-10 minutes.
4. Meanwhile, in a saucepan, add the vegan margarine and sugar over medium-high heat and cook for about 4-5 minutes, stirring continuously.
5. Remove from the heat and transfer into a bowl.
6. In a large-sized bowl, blend the flours.
7. Add the sugar and water mixtures and gently stir to combine.
8. Place about ½-inch thick layer mixture into each prepared muffin cup.
9. Place 3-4 blueberries on top of each cup and gently press them down.
10. Bake for approximately 20-25 minutes.
11. Remove the muffin tin from oven and place onto a wire rack to cool completely before serving.

Per Serving:
Calories: 123| Fat: 8.4g| Carbs: 9.2g| Fiber: 1.2g| Protein: 2.8g

## APPLE TART
**Prep Time: 25 mins.| Cook Time: 1¼ hrs.| Serves: 10**

### For Pastry
- ✓ Non-stick cooking spray
- ✓ 1½ C. all-purpose flour
- ✓ ½ C. chilled vegan butter
- ✓ 3 tbsp. granulated white sugar
- ✓ 1-2 tbsp. cold water

### For Filling
- ✓ 3 tbsp. granulated white sugar
- ✓ 1 tsp. ground cinnamon
- ✓ 1 tbsp. vegan butter, melted
- ✓ Dash of lemon juice
- ✓ Pinch of salt
- ✓ 5-6 apples, cored and cut into 1/8-inch thick slices

1. Preheat your oven to 350 °F. Grease a 9-inch tart pan with cooking spray.
2. For pastry: add all ingredients except for water in a medium-sized-sized bowl and mix until just combined.
3. Add water and mix until well combined.
4. Place the pastry dough into an airtight container and refrigerate for at least 1 hour.
5. Place the pastry dough onto a floured surface and with a rolling pin, to roll into a ¼-inch thick circle.
6. Place the pastry into the prepared tart pan and press in the bottom and sides.
7. Then trim off the excess pastry.
8. With a fork, prick the bottom of the pastry in many places.
9. Bake for approximately 10-15 minutes or until the pastry becomes slightly golden.
10. Remove from the oven and set aside to cool.
11. For filling: add the sugar and cinnamon into a small-sized bowl and mix well.
12. Sprinkle 1 tbsp. of cinnamon sugar in the bottom of the prepared crust.
13. In the bowl of the remaining cinnamon sugar, add melted butter, lemon juice and salt and mix well.
14. Again, set the temperature of your oven to 350 °F.
15. Arrange the apple slices over the crust.
16. With a pastry brush, brush the top of apple slices with cinnamon mixture.
17. Bake for approximately 1 hour until the filling is bubbling.
18. Remove the tart pan from oven and place onto a cutting board to cool before serving.

Per Serving:
Calories: 244| Fat: 10.3g| Carbs: 37.1g| Fiber: 3.3g| Protein: 2.3g

## CHERRY CLAFOUTIS
**Prep Time: 15 mins.| Cook Time: 1 hr. 5 mins.| Serves: 10**

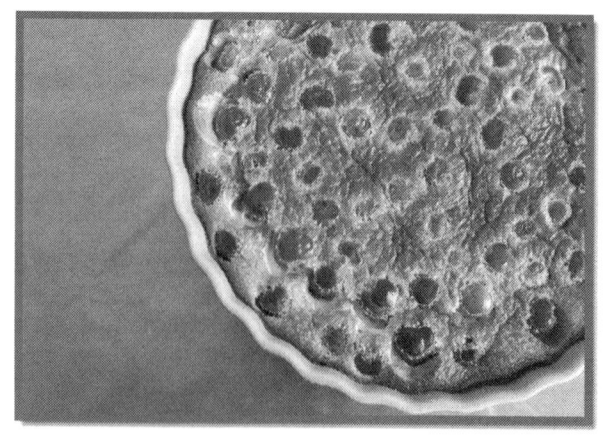

- ✓ Non-stick cooking spray
- ✓ 4 C. frozen cherries, pitted
- ✓ 16 oz. silken tofu
- ✓ ½ C. unsweetened almond milk
- ✓ ¾ C. all-purpose flour
- ✓ ¼ C. almond flour
- ✓ 2 tbsp. cornstarch
- ✓ 6 tbsp. white sugar
- ✓ 2 tbsp. amaretto
- ✓ Powdered sugar for dusting

1. Preheat your oven to 350 °F.
2. Grease a pie plate with cooking spray.
3. In the bottom of the prepared pie plate, place the cherries evenly.
4. Add the remaining ingredients except for powdered sugar in a high-power blender and pulse until smooth.
5. Place the tofu mixture over the cherries evenly.
6. Arrange the baking dish onto a large-sized baking sheet and bake for approximately 45-65 minutes or until the edges are golden and puffy.
7. Serve warm with the dusting of powdered sugar.

Per Serving:
Calories: 151| Fat: 3.2g| Carbs: 24.4g| Fiber: 1.7g| Protein: 5.3g

# CONVERSION TABLES

### Mass

| Imperial (oz.) | Metric (gram) |
|---|---|
| ¼ oz. | 7 grams |
| ½ oz. | 14 grams |
| 1 oz. | 28 grams |
| 2 oz. | 56 grams |
| 3 oz. | 85 grams |
| 4 oz. | 113 grams |
| 5 oz. | 141 grams |
| 6 oz. | 150 grams |
| 7 oz. | 198 grams |
| 8 oz. | 226 grams |
| 9 oz. | 255 grams |
| 10 oz. | 283 grams |
| 11 oz. | 311 grams |
| 12 oz. | 340 grams |
| 13 oz. | 368 grams |
| 14 oz. | 396 grams |
| 15 oz. | 425 grams |
| 16 oz./ 1 lb. | 455 grams |

### C. & Spoon

| C. | Metric |
|---|---|
| ¼ C. | 60 milliliters |
| 1/3 C. | 80 milliliters |
| ½ C. | 120 milliliters |
| 1 C. | 240 milliliters |
| **Spoon** | **Metric** |
| ¼ tsp. | 1¼ milliliters |
| ½ tsp. | 2½ milliliters |
| 1 tsp. | 5 milliliters |
| 2 tsp. | 10 milliliters |
| 1 tbsp. | 20 milliliters |

## Liquid

| Imperial | Metric |
| --- | --- |
| 1 fluid oz. | 30 milliliters |
| 2 fluid oz. | 60 milliliters |
| 3½ fluid oz. | 80 milliliters |
| 2¾ fluid oz. | 100 milliliters |
| 4 fluid oz. | 125 milliliters |
| 5 fluid oz. | 150 milliliters |
| 6 fluid oz. | 180 milliliters |
| 7 fluid oz. | 200 milliliters |
| 8¾ fluid oz. | 250 milliliters |
| 10½ fluid oz. | 310 milliliters |
| 13 fluid oz. | 375 milliliters |
| 15 fluid oz. | 430 milliliters |
| 16 fluid oz. | 475 milliliters |
| 17 fluid oz. | 500 milliliters |
| 21½ fluid oz. | 625 milliliters |
| 26 fluid oz. | 750 milliliters |
| 35 fluid oz. | 1 liter |
| 44 fluid oz. | 1¼ liters |
| 52 fluid oz. | 1½ liters |
| 70 fluid oz. | 2 liters |
| 88 fluid oz. | 2½ liters |

# CONCLUSION

Whether it is ethical or not, veganism has many benefits. Vegan diet offers numerous medical, health and environmental benefits. Vegan diet is currently an ever-growing lifestyle that millions of people are adopting. It can provide countless health benefits, from weight loss to an increased energy level, and it can also be eco-friendly by eliminating the need for products that depend on animal farming.

Vegan is not only a healthy diet but also a diet that reduces carbon footprint on climate change and preserves ecosystems' integrity. Vegan diet prevents loss of biodiversity. Animal products are the largest contributors to water pollution and biodiversity loss and vegan diets are likely to have less environmental impact in general. Although a vegan diet may seem restrictive to some, it can be a healthy and delicious way to eat. Many plant-based foods are nutrient-dense and provide important antioxidants, vitamins, and minerals. A vegan diet has been shown to improve heart health, reduce the risk of cancer, and help with weight loss.

# INDEX

## A

adobo sauce, 41, 49, 52
agar-agar powder, 55, 74, 91
agave nectar, 12, 22, 31, 105
all-purpose flour, 18, 19, 20, 21, 25, 26, 27, 31, 32, 35, 37, 52, 53, 56, 70, 71, 75, 78, 90, 109, 110, 115, 117, 118, 120, 122, 124, 126, 127, 130, 131, 132, 136
almond butter, 20, 35, 101
almond extract, 91, 135
almond flakes, 135
almond flour, 73, 106, 119, 136
almond meal, 135
almond milk, 16, 18, 20, 23, 24, 27, 32, 33, 35, 36, 41, 52, 56, 57, 72, 74, 75, 78, 90, 107, 109, 110, 119, 120, 121, 124, 126, 129, 131, 132, 135, 136
almond yogurt, 105
almonds, 16, 17, 18, 73, 96, 106, 107, 111, 121, 122
amaranth flour, 114
amaretto, 136
ancho chile powder, 41, 46
apple cider vinegar, 23, 31, 33, 36, 50, 84, 111, 118, 133
apples, 16, 22, 37, 54, 121, 136
applesauce, 20, 21, 35, 55, 75, 76
aquafaba, 20, 118
Arborio rice, 65, 66
arrowroot flour, 20, 60, 121
arrowroot powder, 135
arrowroot starch, 113
arugula, 22, 58, 59, 109, 125
asparagus, 23, 65, 66, 67
avocado, 32, 39, 40, 41, 42, 43, 44, 45, 46, 52, 58, 61, 64, 67, 84, 93, 122
avocado oil, 41, 46, 61, 64, 67, 84, 93, 122
avocados, 39, 40, 42, 52

## B

baby greens, 43
baguette slices, 126
baking powder, 18, 19, 20, 21, 31, 32, 33, 35, 36, 53, 55, 56, 75, 109, 110, 118, 119, 120, 121, 122, 132
baking soda, 18, 19, 20, 21, 28, 32, 33, 35, 37, 55, 56, 75, 100, 111, 114, 120, 121, 127, 128
balsamic vinegar, 27, 39, 58, 59, 64, 68, 81
banana, 20, 22, 75, 76, 90, 109, 119, 121
bananas, 16, 21, 34, 90, 97, 119, 134
barley, 16, 63, 65, 116, 117, 118
basil, 30, 47, 58, 61, 66, 67, 68, 69, 72, 81, 82, 131
basmati rice, 103, 104
bay leaf, 24, 26, 28, 63, 64, 65, 102, 103, 104

bay leaves, 25, 29, 68, 101, 102, 115, 116, 126, 127, 128
bean sprouts, 85
beefless tips, 25
beer, 32, 47
beets, 24, 60, 111, 112
bell pepper, 26, 29, 31, 40, 44, 45, 46, 47, 48, 49, 50, 59, 60, 64, 69, 79, 83, 86, 87, 88, 93, 112, 116, 130
bell peppers, 24, 25, 26, 39, 47, 49, 50, 82, 88, 100, 131
biryani masala, 104, 105
black beans, 28, 39, 40, 41, 42, 43, 44, 45, 47, 48, 49, 55, 63, 103
black pepper, 19, 23, 24, 25, 26, 27, 28, 29, 30, 31, 32, 39, 40, 41, 42, 43, 45, 46, 47, 48, 49, 50, 51, 52, 58, 59, 60, 61, 62, 63, 64, 65, 66, 67, 68, 69, 70, 77, 78, 85, 86, 87, 89, 93, 94, 96, 97, 98, 99, 100, 101, 102, 103, 104, 110, 111, 112, 113, 114, 115, 116, 117, 118, 124, 125, 126, 127, 128, 129, 130, 131, 132, 133, 134
blackberries, 22, 36, 73, 119, 121, 134
blackcurrant jam, 135
black-eyed peas, 114
blueberries, 20, 22, 73, 121, 122, 134, 136
bok choy, 83, 88
bread flour, 123
bread roll, 126
bread slices, 22, 122
breadcrumbs, 27, 30, 69, 78, 94, 116, 133, 134
broccoli, 16, 17, 25, 68, 78, 79, 80, 81, 86, 88, 112, 113, 124
broccolini, 87, 88
brown rice, 16, 32, 41, 42, 45, 50, 82, 105
brown rice flour, 32, 105
brown sugar, 28, 31, 33, 35, 63, 78, 80, 81, 87, 96, 119, 120, 136
Brussels sprout, 17, 70, 112, 113
buckwheat flour, 105
bulgur wheat, 124
butterbeans, 116, 117
butternut squash, 26, 64, 127

## C

cabbage, 87, 88, 98, 99, 113, 115, 117
cacao powder, 36, 74, 75, 110
Cajun seasoning, 26
canola oil, 33, 35, 37, 44, 47, 48, 79, 82, 83, 86, 95, 99, 100, 101, 102, 104
caraway seeds, 95, 96
cardamom, 100, 102, 104, 106, 107
carrot, 27, 42, 43, 46, 50, 51, 59, 60, 63, 64, 65, 66, 67, 68, 79, 85, 88, 89, 104, 114, 117, 118, 125
carrots, 16, 24, 25, 26, 27, 40, 45, 46, 50, 51, 58, 61, 62, 63, 68, 77, 80, 83, 85, 87, 88, 89, 94, 100, 104, 105, 106,

141

107, 111, 112, 115, 116, 117, 125, 126, 127, 128, 130, 133, 134
cashew cheese sauce, 42
cashew milk, 18, 19
cashews, 16, 18, 23, 24, 26, 30, 57, 106, 107, 113, 114, 126, 132, 133, 135
caster sugar, 74
cauliflower, 16, 23, 26, 69, 78, 99, 104, 105, 112, 132, 133
celery, 26, 29, 30, 31, 42, 45, 46, 48, 49, 62, 63, 66, 67, 68, 114, 115, 117, 127, 128, 130
chaat masala powder, 95
cherries, 33, 136, 137
cherry pie filling, 120
chervil, 126, 127
chia seeds, 16, 17, 18, 21, 33, 109
chickpeas, 20, 27, 28, 34, 42, 46, 60, 69, 94, 95, 100, 101, 102, 118, 131
chili garlic sauce, 82, 85, 86
chili sauce, 77
chipotle peppers, 41, 52
chives, 60, 66, 125
chocolate, 34, 35, 55, 109, 119, 123, 135
chocolate spread, 123
cilantro, 28, 39, 41, 42, 44, 45, 46, 47, 48, 51, 52, 59, 60, 77, 93, 94, 96, 97, 98, 99, 100, 101, 102, 103, 104, 105
cinnamon, 20, 21, 22, 33, 35, 37, 38, 47, 52, 53, 54, 55, 56, 57, 73, 76, 97, 100, 104, 107, 109, 120, 121, 122, 134, 136
cocoa powder, 35, 36, 37, 54, 55, 56, 74, 110, 120
coconut cream, 19, 56, 57, 60, 73, 74, 91, 92, 102, 103, 118, 126, 127, 133, 134, 135
coconut flakes, 18, 97, 121
coconut flour, 110, 119, 121
coconut milk, 54, 55, 56, 61, 74, 75, 81, 90, 91, 92, 97, 98, 101, 103, 106, 107, 109, 114, 116, 117, 118, 134, 135
coconut oil, 18, 20, 24, 34, 37, 38, 52, 53, 56, 57, 73, 81, 90, 96, 101, 109, 110, 112, 117, 119, 120, 121, 122, 128
coconut sugar, 54, 80, 84, 86, 87, 107, 111
coconut whipping cream, 56
coconut yogurt, 34, 60, 104
coffee, 73, 74, 75
collard greens, 17, 62
confectioners' sugar, 56, 120
cooking spray, 20, 30, 33, 35, 37, 43, 49, 50, 52, 53, 56, 59, 64, 71, 75, 93, 105, 109, 110, 111, 121, 124, 129, 135, 136, 137
coriander, 46, 47, 48, 63, 95, 96, 97, 98, 99, 100, 101, 102, 103
corn, 39, 40, 41, 42, 44, 45, 46, 48, 49, 50, 51, 81, 85, 87, 88, 116
cornbread mix, 50
cornflour, 83, 84, 119
cornmeal, 28, 31, 32, 33, 111
Cornmeal, 110
cornstarch, 23, 24, 37, 38, 50, 54, 74, 78, 79, 80, 81, 84, 85, 90, 119, 120, 121, 122, 129, 136
cranberries, 33
cucumber, 40, 42, 59, 94, 112, 125

cucumbers, 58
cumin, 25, 27, 32, 33, 39, 41, 42, 43, 44, 45, 46, 47, 48, 49, 61, 62, 63, 66, 67, 93, 94, 95, 96, 97, 98, 99, 100, 101, 102, 103, 104, 105, 111
curry leaves, 103
curry powder, 60, 69, 86, 96, 97, 101, 103

# D

dates, 33, 35, 36, 64
desiccated coconut, 98, 109
Digestive biscuit, 119
dill, 60
dragon fruit, 77

# E

egg replacer, 32, 135, 136
eggplant, 79, 97, 100, 116, 130, 131
enchilada sauce, 44
Erythritol, 110, 119

# F

farro, 63
fennel bulb, 24, 133
figs, 64, 75
flaxseeds, 16, 17, 27, 33, 35, 50, 52, 69, 75, 110, 119, 122
frozen pie shell, 124

# G

garam masala, 94, 95, 96, 99, 101, 102, 103
garlic, 19, 21, 23, 24, 25, 26, 27, 29, 30, 32, 39, 40, 41, 42, 43, 44, 45, 46, 47, 48, 49, 50, 51, 52, 58, 59, 60, 61, 62, 63, 64, 65, 66, 67, 68, 69, 77, 78, 79, 80, 81, 82, 83, 84, 85, 86, 87, 88, 89, 94, 95, 96, 97, 98, 99, 100, 101, 102, 103, 104, 105, 109,112, 113, 114, 115, 116, 117, 124, 125, 126, 127, 128, 129, 130, 131, 132, 133, 134
garlic powder, 19, 21, 25, 32, 39, 40, 48, 69, 84, 85, 86, 88, 89, 112, 126, 127
gelatin, 16, 74, 75, 91
ginger, 24, 33, 77, 78, 79, 80, 81, 82, 83, 85, 86, 87, 88, 91, 93, 94, 95, 96, 97, 98, 99, 100, 101, 102, 103, 104, 111, 120, 121
glutinous rice flour, 89
graham cracker crumbs, 56, 57
graham crackers, 74
grapefruit, 111
green beans, 50, 51, 77, 82, 94, 104, 125
green chili, 93, 95, 96, 97, 100, 101, 103
green chilies, 41, 45, 62, 63, 95, 99, 101, 102, 104, 105
green peas, 23, 25, 66, 88, 89, 95, 99, 100, 104, 105, 117
greens, 16, 44, 62, 82, 83, 88
guajillo chile powder, 46
Guinness, 115, 117

## H

habanero pepper, 52
Herbs de Provence, 125, 131, 133, 134
hoisin sauce, 85
hominy, 46
hot sauce, 41, 45, 77

## I

icing sugar, 118, 123, 124
Italian seasoning, 28, 29, 66, 69, 132

## J

jalapeño pepper, 39, 40, 41, 44, 46, 49, 51, 52, 59
jalapeño peppers, 32, 33, 47, 63

## K

kale, 17, 63, 117
ketchup, 28, 29, 43, 84

## L

leek, 61, 113, 114, 115, 116
leeks, 113, 114
lemon, 18, 19, 23, 25, 30, 36, 37, 38, 39, 40, 54, 58, 59, 60, 62, 63, 65, 72, 73, 75, 76, 88, 94, 96, 100, 101, 103, 104, 105, 109, 110, 121, 122, 125, 126, 131, 134, 136
lemongrass, 87
lemon-pepper seasoning, 19
lentils, 16, 17, 29, 45, 46, 62, 63, 64, 66, 67, 95, 101, 114, 117, 125
lettuce, 22, 39, 40, 41, 42, 112, 125
lima beans, 27, 64
lime, 22, 39, 40, 41, 42, 43, 44, 51, 52, 67, 68, 74, 77, 81, 82, 86, 87, 91, 92, 102, 111
liquid smoke, 26, 28

## M

macadamia nuts, 116
macaroni, 29, 30, 31
malt vinegar, 114
mango, 16, 39, 52, 91, 92, 94, 95, 99
mango powder, 94, 95, 99
mangoes, 91
maple syrup, 18, 20, 21, 33, 36, 39, 54, 57, 64, 72, 73, 76, 77, 81, 82, 85, 109, 111, 112, 113, 120, 121, 122, 134, 135
marinara sauce, 64, 66, 69
mayonnaise, 31, 40, 49
millet flour, 21
mint, 23, 59, 65, 73, 77, 94, 96, 104, 105
miso, 68, 86, 112, 113, 124
mixed nuts, 106, 107

mushrooms, 25, 26, 27, 29, 60, 61, 64, 65, 66, 67, 68, 79, 80, 81, 83, 84, 85, 86, 87, 88, 113, 114, 115, 124, 127, 128, 130, 132, 133, 134
mustard, 23, 24, 28, 30, 31, 39, 43, 96, 97, 98, 99, 103, 112, 113, 118, 125, 127

## N

navy beans, 28, 59, 128
noodles, 58, 83, 85, 86, 87, 88
nutmeg, 19, 30, 33, 54, 65, 96, 117, 129, 133
nutritional yeast, 30, 32, 65, 66, 68, 69, 110, 117, 126, 129, 132, 133, 134, 135

## O

oat milk, 31, 55, 68, 106
oats, 16, 20, 21, 28, 29, 33, 34, 35, 43, 109, 121, 122
okra, 96, 97
olive oil, 18, 19, 20, 21, 22, 23, 24, 25, 27, 28, 29, 30, 31, 36, 39, 40, 41, 42, 43, 45, 46, 47, 48, 49, 50, 51, 56, 58, 59, 60, 61, 62, 63, 64, 65, 66, 67, 68, 70, 71, 72, 75, 76, 77, 78, 80, 81, 85, 88, 89, 93, 94, 95, 97, 98, 99, 100, 101, 102, 104, 105, 109, 110, 111, 112, 113, 114, 115, 116, 117, 118, 123, 124, 125, 126, 127, 128, 129, 130, 131, 132, 133, 134
olives, 49, 50, 51, 58, 59, 71
onion, 21, 24, 25, 26, 27, 28, 29, 31, 32, 39, 40, 41, 42, 43, 44, 45, 46, 47, 48, 49, 50, 51, 52, 60, 61, 62, 63, 64, 65, 66, 67, 68, 69, 80, 81, 82, 85, 86, 88, 93, 94, 95, 96, 97, 98, 99, 100, 101, 102, 103, 104, 112, 113, 114, 115, 116, 117, 118, 124, 125, 126, 127, 128, 130, 131, 132, 133, 134
onion powder, 21, 24, 25, 32, 48, 69, 112, 127, 130
onions, 26, 28, 30, 32, 46, 47, 50, 61, 66, 68, 81, 85, 89, 96, 97, 98, 99, 100, 102, 103, 104, 116, 126, 127, 128, 129, 130, 131, 132
orange, 52, 53, 54, 59, 100, 106
orange food color, 106
oregano, 25, 29, 31, 32, 41, 42, 45, 46, 47, 48, 49, 58, 59, 63, 64, 66, 67, 68, 72, 127
oyster sauce, 87, 88

## P

papayas, 77
paprika, 25, 27, 29, 30, 32, 41, 45, 48, 50, 51, 61, 68, 71, 94, 102, 116, 133, 134
parsley, 23, 25, 26, 27, 40, 50, 51, 58, 59, 63, 65, 67, 68, 69, 72, 115, 117, 125, 126, 127, 128, 129, 130, 134
parsnip, 115
parsnips, 24
pasta, 16, 29, 45, 59, 67, 68, 69, 70, 83, 127
pea shoots, 23
peaches, 120, 121
peanut butter, 22, 34, 43, 44, 82
peanut oil, 77, 78, 79, 86
peanuts, 77, 104

pears, 76
pecans, 30, 37, 121
peppermint extract, 135
pine nuts, 58
pineapple, 16, 44, 87
pinto beans, 43, 45, 47, 49
pistachios, 16, 64, 106, 107
pita chips, 49
poblano peppers, 41, 42
pomegranate, 39, 43, 44
poppy seeds, 19
potato, 21, 24, 32, 36, 41, 42, 43, 44, 47, 69, 79, 95, 99, 102, 105, 110, 116, 117, 118, 125, 129, 133
potato starch, 105, 116
potatoes, 16, 21, 23, 24, 25, 26, 31, 32, 46, 54, 62, 63, 94, 95, 96, 98, 99, 100, 102, 110, 113, 114, 115, 116, 117, 118, 125, 126, 127, 128, 129, 130, 133
powdered sugar, 34, 37, 53, 55, 56, 90, 122, 134, 137
Powdered sugar, 53, 136
protein powder, 21, 34, 35, 121, 122
puff pastry, 26, 123
pumpkin puree, 20, 30
pumpkin seeds, 16, 18, 60, 64

## Q

quinoa, 16, 17, 39, 68, 100

## R

raisins, 18, 33, 54, 55, 69, 106, 107
raspberries, 22, 73, 134
red bean paste, 89
red chili powder, 30, 32, 41, 43, 44, 45, 47, 48, 49, 83, 93, 94, 96, 97, 98, 99, 100, 101, 102, 103
red gel food color, 37
red kidney beans, 27, 40, 48, 63, 100, 102, 103
red pepper flakes, 27, 29, 39, 42, 48, 59, 62, 66, 67, 68, 69, 80, 81, 83, 86, 93, 94, 111, 130, 131
red wine, 25, 63, 64, 112, 116, 125, 126, 128, 130
red wine vinegar, 25, 64, 112, 125
refried beans, 49
rice milk, 25, 119, 120
rice vinegar, 78, 80, 81, 83, 85
rice wine, 77, 86, 88
rice wine vinegar, 77
rosemary, 26, 29, 30, 31, 68, 71, 113, 115, 133
rutabaga, 115

## S

saffron, 50, 51, 100, 106, 107, 127, 128
sage, 26, 68, 128
sake, 80
salsa, 40, 41, 42, 47, 48, 51
salt, 18, 19, 20, 21, 22, 23, 24, 25, 26, 27, 28, 29, 31, 32, 33, 35, 36, 37, 38, 39, 40, 41, 42, 43, 44, 45, 46, 47, 48, 49, 51, 52, 53, 54, 55, 56, 61, 62, 63, 64, 66, 67, 68, 69, 70, 71, 72, 73, 74, 75, 77, 78, 79, 83, 84, 87, 88, 89, 93, 94, 95, 96, 97, 98, 99, 100, 101, 102, 103, 104, 105, 106, 107, 109, 110, 111, 112, 113, 114, 115, 116, 117, 118, 119, 120, 121, 122, 123, 124, 125, 126, 127, 128, 129, 130, 131, 132, 133, 134, 135, 136
Salt, 18, 19, 21, 22, 23, 24, 25, 26, 27, 28, 29, 30, 32, 39, 40, 41, 42, 45, 46, 47, 48, 49, 50, 51, 52, 58, 59, 60, 61, 62, 63, 64, 65, 66, 67, 68, 69, 70, 77, 78, 79, 84, 87, 88, 93, 94, 95, 96, 97, 98, 99, 100, 101, 102, 103, 104, 110, 111, 112, 113, 114, 115, 116, 117, 119, 124, 125, 126, 127, 128, 129, 130, 131, 132, 133
scallion, 27, 39, 42, 43, 44, 48, 49, 59, 80, 82, 83, 84, 85, 86, 87, 88, 93, 117
scallions, 42, 43, 77, 78, 79, 82, 83, 85, 86, 87, 88, 93, 112
self-rising flour, 72, 135
semolina, 106
Serrano peppers, 77, 101
sesame oil, 59, 77, 78, 81, 82, 83, 84, 85, 86, 88, 89, 124
sesame seeds, 59, 78, 79, 80, 82, 84, 85, 86, 89, 90, 133
shallot, 30, 77, 111
shallots, 32, 33, 40, 129
shepherd's purse, 84
sherry, 79
smoky sweet glaze, 24
snow peas, 79, 80, 82, 86
soy milk, 16, 21, 30, 32, 35, 37, 40, 50, 54, 55, 60, 74, 90, 91, 111, 119, 122, 123, 133
soy sauce, 25, 29, 43, 60, 68, 70, 77, 78, 79, 80, 81, 82, 83, 84, 85, 86, 87, 88, 109, 115, 124
soy yogurt, 97
spaghetti, 69
spaghetti sauce, 69
spelt flour, 72, 111
spinach, 17, 43, 46, 58, 62, 63, 69, 70, 77, 85, 87, 88, 95, 96, 98, 124, 133
Sriracha, 87
stevia, 18, 34, 73, 75, 121, 122
strawberries, 18, 22, 34, 73, 74, 118, 134
string beans, 129
sugar snap peas, 82, 87
sunflower oil, 72, 97, 112
sunflower seeds, 16, 18, 70, 133
sweet potatoes, 16
Swiss chard, 17, 98, 127

## T

tahini, 17, 23, 25, 26, 59, 85, 116, 124
tamari, 89, 113, 114
tapioca flour, 36, 126
tapioca pearls, 90
tapioca starch, 105
tarragon, 113, 114, 115, 125
tempeh, 12, 16, 17, 41, 84, 85, 128
thyme, 25, 26, 27, 29, 46, 61, 62, 63, 65, 66, 67, 68, 71, 112, 113, 114, 115, 116, 126, 127, 128, 130, 131, 132
tofu, 12, 14, 16, 17, 26, 40, 42, 74, 80, 81, 82, 83, 84, 86, 87, 88, 89, 109, 124, 136, 137

tomatillo, 52
tomato, 27, 29, 40, 41, 42, 43, 44, 46, 47, 49, 50, 51, 52, 59, 63, 64, 66, 67, 72, 77, 78, 93, 97, 99, 101, 102, 103, 109, 115, 116, 127, 130, 131, 134
tomato puree, 44, 47, 72, 99, 102, 103, 116
tomato sauce, 27, 29, 49, 64, 66, 97, 134
tomatoes, 16, 24, 25, 26, 29, 40, 41, 45, 46, 47, 48, 49, 50, 51, 52, 58, 59, 61, 62, 63, 64, 65, 66, 67, 68, 69, 71, 72, 82, 87, 93, 94, 97, 98, 99, 100, 101, 102, 103, 114, 115, 116, 124, 125, 127, 128, 131
tortillas, 43, 44, 46, 49, 54
turmeric, 30, 32, 46, 48, 88, 89, 93, 95, 96, 97, 98, 99, 100, 101, 102, 103, 109, 118, 124, 135
turnip, 16, 115

## U

unsweetened coconut, 18, 21, 61, 73, 74, 96, 97, 109, 121, 134

## V

vanilla bean paste, 74
vanilla extract, 18, 20, 21, 34, 35, 37, 52, 53, 54, 55, 56, 57, 73, 75, 76, 91, 119, 120, 121, 122, 134, 135
vegan butter, 18, 26, 31, 35, 36, 37, 75, 89, 106, 107, 110, 113, 120, 122, 130, 131, 132, 136
vegan cheese, 24, 41, 43, 44, 49, 50, 59, 64, 66, 129, 132
vegan margarine, 119, 135, 136
vegan sausages, 25, 26, 113, 116, 117
vegan whipped cream, 119
vegetable broth, 24, 25, 26, 27, 28, 29, 41, 45, 46, 47, 48, 50, 51, 61, 62, 63, 65, 66, 68, 78, 79, 80, 83, 86, 101, 109, 113, 114, 115, 116, 117, 126, 127, 129, 130, 132, 134

vegetable oil, 19, 26, 27, 44, 51, 54, 56, 69, 85, 87, 88, 89, 90, 94, 95, 96, 98, 100, 103, 106, 119
Vegetable oil, 32, 53
vermicelli, 107

## W

walnuts, 16, 17, 21, 22, 29, 30, 35, 36, 42, 53, 68, 112, 113, 117, 118
water chestnuts, 79, 80
whisky, 112
white beans, 48, 103, 134
white kidney beans, 39, 62
white pepper, 77, 83, 84, 88
white rice, 51, 88, 89, 104, 107, 115
white sugar, 16, 19, 20, 21, 31, 32, 35, 36, 37, 52, 53, 54, 55, 56, 71, 72, 73, 74, 75, 77, 78, 79, 87, 88, 89, 90, 91, 97, 106, 107, 109, 110, 115, 119, 120, 122, 123, 125, 126, 128, 129, 135, 136
white vinegar, 37, 56, 83, 119
white wine, 23, 26, 66, 112, 127
white wine vinegar, 23, 112
whole-wheat flour, 33, 35, 44, 55, 111, 120, 131
whole-wheat pastry flour, 36, 136
wild rice, 29, 41, 66

## Y

yeast, 19, 22, 52, 70, 71, 105, 110, 111, 123
yellow cake mix, 120
yellow squashes, 41, 58

## Z

zucchinis, 46, 48, 58, 59, 61, 64, 131

Printed in Great Britain
by Amazon